CROCHETING FOR THE HOME

Margaret Ramsay
and
Sondra Miller

CREATIVE HOME LIBRARY®
In Association with **Better Homes and Gardens** ®
Meredith Corporation

PHOTOGRAPHY
Arie deZanger

ILLUSTRATIONS
Carol Hines

CREATIVE HOME LIBRARY
© *Meredith Corporation, 1977. All rights reserved. Printed
in the United States of America. First edition. First printing.*

Library of Congress Catalog Card Number:
75-40625

SBN: 696-18300-5

About the Authors

Maggy Ramsay is a former instructor and educational researcher at the University of Wisconsin and New York University. She spent two years traveling in Italy, where she studied crochet and began to create her own designs. Upon her return to the United States, she taught and lectured about crochet at schools and craft shops while she continued to refine her own designs and techniques.

After a brief career teaching English and then producing educational radio shows, Sondra Miller studied crochet seriously with several veteran professional crocheters in the New York City area. She now teaches and lectures at studios and specialty shops in New York.

Maggy and Sondra formed a crochet partnership in 1974 called Madame Defarge Revolutionary Crochet and have shown and sold their designs in galleries, boutiques, and department stores. From their combined academic and craft teaching experiences they have developed an easy, orderly method of showing students how to crochet. This method has become the focus of their book and reflects years of attention to the details and techniques of their well-loved craft.

Contents

---

1 Beginning Skills 7

2 Fancy Stitches 39

3 Special Crochet . . . 83

Foreword

Exciting and versatile, crochet is the perfect craft for home decoration. You can crochet a hammock or a planter, a shower curtain or a lampshade. Crochet is portable, practical, inexpensive, and so easy to do that even if you're a beginner, you'll soon find yourself creating all kinds of fabrics and shapes.

We designed our book to give you a comprehensive and carefully structured course in crochet. It begins with the basics in Chapter 1. Even if you already know how to crochet, we think you'll find it helpful to read this chapter. Every crocheter has slightly different ways of performing the tasks and techniques of crochet. Whether or not you adopt our methods, understanding how we perform the basic skills will enable you to easily follow the more complicated techniques and ideas discussed later on.

Each of the remaining chapters focuses on a different aspect of crochet. Simple stitches are combined into decorative stitches and stitch patterns in Chapter 2. Special kinds of crochet, such as Tapestry stitch, Filet crochet, and Woven crochet are described in Chapter 3. Crochet designs are not limited to straight rows of stitches and, in Chapter 4, you'll learn how to make the elements of many designs—geometric shapes. Finally, in Chapter 5, all the skills and ideas of the first four chapters are integrated into free-form shapes and designs.

The projects in each chapter have been designed to illustrate the concepts and skills of that chapter as well as to be decorative additions to your home. Don't be afraid to make a project just because it looks difficult —looks can often be deceiving and we love to find ways to make projects look unusual. However, please don't begin with a project without knowing exactly what is involved. Too often crocheters are unable or unwilling to find out what they are getting into, and a closet full of incomplete projects is frequently the result.

Read the project before you begin. Look up unfamiliar terms or instructions in the first chapter. Find and read the directions for the stitches or techniques involved, and practice them on small swatches. If your project has motifs, make one before you commit yourself to the entire project. Check the gauge you are getting against ours, and if there is a difference, figure out how that will affect the finished size of the project. The section on yarn selections and gauge in Chapter 1 will tell you how to make any necessary adjustments.

We hope you'll feel free to personalize every project in any way you like. Many design ideas can be easily translated from one functional form to another—a design we have used on a pillow might work best in your home as an afghan, or vice versa. One person's cotton shower curtain can easily become another person's jute room divider or wall hanging. Experiment with color, size, yarn, and even stitches, to find the look that's right for you.

Crochet does not require the extensive instruction or expensive equipment that many other crafts do. This book, a crochet hook, and some yarn are all you need to join the generations of craftspeople who have used crochet to bring beauty and individuality to their homes.

Chapter 1 BEGINNING SKILLS

The best way to learn a craft is to do it. As you read this chapter, make your own practice piece to compare with our step-by-step instructions and diagrams. First you'll learn how to make a slip knot, how to hold the hook and yarn, and how to make a foundation chain. Then you'll make the basic crochet stitch—the single crochet—and its variations: half double, double, treble, and slip stitch. Next we'll show you how to increase and de-

crease, change yarns, edge and join pieces, work in rounds, and block and finish pieces. Finally we'll explain how to follow all sorts of crochet directions. Even if you've never crocheted before, you'll be amazed at how quickly the movements become natural. Once a few skills are mastered, crochet becomes a craft, an art, and a pleasant compulsion that results in something beautiful. We love to crochet and we think you will too.

Slip Knot

All crochet begins with the slip knot. Make a loop about 6 inches from the end of the yarn (Diagram 1), with the long end that leads to the yarn supply (A) lying in front of the short tail (B). Hold the loop in place where the tails cross with the thumb and forefinger of your left hand (C).

With your right hand bring the long end in back of the loop so that it forms a horizontal bar behind the loop (see A in Diagram 2). Pull the horizontal strand of yarn through the original loop (Diagram 3); insert your hook into the newly formed loop and pull so that the loop closes around the hook (Diagram 4). Don't pull the slip knot too tight; it should slide up and down the crochet hook easily.

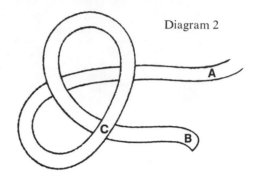

Diagram 2

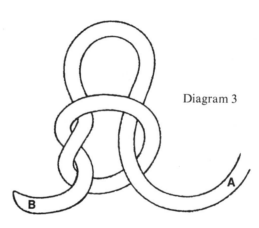

Diagram 3

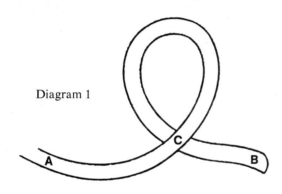

Diagram 1

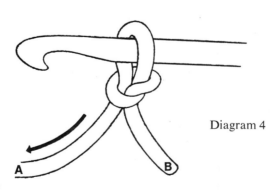

Diagram 4

8

Holding Hook and Yarn

First a word to left-handed readers: All directions in this book are written and illustrated with a right-handed prejudice; that is, the hook is held in the right hand and the yarn is held in the left hand. Most left-handed people can learn to crochet this way, but if you prefer, just reverse the directions.

Hook

You can hold your hook in two ways; the first, shown in Diagram 5, is the more common method. Hold the flattened part of the hook between the thumb and forefinger, with your hand slightly cupped and the bottom half of the hook loosely cradled between the rest of your fingers and the palm of your hand.

The second method, shown in Diagram 6, comes from Europe and is like holding a pencil. Grasp the flattened part of the hook between the thumb, forefinger, and middle finger, allowing the bottom half of the hook to rest above the hand against the gap between the thumb and forefinger.

Yarn

Although there are several positions in which the yarn can be held, yarn tension is always controlled by the index and little fingers of the left hand while the thumb and middle fingers lightly hold the crocheted work. In this way the right hand is completely free to manipulate the hook.

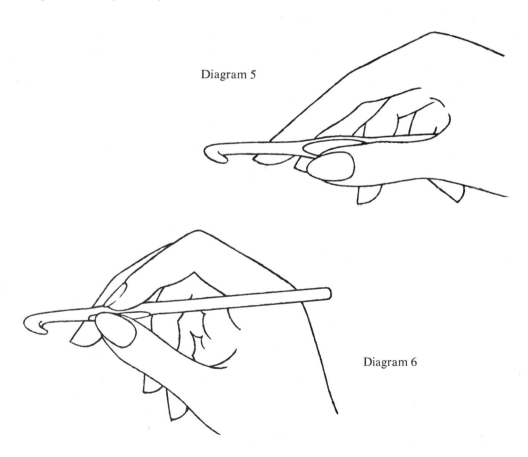

Diagram 5

Diagram 6

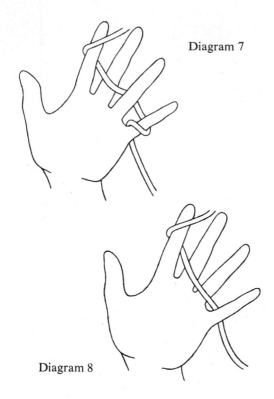

Diagram 7

The little finger of the left hand controls the amount of yarn flowing through your hand; the index finger controls the tautness of the yarn about to be picked up by the hook. If the yarn coming off the index finger hangs loosely, the hook will not easily catch the yarn. If the yarn is too taut, it will be difficult to draw the yarn through a loop to make a stitch.

Try both suggested ways (Diagrams 7 and 8) of holding the yarn to see which is the more comfortable for you. Work with the palm of your left hand facing you, as shown. Following Diagram 7, wrap the yarn around the little finger, under the ring finger, over the middle finger, and then under and over the index finger. Following Diagram 8, bring the yarn under the little finger, over the ring and middle fingers, and then under and over the index finger. With either method the amount of yarn can easily be controlled by squeezing together the little and ring fingers of the left hand.

Hook and Yarn

Diagram 9 shows both hands holding the hook and yarn in a comfortable position, with the slip knot on the hook. The tips of the thumb and middle finger of the left hand lightly grasp the short tail of the yarn.

Diagram 8

Diagram 9

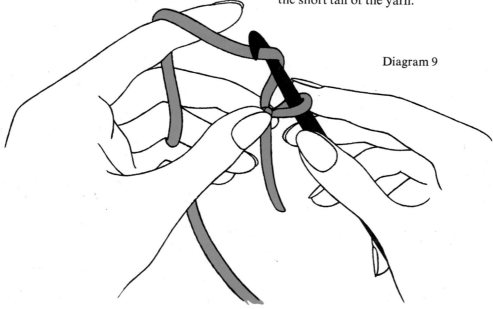

Foundation Chain

You are now ready to make a foundation chain. Position your hands to crochet. Circle the yarn with the hook, bringing it around to the left and then under the yarn. This is called *yarning over* (Diagram 10). Twist the hook slightly toward the yarn and pull the yarn through the loop on your hook (see the arrow in Diagram 10). The new loop on your hook is your first chain stitch. Yarn over again, twist the hook toward the yarn as you catch the yarn, and pull it through the loop on your hook. This is your second chain stitch.

Take some time now to practice making chain stitches. Your chains should be firm and even but still flexible, and you should be able to see each stitch easily. Beginning crocheters often make unworkably tight foundation chains. If the chain stitches are too tight, your hook will fight your yarn on the next row instead of sliding easily into the stitches.

Counting Chain Stitches

Make a chain of 11 stitches and compare your work with Diagram 11. The loop on the hook does not count as a stitch. The chain stitch di-

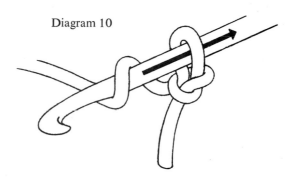

Diagram 10

rectly below the loop on the hook is the first chain from the hook, the chain stitch just below that is the second chain from the hook, and so on. When counting the stitches in your foundation chain, start with the first chain from the hook and stop when you've counted the chain stitch just before the slip knot. The foundation chain in Diagram 11 has 11 chain stitches.

When starting a piece of crochet, you can count the chain stitches as you make them, but if your foundation chain is long, always check the number of stitches by counting backward on the completed chain.

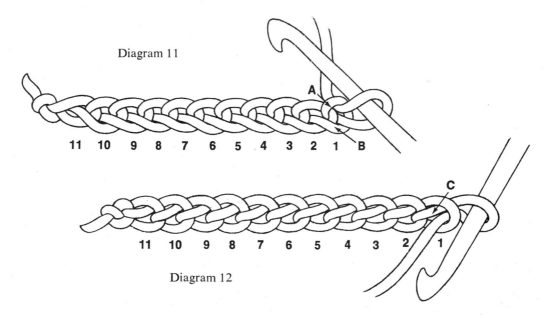

Diagram 11

11 10 9 8 7 6 5 4 3 2 1 B

11 10 9 8 7 6 5 4 3 2 1

Diagram 12

Picking Up Foundation Stitches

Look again at the foundation chain in Diagram 11 on the preceding page. As you can see, the front of each chain stitch has 2 *crossed strands* of yarn (A and B) which together form a V. On the back of the chain there is a third strand that runs up the middle of the stitch (see strand C in Diagram 12). Each of these strands is actually a *loop* of the chain stitch. Strand A will be referred to as the *back loop,* strand B will be referred to as the *front loop,* and strand C will be referred to as the *bottom loop.* The stitches of your first row will be made by inserting your hook under 1 or 2 of these loops: the back loop (Diagram 13), the back and bottom loops (Diagram 14), or the bottom loop (Diagram 15). Inserting your hook through the bottom loop leaves a neat edge on your work. Usually it does not matter which loop or loops you choose *as long as you are consistent.* However, changing loops mid-chain will cause your foundation chain to twist. Some crochet directions, such as those for the Braided Rug (page 70), will tell you which loop of the foundation chain to pick up. Most projects, though, won't specify which loop or loops to pick up. In such cases the choice is entirely up to you.

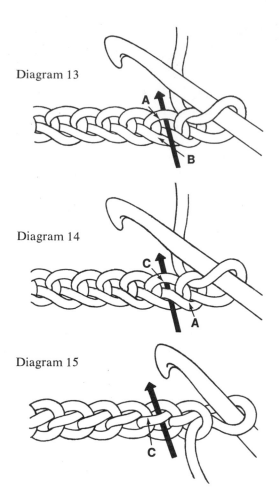

Diagram 13

Diagram 14

Diagram 15

Single Crochet

Now you are ready to make the basic crochet stitch, single crochet, using your 11-stitch foundation chain. The diagrams show the stitch being made through the back loop of the foundation chain stitch, but the directions apply to any method of working off a foundation chain.

Position your hands to crochet, as illustrated in Diagram 16, with the thumb and forefinger of the left hand gently holding the third chain stitch from the hook. Insert your hook through the back loop of the second chain stitch from the hook (Diagram 17). Yarn over and pull the yarn through the loop of the chain

stitch but not through the loop on your hook (Diagram 18). There are now 2 loops on the hook. The loops should be loose; your hook should slide easily up and back through the loops. Yarn over again and pull the yarn through both loops on your hook (Diagram 19). There is now 1 loop on your hook, and you have made 1 single crochet (Diagram 20).

Move the thumb and forefinger of your left hand down 1 chain stitch to the fourth stitch from the hook. Insert your hook into the back loop of the third chain stitch from the hook (see A in Diagram 20); yarn over and pull up a loop; yarn over again and pull a loop

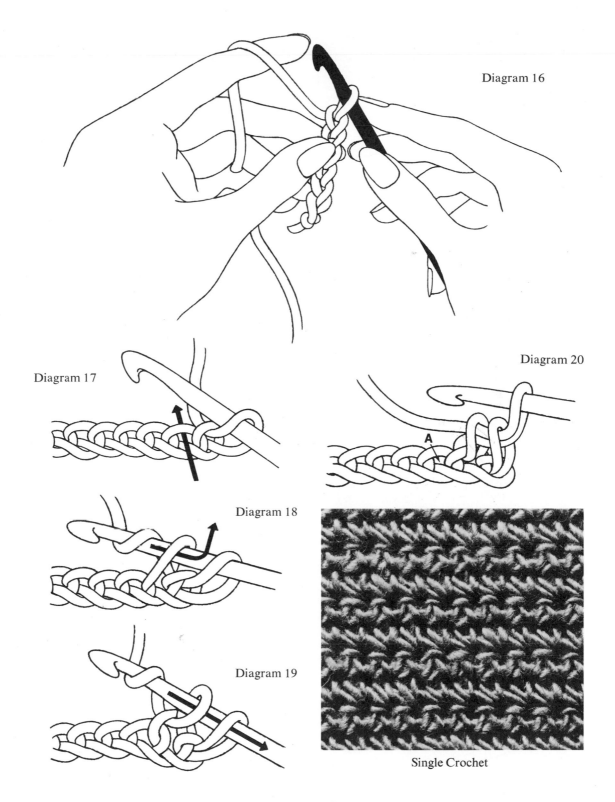

Diagram 16

Diagram 17

Diagram 20

Diagram 18

Diagram 19

Single Crochet

13

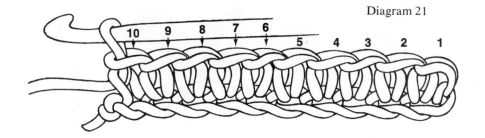

Diagram 21

through both loops on your hook. You have completed your second single crochet.

Do 1 single crochet in each of the remaining 8 chain stitches. When you're done, you should have 10 single crochet stitches and 1 loop on the hook (Diagram 21). If you find, though, that you have made too many stitches, simply rip out the excess stitches. If by some chance you find that you made too many chain stitches as well, don't bother ripping out the entire foundation chain. Just untie the slip knot and undo as many chain stitches as you need, then pull on the tail to close up the chain.

Before you begin another row, examine the stitches you have just made. Every crochet stitch has a *head*. The head consists of 2 loops at the top that together form a V. In Diagram 22 loop A is the loop farthest away from you and loop B is the loop closest to you when the front of a row is facing you. (When you turn your piece over to crochet the next row, loop B will be the loop farthest away and loop A will be the loop closest to you.) In addition to the head, every stitch has a *post*—the vertical strands that connect the newly formed stitch to the row below—which is designated in the diagram by the 2 strands marked C. Look at your practice piece. You should be able to see the heads of the 10 single crochet stitches.

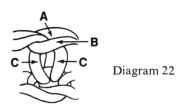

Diagram 22

Make 1 chain stitch at the end of your row of single crochet (Diagram 23) and turn your work over so that you are now looking at the back of the row. (Always turn your work as you would turn the page of a book—move the right end toward you and over to the left.) Chaining up—making a chain stitch or stitches at the end of a row—enables you to get your hook and yarn in the right position for the next row. These chains are referred to as *turning chains*.

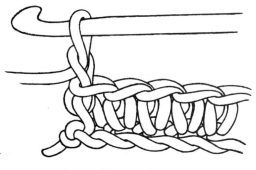

Diagram 23

The heads of the stitches are not easily visible from the back, so study Diagram 24 carefully before making the first stitch of the second row. Make the first stitch by inserting your hook under the head of the first stitch of the previous row (see the arrow in Diagram 24). In case you're getting confused, note that when you turned your work over, what was actually the last stitch of the previous row became the first stitch of the previous row.

Make 1 single crochet in each of the next 8

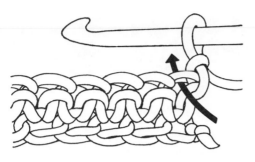

Diagram 24

Diagram 25

single crochets of the row. When making the last single crochet in the row, it is important that you insert the hook in the right spot. Inserting it in the wrong spot may cause an accidental decrease or increase in your work. The last stitch in the previous row has a little "necklace" of yarn where the V of that stitch comes

together (see the arrow in Diagram 25). Be sure to make your single crochet in this last stitch. It is a good idea to check yourself when you are beginning to crochet by counting your stitches after you complete each row. After you have counted, chain 1 and turn the piece in preparation for your next row.

Half Double Crochet

Half double crochet is very much like single crochet and will also be the same height. The only difference between the two stitches is that with half double crochet you yarn over before you insert your hook under the head of the stitch.

Yarn over and insert your hook under the head of the first stitch of the previous row (Diagram 26). Yarn over again and pull up a

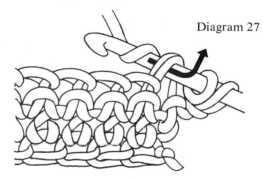

Diagram 27

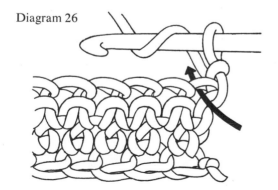

Diagram 26

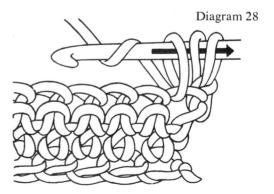

Diagram 28

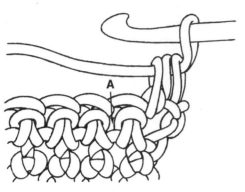

Diagram 29

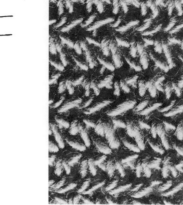

Half Double Crochet

loop (Diagram 27). There are now 3 loops on your hook. Yarn over once again and pull a loop through all 3 loops on your hook (Diagram 28). You have made 1 half double crochet and have 1 loop on your hook (Diagram 29). For the next half double crochet yarn over and insert your hook under the head of the next stitch of the previous row and repeat (see A in Diagram 29).

Make a half double crochet in each remaining stitch of the row. (Notice that there is a third loop—the *post loop*—behind the head of each stitch.) When you reach the end of the row, count your stitches. You should have 10 half double crochet stitches and 1 loop on your hook. Chain 1 and turn your work in preparation for your next row. Make another row of half double crochet for practice.

Double Crochet

As we said earlier, chaining up to turn readies the hook and yarn for the next row of crochet. Double crochet is unique in that there are two ways to get ready to begin a row. You can continue to apply the same principle described for single crochet and half double crochet— that is, chain up, turn your work, and make the first stitch of the row in the first stitch of the previous row. (Note that double crochet is higher than both single and half double crochet. Since it is a higher stitch, you will need to make 2 chains at the end of the previous row instead of 1.) The problem with this method is that the 2 turning chains produce a slight bulge on the side of each row, which some crocheters find unattractive. Since we

Double Crochet

16

edge all our crochet pieces, we don't think the bulge is noticeable and thus prefer this method.

The second method, however, is the more traditional way to begin a double crochet row. Here the turning chain actually becomes the first double crochet of the row. Three chains equal 1 double crochet. Since the chains count as 1 double crochet, you must then skip the first stitch of the previous row and begin working through the second stitch of the previous row. Failure to do so will result in an accidental increase of 1 stitch at the beginning of the row. The disadvantage of this method is that it produces a slightly slanted space between the turning chains and the second stitch of the row. You should try both double crochet methods to see which one appeals to you most. Since you have already become familiar with the first method (see the instructions for beginning the second row of single crochet, page

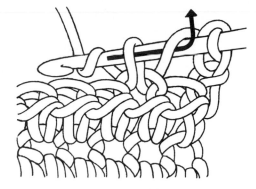

Diagram 32

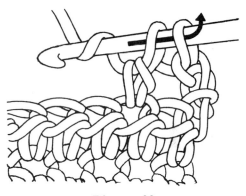

Diagram 33

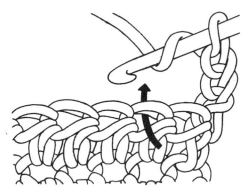

Diagram 30

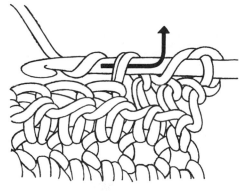

Diagram 31

14), only the second is illustrated on this page.

Start out by chaining 3. This equals your first double crochet. Turn your work. Yarn over and insert your hook into the head of the second stitch of the previous row (Diagram 30). Yarn over again and pull up a loop through the stitch (Diagram 31). There are now 3 loops on your hook. Yarn over and pull a loop through the first 2 loops on your hook (Diagram 32). Now there are 2 loops on your hook. Yarn over again and pull a loop through these 2 loops (Diagram 33). You should now have 1 loop on your hook (Diagram 34), and you have made 1 double crochet. (Note that the head of the double crochet is to the right of its post.) For the next double crochet yarn over, insert your hook into the next stitch of the previous row (see A in Diagram 34), and repeat. Since your turning chain counts as 1

17

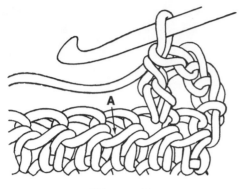

Diagram 34

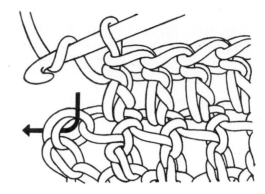

Diagram 35

double crochet, you now have 3 double crochets and need to make 7 more to complete the row. At the end of the row chain 3, turn your work, and do another row of double crochet. Remember that since the last stitch of the previous row is a chain-3, you must make

your last double crochet of the row through the top chain stitch of this turning chain (see the arrow pointing to the top stitch of the turning chain in Diagram 35). Count your stitches to be sure you have 10 double crochets in each row.

Treble Crochet

Now that you have learned how to make the double crochet stitch, you can easily make stitches of any height. The height of the stitch is simply determined by how many times you yarn over *before* you insert the hook through the head of the stitch. You then continue to yarn over and work the loops off your hook in groups of 2.

When you make stitches higher than double crochet, the turning chain *always* counts as the first stitch of the row and you *always* skip the first stitch of the previous row and begin in the second. You have just learned that for double crochet you chain 3 and yarn over once before inserting your hook through the second stitch of the previous row. For each subsequently higher stitch you must yarn over one more time and add 1 more chain stitch to your turning chain. To begin a row of treble crochet, therefore, you will chain 4 and then

yarn over twice before inserting your hook.

Chain 4 and turn your work. Yarn over twice and insert your hook through the second stitch

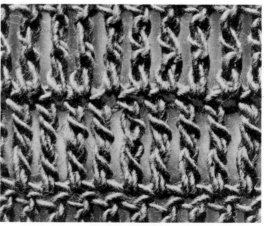

Treble Crochet

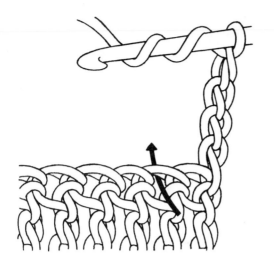

Diagram 36

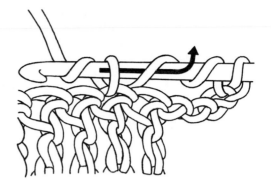

Diagram 38

of the previous row (Diagram 36). Yarn over again and pull a loop through the stitch (Diagram 37). There are now 4 loops on your hook. Yarn over and pull a loop through the first 2 loops on your hook (Diagram 38). There are now 3 loops on your hook. Yarn over and pull a loop through the first 2 loops on your hook (Diagram 39). There are now 2 loops on your hook. Yarn over and pull a loop through the remaining 2 loops on your hook (Diagram 40). You now have 1 loop left on your hook and have made 1 treble crochet (Diagram 41). Since the turning chain counts as 1 treble

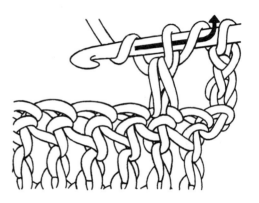

Diagram 39

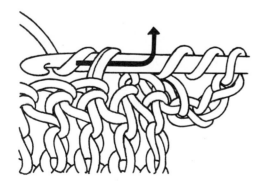

Diagram 37

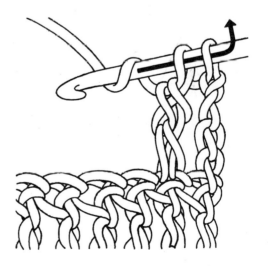

Diagram 40

crochet, you have actually made 2 treble crochets. For the next stitch yarn over twice, insert your hook into the next stitch of the previous row (see A in Diagram 41), and repeat. Complete your row by making 1 treble crochet in each of the next 7 stitches. Chain 4, turn your work, and make another row of treble crochet.

By the way, there is an intermediate step between double crochet and treble crochet called half treble crochet (abbreviated as htr). You will find it in some of the projects here and in other sources. It is done by working a treble crochet until there are 3 loops on your hook. Then yarn over and pull through all 3 loops on the hook.

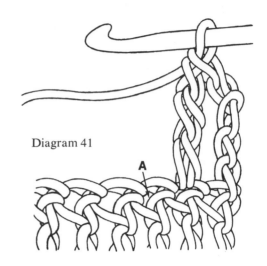

Diagram 41

Basic Stitch Variations

There are two basic ways to change the look of a stitch without really changing the stitch. One has to do with where you insert your hook. Instead of beginning a stitch by inserting your hook under the head (both loops) of the stitch of the previous row, you can pick up either loop A or loop B only (Diagram 22). Simple as this variation is, the loop or loops you use make a marked difference in the texture and appearance of your piece. The two most common basic stitch variations are the *Albanian stitch,* which is made by working rows of single crochet through only loop A of the stitch of the previous row, and the *Ridge stitch,* made by working rows of single crochet through only loop B of the stitch of the previous row. Both variations can be worked in any basic stitch. Practice making a few rows

Albanian Stitch

Ridge Stitch

of Albanian and Ridge stitches and compare them with the 2 rows of single crochet. Note the ribbed effect of the Ridge stitch.

A second way to change the look of a stitch is to change the direction in which it's worked. The Albanian and Ridge stitches look quite different depending on whether they are worked back and forth, as they usually are in rows, or always in the same direction, as they are in rounds. (You can try these variations out when you learn more about rounds on page 27.) If you like the look of a stitch worked always in the same direction but your piece is made in rows, cut your yarn at the end of each row and reattach it on the right end. Keep in mind that stitches worked in the same direction produce a piece with a front and back side; stitches worked back and forth do not.

Slip Stitch

Half double, double, and treble crochet are higher and higher variations of the basic stitch, the single crochet. Now you will end your practice piece with the lowest variation, the slip stitch. It is rarely worked in rows but is a valuable tool in crocheting.

Chain 1 and turn your work. Insert your hook into the first stitch of the previous row. Yarn over and pull a loop through both the stitch *and the loop on your hook*. You have made 1 slip stitch and there is 1 loop on your hook. Make 1 slip stitch in each of the remaining stitches. (Diagram 42 shows the middle of a row of slip stitches.)

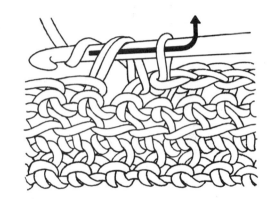

Diagram 42

Ending Off

To end your practice piece, complete the last stitch, and keeping the final loop on the hook, cut the yarn, leaving a tail of 3 to 4 inches. Yarn over with the tail and pull it through the loop on your hook (Diagram 43). Hold onto the crochet piece and pull on the tail to tighten the ending.

You will find that some yarns are too slippery or too stiff to stay closed with this ending. In that case, try making an extra chain after the last stitch is completed and then pull the tail through that chain. If there is another tail nearby, you can knot the tails as close to the ending as possible.

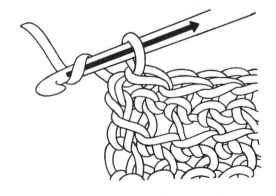

Diagram 43

Unfortunately, there are yarns, notably rayon ribbon, for which even these methods are inadequate. As a last resort end the piece in the manner described above, then using a sharp needle and matching thread, tack the ending to the side or back of the last stitch.

There are a few more skills to learn before starting on an actual project. Since your practice piece is too limited to help further, we will no longer provide directions for it. Do keep yarn and hook nearby, though, so you can learn skills as you read.

Attaching Yarn

Often in crochet work you will have to end off your piece and attach a new piece of yarn in a different place. This is done for example when you are edging a piece. We use two slightly different methods to attach yarn. The first— chaining on—seems best to us because it is easy to rip out and it doesn't require making any knots. However, the same yarns that require extra-secure ending techniques also need something extra when they are attached, and for those yarns the second method—tieing on —is better.

Chaining On

Make a loop in the new yarn about 3 inches from the end and hold the loop behind the stitch of the previous row in which you wish to attach the new yarn (*the attaching stitch*). Insert the hook in the attaching stitch from the

front to back. Pick up the loop and pull it through. Holding the tail of the new yarn and the long end of the new yarn together, yarn over and pull them both through the loop on the hook (Diagram 44). This attachment counts as 1 chain stitch. Drop the tail and continue to chain until you have made the correct number of chain stitches (including the attachment) to count as your first stitch.

Tieing On

Insert the hook through the attaching stitch from front to back and pull the new yarn all the way through. Tie the yarn onto the attaching stitch, leaving a 3-inch tail. Insert the hook

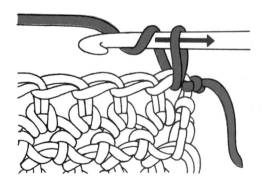

Diagram 45

through the attaching stitch again, yarn over with the long end of the new yarn, and pull up a loop (Diagram 45). Chain as many as needed to count as the first stitch.

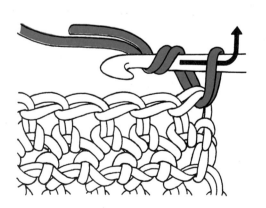

Diagram 44

Changing Yarn

For many of the projects in this book and in other sources you will need to end 1 yarn and begin another in the very next stitch or end 1 row, chain and turn, and begin a new row with a new yarn. Although you could do each task separately—end off and then attach—we think it's easier and neater to combine the two tasks. The method for changing yarn in the middle of a row is different from the method of changing yarn at the end of a row.

Changing in the Middle

Work the final stitch of the old yarn until there are 2 loops left on your hook. Drop the old yarn, yarn over with the new yarn, and pull a loop of new yarn through the 2 loops of old yarn on your hook, leaving a 3- to 4-inch tail of new yarn (Diagram 46). Give the old yarn a

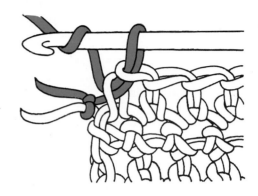

Diagram 47

tug to tighten the stitch, then cut it off, leaving a 3- to 4-inch tail. You now have a loop of the new yarn on your hook and are ready to proceed. (If the yarn is slippery, it's best to tie the tails together.)

Changing at the End

Work the last stitch of the row until there are 2 loops left on your hook. Drop the old yarn and complete the stitch with the new yarn as you did in the preceding method. Give the old yarn a tug and cut it off, leaving a 3- to 4-inch tail. With a loop of the new yarn still on the hook, tie the tails together as close to the side of your piece as possible (Diagram 47). You are now ready to chain up and continue with the new yarn.

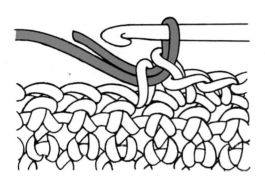

Diagram 46

Hiding Yarn Tails

Once you've finished crocheting a piece, one of the first things you'll want to do is cut off the yarn tails. But cutting off the tails is a dangerous practice. If the ending knot or attaching loop should slip even a little, your crocheting could begin to unravel in the middle. Even if the piece holds together, knots with short or no tails stick out from the work

and leave bumps. On the other hand, however, nobody wants long, ugly tails left on their work. The solution is to leave a tail of at least 3 to 4 inches and learn to hide it.

Although both of the following methods for hiding yarn tails are simple and effective, the first is more efficient. The yarn tails get hidden as you crochet.

Crocheting over Tails

This technique works best when the front of your piece is facing you. If it happens that you change yarns when the back is facing you, wait until the next row to hide the tails. The directions given are for single crochet but apply to any *solid stitch*—this is, any stitch or pattern of stitches that does not form a lacy, open-work design.

Change from the old yarn to the new yarn. You will have 2 yarn tails hanging from the work and a loop of the new yarn on your hook. Place the 2 tails together on the back of the work, directly behind the heads of the stitches about to be worked on, and position your hands to crochet. The third finger and thumb of your left hand will hold the yarn in place while holding the crochet piece.

Insert the hook into the first stitch so that the yarn tails are above the hook. Yarn over and pull a loop through. The yarn tails are now cradled between the loop on the hook and the rest of the new yarn (Diagram 48). Yarn over and close the stitch over the tails. Continue in the same way until all of the tails are covered.

Weaving Tails In

There will be times when you simply won't be able to crochet over the tails; perhaps the piece is complete, or you are using an *open-work stitch*. In these cases you can use the more traditional way of hiding yarn ends. When you use this method, weave in your ends as you go along; don't wait until your project is completed. You will have a much better sense of how your work looks without random pieces of yarn hanging from it, and you won't face the disagreeable job of weaving in seemingly hundreds of tails at the very moment when you should be able to sit back and enjoy your completed product.

Use either a blunt tapestry needle or a small crochet hook to weave in the yarn tails. If you use a crochet hook, though, be sure to use one that is smaller than the hook used to make the piece.

With a blunt yarn needle: End the yarn and thread the tail into the needle. With the back of the piece facing you, draw the needle through the back vertical loops of successive stitches. Do not pierce the strands themselves (see Diagram 49). Repeat with the other tail if there is one.

With a small crochet hook: End the yarn. With the back of the piece facing you, insert a small crochet hook through the back vertical loop of the stitch nearest to the tail, yarn over with the tail end, and pull the tail through the loop. Continue this process until the tail is completely hidden. If there is a second tail, repeat the procedure.

Diagram 48

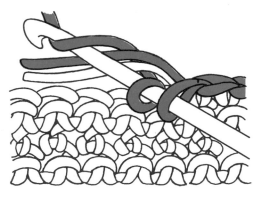

Diagram 49

Edging Piece

Crocheting a row of single crochet around the outside of a piece gives it a smooth, uniform appearance. We make it a habit to edge our pieces. Almost every piece of crochet should be edged; not only will your work look better, but also joining pieces of crochet to each other is simplified when there are distinct, countable stitches on the outside edges of each piece.

Most edging is done with single crochet stitches alone, but variations such as picots and bumps (see pages 50 and 46) can sometimes be effective. Decorative borders, however, are usually added after the basic edging round is put on.

Work with the piece facing you. Attach the yarn in the side of the stitch at the top left-hand corner and crochet down the left side. It is hard to be precise about working down the sides of a piece. In general, make 1 single crochet in the side of each single crochet or half double crochet row and 2 single crochets in the side of each double crochet row to edge a piece evenly. To edge treble crochet, you will need to make roughly 3 single crochets in the side of each row. (When you are edging the sides of double crochet rows or higher stitches, take care to insert your hook *into* the post of the stitch closest to the edge rather than working the edging stitch *over* the post. The latter would pull the entire stitch toward the edge, leaving a rather obvious hole. Since each double crochet stitch consists of several strands of yarn, your hook can slide easily between these strands.) Remember that too many edging stitches will cause a piece to ruffle; too few will make it cup or gather. Since it is often difficult to space stitches precisely in the side, it is best to edge a piece first with its own color. Then if you wish, you can edge the piece a second time with a new color and the stitches of the new color will look even.

As a general rule, after you have edged the left side, make 3 single crochets in the corner stitch and crochet across the bottom, making 1 single crochet in every stitch. (Remember that when you made the first row of your piece you picked up 1 or 2 strands of the foundation chain. The remaining strands of the chain then became the bottommost edge of the piece. It is not a good idea to use these leftover strands for making edging stitches since they tend to be loose and to pull away from the piece. Instead, work over the entire foundation chain and into the bottom of Row 1.) When you come to the corner, make 3 single crochets, crochet up the right side, make 3 single crochets in the corner, and crochet across the top. After you have made 3 single crochets in the top left-hand corner, insert your hook in the first stitch you made and pull a loop through both the stitch and the loop on your hook. Cut your yarn and end off. (In many instances it will not be necessary to make 3 single crochets in the corner. If your corner is not as sharp as a right angle, you can work 2 single crochets instead of 3. On subsequent rounds, make your 2 single crochet increase group in the second stitch of the increase group of the previous round.)

Do subsequent rounds of edging in the same manner. When you come to the corners, however, make 3 stitches in the center stitch of the 3-stitch group of the previous round. (Refer to the arrow in Diagram 50.) Remember that the head of the center stitch is to the right of the post.

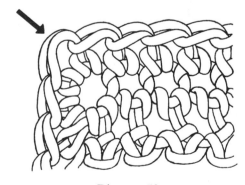

Diagram 50

Increasing and Decreasing

The best and easiest way to shape a piece of crochet is by increasing or decreasing the number of stitches in a row. When you decrease, the work becomes narrower; when you increase, it widens. Increasing and decreasing can be done at the beginning, in the middle, or at the end of a row, but when they are done at either end, the effect is more pronounced. If you are going to add or eliminate more than 2 stitches, try to space the changes evenly across the row as you crochet.

Increasing

Increasing is quite simple: To make 1 increase, just make 2 stitches in 1 stitch of the previous row. This works for all basic stitches; pattern stitches, though, require special handling (see page 40).

Sometimes, particularly when you turn corners, you will want to increase 2 stitches at once. Rather than making 2 regular increases you would then make a 3-stitch increase; that is, you would make 3 stitches in 1 stitch of the previous row.

Decreasing

You can decrease in two ways. Both methods can be used for single crochet; the second can be used for both single crochet and the higher stitches.

Method 1: The first method might be called *Skip-A-Stitch,* and it is exactly that. To de-

Diagram 51

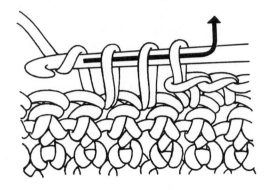

Diagram 52

crease 1 stitch, just skip a stitch and do a single crochet in the next stitch (Diagram 51). This method is the easiest. However, it leaves a small hole in the fabric which may or may not be noticeable, depending on the yarn you are using and the size of the stitches. For this reason we usually prefer to use the next method.

Method 2: Here you will combine 2 stitches into 1. Insert your hook into the stitch, yarn over, and pull a loop through. There are now 2 loops on your hook. Instead of yarning over to complete the stitch, insert the hook into the next stitch, yarn over, and draw the yarn through. There are now 3 loops on the hook. Yarn over and pull through all 3 loops (Diagram 52). The 2 stitches have become 1. A 3-stitch decrease works in the same way. Draw up a loop in each of 3 stitches, yarn over, and close them all together. You have combined 3 stitches into 1—a loss of 2 stitches.

The principle of combining 2 stitches into 1 can also be used to decrease higher stitches. Work your first stitch until there are 2 loops left on the hook. Now instead of completing the stitch, yarn over to begin the next stitch. Work the new stitch until there are 3 loops left on the hook. Then yarn over and pull a loop through all 3 loops. You now have 1 loop on your hook and have combined 2 stitches into 1 or, in other words, decreased 1 stitch.

Working in Rounds

Sometimes instead of working back and forth in rows, you will work around and around in the same direction. A variety of shapes—circles, hexagons, tubes, and others—are made by working in rounds. These shapes will be taught in Chapter 4. Here we'll teach you how to start the round and how to move from one round to the next.

Starting Out

Begin by making a foundation chain of 5 to 10 stitches. Actually, the number of chains to make depends on how small a circle you want in the center and how many stitches you will want on Round 1. Next, insert the hook through the head of the *first* chain stitch you made, yarn over, and pull a loop through the first chain and the chain on your hook (Diagram 53). This is called joining with a slip stitch. Then, if you are working in single crochet, chain 1 (chain more for higher stitches). You are now ready to work the first round of stitches. Don't try to work the stitches into the chains—it's too difficult, and in any event you'll need to make more stitches than you have chains. Instead, make your stitches over the chain and into the ring itself (Diagram 54). Work 8 to 12 single crochets into your ring so that the ring is just covered all around with

stitches. (If you have chained 2 or more stitches at the beginning, count that chain-2 as the first stitch of the round.)

Starting Round 2

The way you complete Round 1 and begin Round 2 depends on whether you are going to *join* your rounds or *spiral* them. It is much easier to make patterns and to increase evenly on joined rounds. Unfortunately, joined rounds always have a slight seam visible in the place where one round ends and another begins. You can minimize this seam, but you can't eliminate it. So when it's not necessary to keep close count of where you are, spiral.

To join rounds: After you have completed the final stitch of Round 1, insert your hook into the first stitch of Round 1, yarn over, and pull a loop through that stitch and the loop on your hook (Diagram 55). You have closed the round with a slip stitch. For single crochet, chain 1 and make your first stitch of Round 2

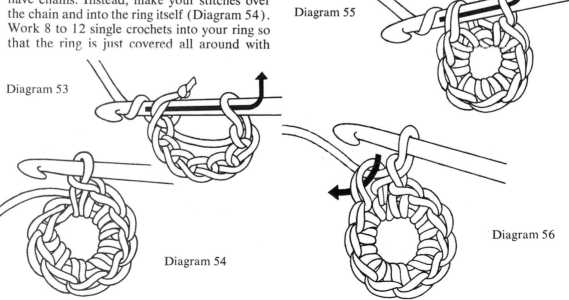

Diagram 53

Diagram 54

Diagram 55

Diagram 56

into the first stitch of Round 1—that is, into the same stitch in which you made the slip stitch (Diagram 56). On subsequent rounds make sure you don't make a stitch in the joining slip stitch or the chain-1 of the previous round. (In Diagram 57, point A is the slip stitch of the previous round, point B-B is the chain-1 made at the beginning of the round, and point C-C is the first stitch of the round.)

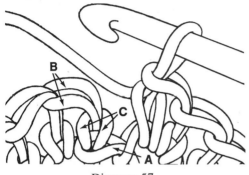

Diagram 57

For double crochet and the higher stitches, chain the necessary number. Remember to count the chain group as 1 stitch. When you come back around, you will join the round into the top chain of the chain group.

To change yarns in joined rounds, work the last stitch of a round until there are 2 loops on your hook. Complete the stitch with the new yarn, tug on the old yarn, and drop it. Join and chain up with the new yarn.

To spiral rounds: After you have made the final stitch of Round 1, simply make a stitch

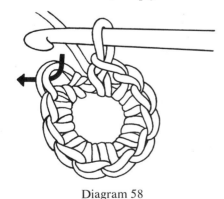

Diagram 58

in the first stitch of Round 1 (Diagram 58). The first time you do this, you will need to pull a bit to reach the stitch comfortably, but then the division between rounds disappears, and you can go around and around. This can be a problem. It's so easy to lose track of where the rows begin and end that it is difficult to increase correctly. To help you keep track of where you are, put a piece of yarn or a safety pin in the first stitch of the first round.

To end a spiraled piece find the stitch of the round you're working that's directly over the stitch with the marker. When you reach that stitch, slip-stitch into it and break the yarn. If you are working in a high stitch, make lower and lower stitches (single crochets and slip stitches) as you approach the joining stitch, then slip-stitch into that.

To change yarns complete the stitch directly before the joining stitch with the new color, and with the new color, slip-stitch into the joining stitch, chain 1, and begin as you would for a joined round.

Chaining for a Larger Center

In some instances, you'll want to start with a larger center. Start by chaining the number of stitches you'll need. Remember that chains have no give; if the opening must fit over something, so must the chain. Since it's crucial that the chain not be twisted when you join one end to the other, we feel it's easier to work the first round as a row. When your chain is complete, go into the appropriate chain for the stitch you are making and make a stitch in every chain. You will now be able to see clearly whether the piece is twisted or not before you join it.

Straighten your piece and bring the 2 ends together. Insert your hook into the first stitch and the loop on your hook. You have joined the piece with a slip stitch and are ready to chain up and begin the second round.

Joining Pieces

Few crochet projects are made in one piece. Usually pieces are made separately and then joined. The techniques you'll learn in this section are appropriate for joining any solid pieces of crochet.

Edge-to-Edge Joining

Whether you eventually sew, slip-stitch, or single crochet the pieces together, all edge-to-edge joining begins in the same way.

First edge each piece. These edging stitches will be joined together. How obvious should your seam be? Traditionally seams are made on the back of the work. But since all edge-to-edge joinings are visible to some extent, it is often desirable to make the seam an integral part of the overall design by joining your pieces on the front side.

Hold or pin the pieces one on top of the other so that either the two fronts or the two backs are both facing out. The seam will be most visible on the sides that face out at this point.

Look at the edges being joined in Diagram 59. The two fronts of the pieces are facing out; the seam will be on the front. The heads of the edging stitches are lined up side by side in opposing pairs.

Joining is done through each pair of opposing stitches. Each pair has 4 loops—2 from each stitch—that are available for joining. Joining through all 4 loops produces the strongest seam. However, we prefer the look of joining through the 2 center loops as shown in Diagram 59, particularly for joining on the front side. Use the 2 outside loops where you want your pieces to lie at an angle to each other; in this case, the sides that face out while the joining is done will face in when it is complete.

You must have the same number of edging stitches on each piece. If the pieces are supposed to be identical but one somehow has more edging stitches than the other, you can correct this as you go along. Every so often,

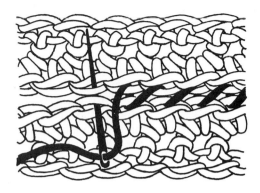

Diagram 59

after you have made a stitch through a pair of opposing stitches, go back through the *same* stitch of the shorter piece and the next stitch of the longer piece and then make a stitch. It is a good idea to figure out ahead of time how many times you will need to do this; then space your corrections evenly across the joining.

You can either sew or crochet your pieces together.

To sew pieces together: Thread a blunt yarn needle, insert it through 1 or both loops of the first opposing pair of stitches, and tie a knot. Continue to insert the needle through the same loops of each subsequent pair of stitches, always inserting it in the same direction, either back to front or front to back (Diagram 59). Try not to pierce the yarn. When you reach the end of the joining, make several stitches in the same place, then knot and break the yarn.

To slip-stitch pieces together: With your crochet hook and yarn, pull a loop all the way through the first pair of stitches and tie a knot. Insert the hook through both stitches, yarn over, and pull up a loop. Yarn over above the work and pull a loop through the loop on your hook. This attaches the joining yarn to the pieces.

Insert your hook through the next pair of stitches, yarn over, and pull the loop through both stitches and the loop on your hook. You have made 1 slip stitch. Continue across the edges. If the pieces start to buckle, you are making your stitches too tight. End off as you would any crocheting and tie a knot in the tail. (The knot should be as close to the piece as possible.)

To single crochet pieces together: Attach the yarn just as you did for the slip stitch method. You should have a loop on your hook and be ready to join the second pair of stitches.

Insert the hook through both stitches of the next pair, yarn over, and pull a loop through. There are now 2 loops on your hook. Yarn over and pull a loop through these 2 loops. You have made 1 single crochet joining stitch. Continue in the same way. Single crochet joining makes a ridge on the work and is most useful for joining that will show on the front.

Overlap Joining

On occasion you will want to hide one of the edges to be joined, or perhaps you will not want the definitive boundary that is inevitable with edge-to-edge joining. In such situations overlap joining is a useful method. We used overlap joining in the Peacock's Eye Pillow (page 128) because edging each motif would have required changing the color of the yarn every few stitches.

Edge the piece that is to go on top. It is not necessary to edge the bottom piece. However, the bottom piece must extend under the top piece for at least 1 row. If you don't want to hide 1 row of the bottom piece, edge it and hide the edging row.

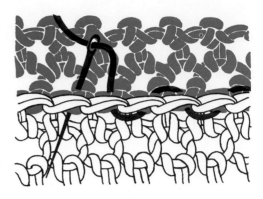

Diagram 60

Hold or pin the two pieces together so that they lie flat, fronts facing up, with the edge of the top piece slightly overlapping the bottom piece. Thread a blunt needle with the same color yarn that you used to edge the top piece. Bring the needle up through the bottom piece and in between the first 2 stitches of the edging on the top piece. Bring it over the post of the second stitch and pass it back out between the second and third stitches (Diagram 60). On the next stitch the needle should come up through the bottom pieces and out between the third and fourth stitches, across the fourth stitch, and back out between the fourth and fifth stitches. Continue across the piece, turn, and work back in the opposite direction. This time the stitches should be brought across the front of the odd-numbered, rather than the even-numbered stitches. Work back to the beginning, ending on the back of the work. Cut the yarn and knot the tail close to the piece.

Reading Crochet Directions

When you made the practice piece at the beginning of this chapter, we explained what to do in complete sentences. If we were to continue to write the directions for this book in sentences, we would have room for very few projects. Moreover, as you became more comfortable with crochet, you would find such detailed explanations both unnecessary and annoying. Standardized crochet abbreviations save both time and space.

All crochet directions follow a similar format and use the same abbreviations. But it's often hard to agree about the clearest way to

explain something, and you can expect to find variations in style and format as you go from one crochet publication to another.

Let's see how some instructions would look if written in abbreviated form. Under each line of crochet directions we'll give you a "translation" of the line and explain how to read the format. (Refer to the box on this page for a list of abbreviations and their meanings.) If directions for your practice piece had been written in abbreviated form, the foundation chain directions would have looked like this:

Foundation chain: Ch 11.
Translation: Make a slip knot, then make 11 chain stitches.

You are never told to make a slip knot, but it is assumed that you will do so. The foundation chain does not count as a row; the stitches you will be making into the chain will be your first row.

Row 1: 1 sc in 2nd ch from hk, *1 sc in next ch. Repeat from *, ending with 1 sc in last ch. Ch 1, turn [10 sts].
Translation: Make 1 single crochet in the second chain stitch from the hook. Make 1 single crochet in each chain stitch until you have made 1 single crochet in the last chain stitch. Chain 1 (your turning chain) and turn your piece. This row should have 10 single crochet stitches in it.

Each line of directions has several parts; don't try to understand and absorb the entire line at one time. Let's divide the line into its parts, then look at each part separately.

1 sc in 2nd ch from hk: The directions that come *before* the asterisk (*) tell you how to make the first stitch (or stitch pattern) of the row and in what stitch of the previous row to make it. The first stitch (or stitch pattern) is set off from the rest of the row, even if it is the same as the rest of the row.

***1 sc in next ch. Repeat from *:** The directions *after* the asterisk give you the stitch (or stitch pattern) that is to be repeated across the row. That is, you are to repeat the directions that

Crochet Abbreviations

beg . . . . beginning
ch . . . . chain
dc . . . . double crochet
dec . . . . decrease
dtr . . . . double treble crochet
hdc . . . . half double crochet
hk . . . . hook
inc . . . . increase
lp . . . . loop
pat . . . . pattern
rnd . . . . round
sc . . . . single crochet
slst . . . . slip stitch
sp . . . . space
st . . . . stitch
thru . . . . through
tog . . . . together
tr . . . . treble crochet
yo . . . . yarn over
* . . . . . repeat the instructions following
        the asterisk to the end of the row
( ) . . . repeat the instructions in parentheses the number of times specified following the parentheses
[ ] . . . . brackets are used to give information
= . . . . equals
. . .. . . repeat pattern from ** to **

31

follow the asterisk over and over until you reach the final stitch or stitches of the row.

Ending with 1 sc in last ch: Usually you will be given separate directions for the final stitch (or stitch pattern) of the row, even if it is the same as the rest of the row.

Ch 1, turn: The directions for going from one row to the next may come either at the end of the row you have just completed or at the beginning of the new row.

[10 sts]: Brackets are used to give you descriptive information. Here the information in brackets helps you check your work by telling you how many stitches (or stitch patterns) you should have at the end of a row. Bracketed information is usually given only once or twice, then is not repeated as long as it remains constant. If the number of stitches in each row were to change as a result of increasing or decreasing, then the new number would be given in brackets at the end of the row in which the increasing or decreasing occurred.

Notice that you were not told how to make a single crochet. It is assumed in crochet directions that readers can make all the basic stitches. These stitches are taught only in stitch glossaries. The rows of the practice piece are quite simple—only 1 kind of stitch is made in each row. A row of crochet is often made up of several stitches put together to form a pattern. The pattern may be repeated across the row, or it may be combined with other stitches or patterns of stitches into a more complex pattern. Here is Row 2 from a panel of the Hammock and Two Pillows (page 56):

Row 2: 1 sc in 1st st, *ch 1, skip 1 st, 1 sc in next st. Repeat from *, ending with ch 1, skip next-to-last st, 1 sc in last st. Ch 1, turn.

Translation: Make 1 single crochet in the first stitch. Chain 1, skip the next stitch, and make 1 single crochet in the next stitch. Chain 1 again, skip the next stitch, and make 1 single crochet in the next stitch, Repeat this pattern until you reach the last 2 stitches of the row. Chain 1, skip the next-to-last stitch, and make 1 single crochet in the last stitch. Chain 1 and turn your piece.

As long as there is only one pattern per row, the row is no more complicated than those in the practice piece. However, if after every 3 chain-1 patterns you were to make 1 Hazelnut stitch (the Hazelnut stitch is taught on page 45) and then 1 single crochet, the directions would look like this:

Row 2: 1 Hazelnut in 1st st, *(ch 1, skip 1 st, 1 sc in next st) 3 times, 1 Hazelnut in next st, 1 sc in next st. Repeat from *, ending with 1 Hazelnut in next-to-last st, 1 sc in last st. Ch 2, turn.

Translation: Make 1 Hazelnut stitch in the first stitch. Chain 1, skip 1 stitch, and make 1 single crochet in the next stitch. Chain 1 again, skip 1 stitch, and make 1 single crochet in the next stitch. Chain 1 again, skip 1 stitch, and make 1 single crochet in the next stitch. Make 1 Hazelnut in the next stitch. Make 1 single crochet in the next stitch. Now you are ready to repeat the entire pattern again, beginning with the first chain-1. Continue to repeat the entire pattern across the row. The final pattern should end with 1 Hazelnut in the next-to-last stitch and 1 single crochet in the last stitch. Chain 2 and turn your piece.

Parentheses are used to set off the part of the pattern that is to be repeated. Directly after the closing parenthesis you will be told how many times to repeat the pattern. In this case it was 3 times. Parentheses are also used to group stitches all made in the same stitch of the previous row:

Row X: Ch 3 [= 1 dc], skip 1st st, *(1 dc, ch 1, 1 dc) in next st, skip 2 sts. Repeat from *, ending with (1 dc, ch 1, 1 dc) in next st, skip 1 st, 1 dc in last st.

Translation: Chain 3; this equals 1 double crochet. Skip the first stitch. Make 1 double crochet in the next stitch, chain 1, then make 1 more double crochet in the same stitch. Skip 2 stitches. Repeat the pattern, beginning with 1 double crochet, chain 1, and 1 more double crochet all in the same stitch. Continue to repeat the pattern until there are 3 stitches left. Make 1 double crochet, chain 1, and make 1 more double crochet in the same stitch. Skip the next-to-last stitch, and make 1 double crochet in the last stitch.

Here the brackets are used to explain that the 3 chains are not only turning chains, but are also the first double crochet of the next row. Sometimes after a short pattern has been given stitch by stitch, it will be named in brackets. From then on in that project, when that pattern is used, you will not be given stitch-by-stitch directions for it but just its name. For instance, the row we just gave you might have looked like this:

Row X: Ch 3 [= 1 dc], skip 1st st, *(1 dc, ch 1, 1 dc) in next st [1 V-st formed], skip 2 sts. Repeat from *, ending with 1 V-st, skip 1 st, 1 dc in last st.

Translation: Of course, the translation of this is identical to the first one given for Row X.

The patterns discussed thus far are repeated across the entire row or round. Sometimes repeated patterns are interrupted by other patterns that are *not* repeated. In such situations a single * doesn't work. For example, the first row of edging for the Filet Curtain (page 106) is worked down one side of the curtain, then a corner is made, then a slightly different pattern is worked across the bottom of the curtain, then there is another corner, and finally the side pattern is repeated. Double asterisks are put at both ends of the repeated pattern:

Row 1: Ch 2 [= 1 sc], 1 sc in side of 1st dc in upper left-hand corner, **2 sc in side of next dc. Repeat from ** to ** until corner. 4 sc in corner. 1 sc in each ch-1 sp of 1st row, 4 sc in next corner. Repeat from ** to **, ending with 2 sc in side of last dc in upper right-hand corner. Ch 1, turn. [Do not work across top of panel.]**

Translation: Chain 2; this equals 1 single crochet. Make 1 single crochet in the first stitch. Make 2 single crochets in the side of the next double crochet. Continue to make 2 single crochets in the side of each double crochet until you reach the corner. Make 4 single crochets in the corner. Make 1 single crochet in each chain-1 space of the first row until you reach the next corner. Make 4 single crochets in that corner. Now you can repeat the pattern within the double asterisks on the other side of the curtain: Make 2 single crochets in the side of each double crochet until you reach the top right-hand corner. Chain 1 and turn your piece. Don't work across the top of the curtain.

Once in a great while directions are so complex that brackets have to be used to set off repeated patterns that include *other* repeated patterns:

Round 1: 1 sc in 1st st, *[(ch 3, skip 2 sts, 1 sc in next st) 3 times, 1 Hazelnut in next st, 1 sc in next st] 2 times, skip 2 sts, 5 dc in next st [1 Shell formed], skip 2 sts, 1 sc in next st. Repeat from *, ending with 1 Shell, skip 2 sts, join to 1st sc with slst. Ch 1.

Translation: Make 1 single crochet in the first stitch. Chain 3, skip 2 stitches, and make 1 single crochet in the next stitch. Chain 3 again, skip 2 stitches, and make 1 single crochet in the next stitch. Once again, chain 3, skip 2 stitches, and make 1 single crochet in the next stitch. Make 1 Hazelnut stitch in the next stitch and 1 single crochet in the stitch after that.

Now return to the beginning and repeat the pattern, beginning with the first chain-3. After you have made this pattern for the second time, skip 2 stitches and make 5 double crochets in the next stitch. These 5 double crochets make 1 Shell stitch. Skip 2 more stitches and make 1 single crochet in the next stitch.

You have now made 1 complete pattern. Return to the beginning and repeat the entire pattern, starting with the first chain-3. Continue to repeat the entire pattern until you reach the end of the round. To end the round make 1 Shell stitch, skip 2 stitches, and join to the first single crochet with a slip stitch. Chain 1.

When you read a complicated pattern, don't try to understand the entire pattern right away. Look at only one part at a time, complete that part, then go on to the next part. You might find it helpful to cover the directions with a blank piece of paper, then uncover one line at a time so that only the line you are working is exposed.

Remember too that crochet directions are written to be worked and are much more difficult to understand when simply being read than they are when you are actually making a piece. If you try to understand directions out of context, you may very easily be confused by something that would be quite obvious if you had made the piece up to that point, following the directions as you worked.

Gauge and Finished Size

The yarn you select, the hook you use, and the tension you maintain on the yarn as you crochet will each affect the size of the stitches you make. The size of the stitches, or the *gauge,* in turn determines the size of your finished piece. Gauge is described by two measurements: The number of stitches per inch in a row indicates the width of the stitches, and the number of rows per inch indicates the height.

Before you begin a project, it's a good idea to make a sample piece in the same stitch that is used in the project and compare your gauge to the gauge given in the directions. Be sure you use the same hook and yarn that you will use to make the project. If your gauge is different, it doesn't mean that you are doing something wrong. It does mean, however, that your finished piece will not be the same size as that given for the project. The stiffness of the fabric will be affected as well.

If you have *more* stitches or rows per inch than the number given in the directions, your gauge is tighter than ours, and your piece will be proportionately stiffer and smaller. If you have *fewer* stitches or rows per inch, your gauge is looser than ours, and your piece will be proportionately softer and larger.

As long as you are aware of these differences and don't mind them, there is no particular reason to match your gauge to ours. Should you want to adjust your gauge to ours, however, the easiest way to do so is to change the size of the hook you use. A smaller hook will produce a tighter gauge; a larger hook will produce a looser gauge.

Gauge is determined to a remarkable degree by the amount of tension you maintain in the uncrocheted yarn as you work. If your left hand holds yarn tightly, producing a lot of tension, each time you pull up a loop with your hook, the tension will pull the hook back toward the piece. The loops you pull up will be short, and your stitches will be made close to the piece, creating a tight gauge. Less tension will allow you to pull up longer loops and to complete your stitches well above the piece; big stitches—a loose gauge—will result.

There is no "correct" amount of tension that should be maintained by every crocheter in every project. Consistency within a project is much more important. However, you will have much more freedom to create projects that look the way you want them to if you can adjust your tension to suit the piece. With practice, you can learn to control the tension as you work, just as you control the other factors that produce gauge, the hook and yarn.

Yarn Substitution and Selection

We have listed the brand name of the yarn we used for most of our projects so that we could provide exact amounts and colors. We have also usually suggested a broad category of yarn that can be substituted for the brand specified. These categories, such as bulky and sport yarn, are at best general descriptions, and substitutions within a category will not be identical. Your yarn may be thicker or thinner, stiffer or softer, smoother or rougher, than the yarn we used, producing a different gauge. Yardage per skein varies from yarn to yarn, so you may need more or fewer skeins to make the project than we used.

None of this, however, should deter you from using any yarn you like to make any project. Consider our choices only suggestions. There are so many beautiful yarns available that yarn-hunting can be one of the most exciting parts of making a project. Find one that you like and adjust the project accordingly (if your motifs are smaller than ours, for example, you can always crochet a few more motifs).

Don't limit yourself to only a few kinds of yarn. Fabrics for the home lend themselves particularly well to yarn traditionally reserved for weaving and needlepoint, so get to know nearby shops that specialize in such yarn. Your local hardware store is a good source of twine, jute, sisal, and wire. The yarn companies listed on page 204 will provide lists of outlets for their yarns, and many will deal directly with retail customers.

Invest the same careful thought in yarn se-lection that you would in any important pur-chase for your home. There is no substitute for good-quality yarn, and no amount of work can compensate for poor yarn. Yarn of high qual-ity, whether acrylic or natural fiber, is strong, good-textured, and durable, with vibrant, com-plex colors reminiscent of nature. Poor-quality yarn splits, breaks, has one-dimensional color and an unpleasant texture. Good yarn may cost more, but the increased beauty and dur-ability of your finished project will be more than worth the difference.

Blocking

Blocking gives uniform shape to your cro-cheted piece, corrects mistakes, and can ex-pand or contract the size. We usually block on an ironing board; however, any flat surface, such as a table or piece of wood, can be cov-ered with toweling and then an old sheet se-cured with some string and utilized as a blocking board. Circular crocheted pieces should be blocked from the center out, and if possible, on the surface they will cover.

Pin your piece to the blocking board so that the measurements are correct and the sides are straight. We use either stainless steel T-pins or plastic-tipped straight pins available in any hardware store. Dampen a thin cloth and lay it on top of the piece. Set your iron to a medium-hot temperature and lightly press over the dampened cloth. Be careful not to allow the iron to sit on any one spot. It should barely touch the cloth. If your piece has textured stitches, such as Hazelnut or Popcorn stitches, do not place the iron directly on these stitches or they will be permanently flattened. Remove the dampened cloth and allow the piece to dry completely before unpinning it from the block-ing board.

Fringes and tassels can be blocked in the same way; however, after blocking, run your fingers through the strands while they are still damp to straighten and separate them.

Washing and Cleaning Instructions

Read the label of each yarn for specific instruc-tions. Most cottons, wools, and acrylics can be washed by hand and some can be washed by machine; do not wash jute. There are several good cold water detergents on the market. Cold or lukewarm water will inhibit shrinkage. Do not use bleach, strong soap, or detergent. Be sure you rinse thoroughly and squeeze out all excess water. (Do *not* twist—this can cause misshaping.) Place the piece on an ironing board or any surface where it can be shaped to its correct measurements and pin in place. Let the piece dry thoroughly before unpinning. Never hang a crocheted piece to dry. If the project needs ironing, follow the directions for blocking (above).

If you decide to dry-clean the project, try to locate an establishment that specializes in knit-ted fabrics. Give the dimensions so that it can be blocked correctly.

Special Skills

As you crochet you'll need to learn a few related skills. By applying these simple techniques you'll give your work a more complete, professional look.

Lining

You may line a project to prevent stretching, or you may want to hide the crossed strands and unsightly knotting that some crochet techniques, such as Tapestry stitch, produce.

Cut the piece of lining fabric slightly larger than your crocheted piece (approximately ⅛ inch on all sides). Fold each edge of the lining ¼ inch to the back and pin it in place. (If your lining is curved, mark the curve on the lining fabric ¼ inch in from the edge. Then at 1-inch intervals cut a ¼-inch vertical slit from the edge to the marked line. Fold each section in ¼ inch and pin in place.) After pinning the edges down, baste the edges just above the pins with ½-inch-long basting stitches. These basting stitches will hold the folded edges in place until you are ready to attach the lining to the crocheted piece.

Place the back sides of the lining and crocheted piece together so that the front sides face out. The crocheted piece should extend slightly beyond the lining on all sides. Blind-stitch the lining to the piece (see page 38).

Muslin Casings and Stuffing for Pillows

Although pre-made pillow forms, both stuffed muslin and shaped foam, are available in many stores, they come in only a few standard sizes. If you can't find one to suit your needs, you will have to make the pillow form yourself—an easy task. We use unbleached muslin and polyester filling. There are other fillers available, but polyester combines ease and durability for the least amount of money.

All of the pillows in this book are knife-edged. The finished size at the beginning of each pillow project refers to the size of the crocheted piece. Your muslin casing should be 1 inch longer and wider than the crocheted piece to ensure a tight-fitting pillow. Add 1 inch to the length and width of the crocheted pillow. Fold the muslin so that you have two thicknesses, one on top of the other. Mark the muslin casing dimensions on the double thickness of muslin. If your crocheted pillow is 18 by 20 inches, the dimensions for each thickness of the muslin should be 19 by 21 inches. Cut out the pieces of muslin. Sew the muslin pieces together ½ inch from the edge. If you are using a sewing machine, set the stitch gauge to 10 stitches to the inch; if you are working by hand, use a backstitch (see page 38). Leave a 5- to 10-inch opening on one side for stuffing. The ½-inch seam allowance along this opening should be pressed down with an iron or pinned in place until you are ready to close the opening after stuffing. The ½ inch of excess fabric between the seam line and the edges of the muslin should be clipped diagonally across each corner so that you can push the corner out to form a sharp point when you reverse the muslin. Turn the muslin casing inside out (to the front side). Push the corners out with your fingernail. Fill the casing with stuffing, using approximately 1 pound of stuffing per square foot of pillow. You may want to use more or less, depending on the fullness you desire. Sew the opening closed, using an overcast stitch (see page 38).

Backing and Completing Pillows

In order to complete your pillow you will have to make a backing for the crocheted piece, insert the stuffed muslin casing into the pillow, and close the pillow.

Directions for most of the pillows in this book are for one side of the pillow only. You can duplicate the design on the other side of the pillow, you can crochet a plain piece the same size, or you can use fabric that coordinates with the crochet, as we did for several of the pillows. Cut the backing fabric slightly larger than the crocheted piece. Fold the edges of the piece ¼ inch to the back and pin them in place. Baste the edges down with ½-inch-long basting stitches just above the pins, then remove the pins. The basting stitches will hold the folded edges in place until you are ready to attach the backing to the crocheted piece. Place the backing on top of the crocheted piece so that the front sides face each other. Either machine stitch or backstitch (by hand) the two pieces together ⅛ inch from the edges on three sides. Leave the fourth side open to insert the pillow form. Turn the crocheted piece and backing front sides out. Push out the corners with your fingernail. Insert the stuffed muslin casing into the pillow and blind stitch the fourth side closed.

Fringes

Cut a piece of heavy cardboard a little longer than the length of fringe you want. Wrap your yarn around the cardboard until you have a good-sized bunch. Cut it at one end. You'll probably need to repeat this step several times before you have enough fringe. Don't let the cardboard buckle when you wrap, or some strands will be longer than others.

Divide the fringe into groups with approximately the same number of strands in each group. Work with the back of the piece facing you. You can use either your fingers or a crochet hook to attach the fringe. Pick up a group of fringe strands and double them. Try to be accurate—the more evenly you attach your fringe, the less you'll lose when you trim it.

Insert the loop of the doubled fringe group through the attaching space from back to front. Then insert the cut ends of the fringe group through the loop (see Diagram 61). Pull on the cut ends to tighten the fringe. (The V formed by this process is on the back side of the piece.)

The number of strands in each fringe group and the number of fringe groups in each attaching space will depend on the yarn and the look you want. Heavy fringe takes more yarn but is usually more effective. After you have attached all the fringe, you can block it if necessary. Then place the project so that the fringe hangs evenly. Run your fingers through the fringe to straighten it out and separate the strands. Trim any uneven ends.

Tassels

Cut a piece of heavy cardboard a little larger than the length of the tassel you want. Wrap your yarn around the cardboard until you have enough for a tassel, then cut it at one end. Tie the tassel securely in the exact center with a piece of yarn about 5 inches long (point C in Diagram 62). This piece of yarn will later serve to tie the tassel to the project. Double the tassel at the point where this yarn is tied.

Cut another piece of yarn approximately twice as long as the rest. You will wrap this strand around the top few inches of the tassel. Make a loop in the wrapping strand about one fourth of the distance along the strand. Place this loop against the tassel so that it is even with the loop formed by doubling the tassel.

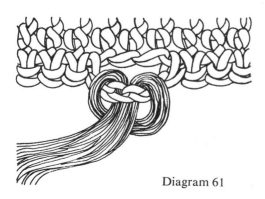

Diagram 61

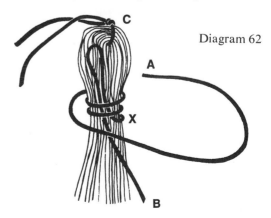

Diagram 62

Grasp the tassel and the wrapping strand loop with your left hand about 1½ to 2 inches from the top of the tassel (point X in Diagram 62). Let the short end of the wrapping strand hang (point B in Diagram 62). Begin wrapping the long strand (end A in Diagram 62) tightly around both the tassel and the wrapping strand loop at point X. Continue to wrap, working toward the top of the tassel. When you reach the top, a small piece of the wrapping strand loop should still be visible. Insert end A of the wrapping strand through the wrapping strand loop. Then pull hard on end B. The loop and end A will disappear under the wrapping. The tassel will be quite secure; knots are unnecessary. Trim the tassel.

Hand Stitches

The following basic hand stitches will be needed occasionally for your crochet work.

Blind Stitching: Holding the edges of your fabric and crocheted piece together, make a small horizontal stitch through one or two threads of the fabric, then pick up several threads of the crocheted piece diagonally above and pull closed (see Diagram 63). The stitches should be close together.

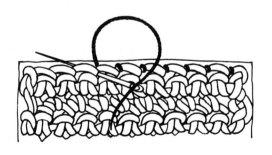

Diagram 63

Backstitching: Bring your needle through the fabric for about $\frac{1}{16}$ inch on the seam line. Bring the needle back to the right about $\frac{1}{16}$ inch, insert it into the fabric, and bring it out about $\frac{1}{16}$ inch in front of the point where the thread emerges from the fabric on the seam line (see Diagram 64). Continue inserting the needle in the end of the last stitch made and bringing it out $\frac{1}{16}$ inch ahead.

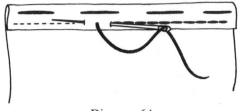

Diagram 64

Overcast Stitching: Make small diagonal stitches over both edges of your fabric, spacing them evenly and making them uniformly $\frac{1}{8}$ to $\frac{1}{4}$ inch deep (see Diagram 65).

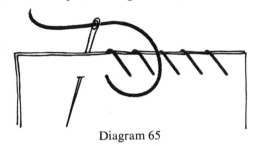

Diagram 65

Blanket Stitching: This stitch is always worked from left to right, holding the edge of the fabric toward you. Insert the needle near the edge, from back to front, for the first stitch. Then insert the needle through the front side of the fabric about $\frac{1}{8}$ to $\frac{1}{4}$ inch above the edge and an equal distance from the preceding stitch. As you work, be sure to keep the thread beneath the edge of the fabric and under the needle (see Diagram 66).

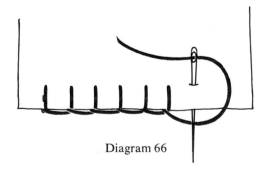

Diagram 66

Chapter  2 FANCY STITCHES

Even the most complicated crochet stitches and patterns are only variations of stitches and patterns you have already learned—which tells you a lot about the versatility of the basic stitches and the ingenuity of crocheters. The Shell stitch, for instance, is a variation of the double crochet. Its variations include a Pointed Shell, a Treble Shell, a Tilted Shell, a Circle Shell, and more. Any of these versions of the Basic Shell can be used alone or (with some adjustments in the count) in a Shell pattern. The emphasis in this chapter is on the stitches themselves rather than on complex, multi-row patterns. In the Glossary of Fancy Stitches we've given you row-by-row directions for 23 stitches. Many of these will be incorporated in projects in this chapter and the rest of the book. So make these stitches your own and learn to adapt and adjust them.

Notes on Fancy Stitches

When you make a row of a basic stitch (single crochet, half double crochet, double crochet, or treble crochet), you put 1 stitch in every stitch of the previous row. When you make fancy stitches, you use several stitches of the previous row to make each complete fancy stitch. We'll use the Shell stitch once more to illustrate what we mean. A Shell begins with 1 single crochet. You skip 2 stitches on the previous row and work 5 double crochets all in the next stitch. Then you skip 2 more stitches and are ready to begin the next Shell with another single crochet. You have used 6 stitches of the previous row to make 1 Shell. Of course, this "stitch" is really a small pattern composed of 6 stitches—1 single crochet and 5 double crochets—so there has been no change in the actual number of stitches.

Starting Fancy Stitches

It's helpful to know how many stitches a fancy "stitch" needs before you begin a row or round. The directions for each stitch in the stitch glossary that follows will tell you to chain a multiple of the number of stitches it takes to make 1 complete fancy stitch. Directions for the Shell stitch, for example, begin, "Ch a multiple of 6 . . .".

When you work in rounds, it's a good idea to figure out beforehand whether or not the particular fancy stitch will fit evenly on the round you are about to begin. There is a simple way to determine this using the multiple number: If the total number of stitches you will have in the round can be divided evenly by the multiple number, you will have no leftover stitches at the end of the round. For example, if you will have 72 stitches (or any other number of stitches evenly divisible by 6) in your round, the final Shell stitch of the round will use up the final 6 stitches. If, instead, you will have 76 stitches in the round, you will have 4 leftover stitches when you reach the end. Conclusion: It might be better to try another stitch on that round.

Rows of fancy stitches often begin and end with partial patterns. This keeps the sides of your piece straight, makes it easier to begin subsequent rows, and provides anchors for adjoining complete stitches. A row of Shells begins with 3 double crochets—half of a Shell—in the first stitch and ends with 3 double crochets in the last stitch. The number of extra chain stitches you need to make these partial patterns and the number of chain stitches you need to turn and begin the next row must be included in your foundation chain. Ten extra stitches are needed for the partial patterns and turning chain in a row of Shell stitches—6 at one end and 4 at the other. Six of these chain stitches are accounted for in whatever multiple of 6 you chain. The other 4 are given separately after the multiple number is given. So the complete directions for making a foundation chain for the Shell stitch read, "Ch a multiple of 6, plus 4."

Increasing and Decreasing Fancy Stitches

It is often extremely difficult, if not impossible, to increase or decrease while making several rows of a fancy stitch. To do so, you would need to add or eliminate a complete "stitch" at one time, which could consist of as many as 6 individual stitches. Two-stitch fancy stitches, such as the Daisy, are a bit easier, since you can usually add or subtract 2 stitches at a time without distorting the piece. When we have found a way to increase and decrease a fancy stitch, we have included the directions under the variations of the stitch. Fortunately, many fancy stitches are made in a 2-row pattern; first a row or round of the fancy stitch, then a row or round of single crochet. In this case always make your increases and decreases in the single crochet row.

If you don't mind your piece fanning out, you can increase or decrease at the ends of the row as well by gradually completing the partial patterns and starting new ones.

Glossary of Fancy Stitches

V-Doubles

Ch an odd number of sts.

Row 1: 2 dc in 4th ch from hk, *skip 1 ch, 2 dc in next ch. Repeat from *, ending with 2 dc in next-to-last ch, 1 dc in last st. Ch 3, turn.

Row 2: 2 dc in sp between the 1st 2 dc, *2 dc in sp between the next 2 dc. Repeat from *, ending with 1 dc in top of turning ch. Ch 3, turn.

Repeat Row 2 for pat.

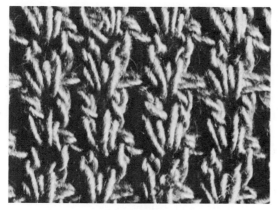

V-Doubles

Variation: This st can also be worked in hdc or tr.

Crossed Double Crochet

Ch an even number of sts.

Row 1: 1 dc in 5th ch from hk. Holding hk behind dc just made, yo, insert hk in the 4th ch from hk from *front to back,* yo, pull up a lp, and complete the dc [1 Crossed dc formed]. *Skip next st, 1 dc in next st. Holding hk behind dc just made, yo, insert hk in *st just skipped* from front to back, yo, pull up a lp, complete dc. Repeat from *, ending with 1 dc in last st. Ch 3, turn.

Row 2: Skip 1st and 2nd dc, 1 dc in 3rd st of previous row. Holding hk behind dc just made, make 1 dc in 2nd st of previous row. Repeat from * of Row 1, ending with 1 dc in top of turning ch. Ch 3, turn.

Repeat Row 2 for pat.

Note: To inc or dec this st you must always add or eliminate 2 sts [1 Crossed dc] each time. *To increase:* *Do *not* skip st after completing Crossed dc, work 1 dc in next st, yo, insert hk thru same st as nearest dc in last Crossed dc, yo and pull up a lp, complete dc. Repeat from * once. *To decrease:* *Skip 2 sts after completing a Crossed dc, 1 dc in next st, insert hk

Crossed Double Crochet

in dc and make dc in 2nd skipped st. Repeat from * once.

Variation: The cross can be made in back of the 1st dc in order to achieve more of a raised effect.

Judith Stitch

Ch a multiple of 4, plus 3.

Foundation Row: 1 sc in 2nd ch from hk, *1 sc in next ch. Repeat from * to end. Ch 3, turn.

Row 1: Skip 1st st, *skip next st, 1 dc in each of next 3 sts. Put hk in front of 3-dc and then thru skipped st from front to back. Yo and pull up a *long, loose* lp thru the skipped st and across the front of the 3-dc until it is even with the top of the 3rd dc, yo and pull a lp thru both

Judith Stitch

Basic Shell Stitch

lps on hk. Repeat from *, ending with 1 dc in last st. Ch 1, turn.

Row 2: 1 sc in 1st st, *1 sc in next st. Repeat from *, ending with 1 sc in top of ch-3. Ch 3, turn.

Repeat Rows 1 and 2 for pat.

Note: The Judith st will be more distinct if, on the sc row, the sc that comes between complete Judith sts is worked *over all lps* into the sp rather than into the st itself.

Variation: The st may be worked with a 2-dc group in each Judith st instead of a 3-dc group. Adjust the ch to a multiple of 3, plus 3.

Basic Shell Stitch

Ch a multiple of 6, plus 4.

Row 1: 2 dc in 4th ch from hk, *skip 2 chs, 1 sc in next ch, skip 2 chs, 5 dc in next ch [Shell]. Repeat from *, ending with skip 2 chs, 3 dc in last ch [½ Shell]. Ch 1, turn.

Row 2: 1 sc in 1st dc, *5 dc in next sc, 1 sc in center dc on next Shell. Repeat from *, ending with 1 sc in top of turning ch. Ch 3, turn.

Row 3: 2 dc in 1st sc, *1 sc in center dc of next Shell, 5 dc in next sc. Repeat from *, ending with 3 dc in last sc. Ch 1, turn.

Repeat Rows 2 and 3 for pat.

Variations: *To make Pointed Shell Stitches:* Instead of making a 5-dc Shell, work (1 sc, 1 hdc,

1 dc, 1 hdc, 1 sc) in the same st. On the next row put your sc in the dc of this Shell.

To make Treble Shells: Work 7 tr instead of the 5-dc group and skip *2 chs* between each Shell on Row 1. On Rows 2 and 3 again substitute 7 tr for the 5-dc group and ch 4 at the end of Row 2.

Repeat Rows 2 and 3 for pat.

Tilted Shell Stitch

Ch a multiple of 7, plus 5.

Row 1: 1 sc in 2nd ch from hk, skip 2 chs, 3 dc in next ch, *ch 3, skip 3 chs, 1 sc in next ch,

Tilted Shell Stitch

skip 2 chs, 3 dc in next ch. Repeat from * to end. Ch 1, turn.

Row 2: 1 sc in 1st dc, 3 dc in next sc, *ch 3, 1 sc under ch-3, 3 dc in next sc. Repeat from * to end. Ch 1, turn.

Repeat Row 2 for pat.

Circle Shell Stitch

Ch a multiple of 6, plus 2.

Row 1: 1 sc in 2nd ch from hk, *skip 2 chs, work 7 dc [Shell] in next ch, skip 2 chs, 1 sc in next ch. Repeat from * to end. Ch 2, turn.

Row 2: [Front side] *Yo, pull up a lp in next dc, yo, and pull a lp thru 2 lps.* Repeat from * to * in each of next 2 dc, yo, and pull a lp thru all 4 lps on hk, ch 1 for eye of inverted Shell, ch 2, 1 sc in next dc, **ch 2, repeat from * to * in each of next 3 dc, the sc, and the next 3 dc, yo and pull a lp thru all 8 lps on hk, ch 1 for eye, ch 2, 1 sc in next dc.** Repeat from ** to **, ending with ch 2, 1 sc in next dc, repeat from * to * in each of last 3 dc and in last sc, yo and pull a lp thru 5 lps on hk [½ Shell], ch 1 for eye. Ch 2, turn.

Row 3: 3 dc in eye of inverted Shell, *1 sc in next st, 7 dc in eye of next Shell. Repeat from *, ending with 1 sc in sc, 4 dc in eye of last Shell. Ch 1, turn.

Row 4: 1 sc in 1st dc, repeat from ** to ** of Row 2, ending with 1 sc in top of turning ch. Ch 1, turn.

Circle Shell Stitch

Row 5: Repeat from * to * of Row 3, ending with 1 sc in last sc. Ch 3, turn.

Repeat Rows 2–5 for pat.

Double Crochet Arches

Ch a multiple of 6, plus 2.

Row 1: 1 sc in 2nd ch from hk, 1 sc in next st, *ch 3, skip 3 sts, 1 sc in each of next 3 sts. Repeat from *, ending with ch 3, skip 3 sts, 2 sc in each of next 2 sts. Ch 2, turn.

Row 2: 1 sc in 1st st, *5 dc under next ch-3, skip 1 sc, 1 sc in next st. Repeat from *, ending with skip 1 sc, 1 sc in last st. Ch 3, turn.

Row 3: *1 sc in each of 3 center dc of 5-dc group of previous row, ch 3. Repeat from *, ending with ch 2, 1 sc in last st. Ch 3, turn.

Row 4: Work 2 dc under ch-2, *1 sc in center sc of 3-sc group of previous row, 5 dc under next ch-3. Repeat from *, ending with 1 sc into center sc of 3-sc group, 3 dc in last sp. Ch 1, turn.

Row 5: 1 sc in each of 1st 2 sts, ch 3. Repeat from * of Row 3, ending with ch 2, 1 sc in last st, ch 3, turn. Repeat Rows 2–5 for pat.

Double Crochet Arches

Post Stitch

Ch any desired number of sts.

Row 1: 1 sc in 2nd ch from hk, *1 sc in next ch. Repeat from * to end. Ch 1, turn.

Row 2: Insert hk from back to front in the sp between the 1st and 2nd sc of previous row,

43

Post Stitch

Chevron Stitch

across the post, and out to the back between the 2nd and 3rd sts, yo and pull a lp thru 2 lps on hk [1 sc "post" st made]. Insert hk between 2nd and 3rd sts and repeat. Continue to work around post in this manner, ending by inserting hk in sp between last and next-to-last st and making 1 sc. Ch 1, turn.

Repeat Row 2 for pat.

Variations: You can go around the post from front to back as well as from back to front. You can even alternate the direction in which you insert your hk for a unique textured look. When you work around the post of a st, the head of the st being worked will tilt in the direction opposite to the way the post is being pulled.

In addition to sc, the Post st can be made with any 1 of the basic sts.

Chevron Stitch

Ch a multiple of 11, plus 10.
Row 1: 1 sc in 2nd ch from hk, 1 sc in each of next 3 chs, 3 sc in next ch, *1 sc in each of next 4 chs, skip 2 chs, 1 sc in each of next 4 chs, 3 sc in next ch. Repeat from *, ending with 1 sc in each of last 4 chs. Ch 1, turn.
Row 2: Skip 1st sc of row, 1 sc in each of next 4 sc, 3 sc in next sc, *1 sc in each of next 4 sc, skip next 2 sc, 1 sc in each of next 4 sc, 3 sc in next sc. Repeat from *, ending with 1 sc in

each of next 3 sc, skip next sc, 1 sc in last sc. Ch 1, turn.

Repeat Row 2 for pat.

Variation: You can make Chevrons of any height by changing the number of scs that come before and after the 3-sc group [the point of the Chevron]. Be sure that the number of scs that comes before the 3-sc group is the same as the number of scs that you work after the 3-sc group. Then skip 2 sc and continue in the same way.

Moss Stitch

Ch an uneven number of sts.
Row 1: 1 sc in 2nd ch from hk, 1 sc in next ch, *ch 4, slst in 4th ch from hk [picot], 1 sc in each of next 2 chs. Repeat from *, ending with 1 sc in each of last 2 chs. Ch 1, turn.
Row 2: 1 sc in 1st sc, *1 sc in next sc at base of picot [hold the picot to front of work, keeping yarn in back of picot], 1 sc in next sc. Repeat from *, ending with 1 sc in each of last 2 sc. Ch 1, turn.
Row 3: 1 sc in 1st sc, *ch 4, slst in 4th ch from hk, 1 sc in each of next 2 sc. Repeat from *, ending with ch 4, slst in 4th ch from hk, 1 sc in last sc. Ch 1, turn.
Row 4: *1 sc in sc at base of picot, 1 sc in next sc. Repeat from *, ending with ch 1, turn.
Row 5: 1 sc in each of 1st 2 sc, *ch 4, slst in

4th ch from hk, 1 sc in each of next 2 sc. Repeat from *, ending with 1 sc in each of last 2 sc. Ch 1, turn.

Repeat Rows 2–5 for pat.

Check Stitch

Ch a multiple of 4, plus 1.

Row 1: 1 dc in 4th ch from hk, 1 dc in next ch, *ch 1, skip next ch, 1 dc in each of next 3 chs. Repeat from *, ending with 1 dc in each of last 3 chs. Ch 4, turn.

Row 2: Skip 1st 2 sts, *1 dc in next st, 1 dc in ch-1 sp, 1 dc in next st, ch 1, skip 1 st. Repeat from *, ending with ch 1, skip last st, 1 dc in top of ch-3 turning ch. Ch 3, turn.

Row 3: Skip 1st st, 1 dc in 1st ch-1 sp, 1 dc in next st, *ch 1, skip next st, 1 dc in next st, 1 dc in ch-1 sp, 1 dc in next st. Repeat from *, ending with ch 1, skip next st, 1 dc in last st, 1 dc over ch-4 turning ch, 1 dc in 3rd ch of ch-4 turning ch. Ch 4, turn.

Repeat Rows 2 and 3 for pat.

Hazelnut Stitch

Ch a multiple of 3, plus 2.

Row 1: 1 sc in 2nd ch from hk, *1 sc in next ch. Repeat from *, ending with 1 sc in last ch. Ch 1, turn.

Row 2: 1 sc in 1st st, *in next st (yo, insert hk in st, pull up a lp, yo and pull thru 2 lps) 5 times, push the middle finger of your left hand into the back of the st group, yo and close all 6 lps tog [1 Hazelnut formed], 1 sc in each of next 2 sts. Repeat from *, ending with 1 Hazelnut in next st, 1 sc in each of last 2 sts. Ch 1, turn.

Row 3: 1 sc in 1st st, *1 sc in next st. Repeat from * to end. Ch 1, turn.

Row 4: 1 sc in each of 1st 2 sc. Repeat from * of Row 2, ending with 1 Hazelnut in next-to-last st, 1 sc in last sc. Ch 1, turn.

Row 5: Repeat Row 3.

Repeat Rows 2–5 for pat.

Note: The Hazelnut has a back and front side—the bump makes a hole on the back side. The sc that follows a Hazelnut should be tight; it keeps the bump puffed out.

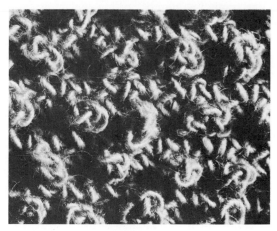

Moss Stitch

Check Stitch

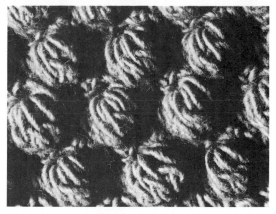

Hazelnut Stitch

Variation: The number of incomplete dcs you make for each Hazelnut can vary. The thicker the yarn, for example, the fewer yos necessary. You can also vary the number of scs between Hazelnuts. The ch multiple, of course, must be adjusted accordingly.

Bump Stitch

Ch an even number of sts.
Row 1: [Front; see Note] 1 sc in 2nd ch from hk, 1 tr in next st, *1 sc in next st, 1 tr in next st. Repeat from *, ending with 1 sc in last st. Ch 1, turn. .
Row 2: 1 sc in 1st st. Repeat from * of Row 1, ending with 1 sc in each of last 2 sts. Ch 1, turn.

Repeat Rows 1 and 2 for pat.

Note: On Row 2 the bumps should be pushed out so that they puff on the same side as Row 1.

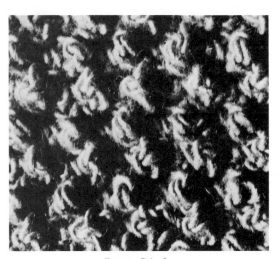

Bump Stitch

Cluster-Stitch

Ch an even number of sts.
Row 1: (Yo, insert hk in 4th ch from the hk, pull up a lp, yo and pull thru 2 lps) 3 times, yo and pull thru all 4 lps [1 Cluster made], ch 1, skip 1 st. *(Yo, insert hk in next st, pull up a lp, yo and pull thru 2 lps) 3 times, yo and pull thru all 4 lps, ch 1, skip 1 st. Repeat from

Cluster Stitch

*, ending with skip 1 ch, 1 dc in last st. Ch 3, turn.
Row 2: 1 Cluster in 1st ch-1 sp, *ch 1, skip 1 Cluster, 1 Cluster in next ch-1 sp. Repeat from *, ending with 1 Cluster in last ch-1 sp, ch 1, skip last Cluster, 1 dc in top of turning ch. Ch 3, turn.

Repeat Row 2 for pat.

Variation: Make a row of sc between each row so that the st can be increased, the fabric is more solid, and all the Clusters face the same side. Ch 1 and turn at the end of the Cluster row and sc in each st of the row. At the end of the row, ch 3, turn, skip 1st sc, and make the 1st Cluster in the 2nd st of the previous row.

Slanting Clusters

Ch a multiple of 3, plus 2.
Row 1: (Yo, pull up a lp in 4th ch from hk) twice, yo and pull up a lp thru 5 lps on hk, ch 1 to form eye [½ pat], ch 1, skip 1 ch, in next ch (yo and pull up a lp) twice, *skip 2 chs, in next ch (yo and pull up a lp) twice, yo and pull a lp thru 9 lps on hk, ch 1 to form eye [1 pat], ch 2, (yo, insert hk into same ch as last half of last pat and pull up a lp) twice. Repeat from *, ending with (yo and pull up a lp in same ch as last half of last pat) twice, yo and pull a lp thru 5 lps on hk, ch 1 to form eye,

Slanting Clusters

Popcorn Stitch

ch 1, skip 1 ch, 1 dc in last ch. Ch 2, turn.
Row 2: (Yo, pull up a lp in 1st eye) twice, yo and pull a lp thru 5 lps on hk, ch 1, *ch 2 (yo, pull up a lp in same eye as last half of pat) twice, skip ch-2, (yo, pull up a lp in next eye) twice, yo and pull a lp thru 9 lps on hk, ch 1. Repeat from *, ending with ch 1, 1 dc under turning ch. Ch 2, turn.
Row 3: Work ½ pat (yo, pull up a lp) twice in ch-1 sp, ch 2, (yo, pull up a lp in 1st eye) twice, (yo, pull up a lp in next eye) twice, yo and pull a lp thru 9 lps on hk, ch 1. Repeat from * of Row 2, ending with yo and pull a lp thru 9 lps on hk, ch 1 to form eye, ch 1, 1 dc under turning ch. Ch 2, turn.
Repeat Rows 2 and 3 for pat.

Popcorn Stitch

Ch an odd number of sts.
Row 1: 5 dc in 4th ch from the hk, remove hk and insert it under both lps of 1st of the 5 dc, pick up dropped lp and pull it thru [1 Popcorn made], ch 1, skip 1 st. *5 dc in next st, remove hk and insert it under both lps of 1st of the 5 dc, pick up dropped lp and pull it thru, ch 1, skip 1 st. Repeat from *, ending with 1 Popcorn, *do not skip a st,* 1 dc in last st. Ch 1, turn.
Row 2: 1 sc in 1st dc, *1 sc in top of Popcorn, 1 sc in ch-1 sp. Repeat from *, ending with 1 sc in top of turning ch. Ch 3, turn.

Row 3: Skip 1st st. Repeat from * of Row 1. Repeat Rows 2 and 3 for pat.

Note: The Popcorn has a front side and a back side. The st looks better when you puff out the back side; the back then becomes the front.

The number of dcs for each Popcorn will vary, depending on the yarn you are using.

Pineapple Stitch

Ch an odd number of sts.
Row 1: (Yo, insert hk in 4th ch from the hk and pull up a *long* lp) 4 times in same st [9 lps

Pineapple Stitch

47

on hk], yo and pull thru 8 lps, yo and pull thru 2 lps [1 Pineapple formed], ch 1, skip 1 st. *(Yo, insert hk in next st and pull up a *long* lp) 4 times in same st [9 lps on hk], yo and pull thru 8 lps, yo and pull thru 2 lps, ch 1, skip 1 st. Repeat from *, ending with 1 Pineapple, *do not skip a st,* 1 dc in last st. Ch 3, turn.

Row 2: 1 Pineapple in 1st ch-1 sp, *ch 1, skip next Pineapple, 1 Pineapple in next ch-1 sp. Repeat from *, ending with 1 Pineapple in last ch-1 sp, ch 1, 1 dc in top of turning ch. Ch 3, turn.

Repeat Row 2 for pat.

Note: If you don't pull up long, loose lps, you'll have trouble getting your hk thru all 8 lps. The number of lps needed to make a solid Pineapple will vary, depending on the thickness of the yarn you are using.

Variation: You can replace the ch-1 sp with hdcs or dcs.

Loop Stitch

Ch any desired number of sts.

Row 1: 1 sc in 2nd ch from hk, *1 sc in next ch. Repeat from *, ending with 1 sc in last ch. Ch 1, turn.

Row 2: Insert your hk into the 1st st of the previous row, raise the index finger of the left hand, and wrap the yarn around the raised index finger from back to front. Bring the hk

to the right of the strand that lies behind your index finger. Twist the hk so that it catches the strand behind your index finger and the strand that comes over your finger and lies in front of it. Pull both strands thru the st in 1 motion. Drop the lp, yo and pull a regular lp thru 3 lps on hk. Repeat in next st.

Repeat Rows 1 and 2 for pat.

Note: The lps formed in Row 2 will fall to the front of your work. To make lps of uniform length and evenness, pass the yarn over a band of cardboard (of the desired size) instead of your finger(s).

Variation: If you wish, the lp can be made longer by passing the yarn over the 2nd and 3rd fingers of the left hand as well as the index finger.

Simple Looping Stitch

Ch an even number of sts.

Row 1: Skip 1st ch, *1 sc in next ch, repeat from * ending with 1 sc in last ch, ch 2, turn.

Row 2: Skip 1st sc, *yo, insert hk into next sc, pull up a lp, yo, insert hk into next st and pull up a lp, yo and pull a lp thru all 5 lps on your hk, ch 1, repeat from * to end, ch 1, turn.

Row 3: 1 sc in 1st st, *1 sc in next ch-1 sp, 1 sc in next st, repeat from * ending with 1 sc in top of turning ch, ch 2, turn.

Repeat Rows 2 and 3 for pat.

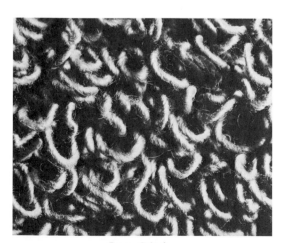

Loop Stitch

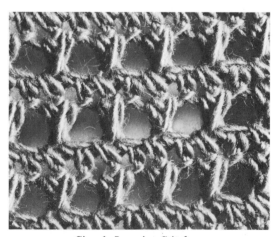

Simple Looping Stitch

Daisy Stitch

Ch an odd number of sts.

Round or Row 1: Press the thumb and middle finger of your left hand tog above the 1st ch from the hk. Ch 1 around your thumb and middle finger, using them to keep the eye of the ch open. [The eye is the sp between the top 2 lps and the bottom lp of the ch.] Insert your hk thru the eye from front to back and pull thru a lp [2 lps on hk]. Insert hk thru 2nd ch from hk and pull up a lp [3 lps on hk]. Pull up a lp thru each of next 2 chs [5 lps on hk]. Yo and close all lps tog. *Press thumb and middle finger tog above last st between hk and uncrocheted yarn. Ch 1 around thumb and middle finger, insert hk thru eye and pull up a lp [2 lps on hk], insert hk thru same st as final lp of just-completed Daisy and pull up a lp [3 lps on hk]. Pull up a lp thru each of the next 2 sts [5 lps on hk]. Yo and pull thru all 5 lps on hk. Repeat from *, ending with yo and pull thru all 5 lps on hk.

Complete row or rnd according to the following directions:

If working in rows: Ch 1, insert hk thru eye, pull up a lp thru eye *and* lp on hk. Break yarn.

Row 2: Reattach yarn in 1st st [not an eye]. Ch 1, press thumb and middle finger tog above ch-1, and ch 1 around thumb and finger. Insert hk thru eye, pull up a lp, insert hk thru attaching st, pull up a lp [3 lps on hk], insert hk thru next st [1st eye] and pull up a lp [4 lps on hk], yo and pull thru all lps. Repeat from * in Row 1, making sure that the 1st and last lps of each new Daisy are worked thru the eyes of Daisies in the previous row.

If working in spiral rounds: Insert hk thru eye, pull thru a lp [2 lps on hk], insert hk thru same st as final lp of last Daisy, pull up a lp [3 lps on hk], insert hk thru 1st st of previous rnd [*not* an eye], pull up a lp [4 lps on hk], insert hk thru 2nd st of previous row [1st eye] and pull up a lp [5 lps on hk], yo and pull thru all 5 lps. Repeat from * in Round 1, making sure that the 1st and last lps of each new Daisy are worked thru the eyes of Daisies in the previous rnd.

If working in joined rounds: Insert hk thru eye

Daisy Stitch

and 1st st of previous rnd [not an eye], pull a lp thru 1st st, eye, and lp on hk. Beginning with ch 1, follow directions for Row 2 under directions for working in rows.

Note: The Daisy can *only* be worked in 1 direction—not back and forth. If you are not working in rnds, you must cut the yarn at the end of each row and reattach it on the right end.

This st can be increased or decreased. *To increase:* You must inc 2 sts [1 complete Daisy] every time you inc. *Press thumb and middle finger tog, ch 1 around them, insert hk thru eye of ch and pull up a lp [2 lps on hk], yo, pull up a lp in same st as just-completed Daisy [4 lps on hk], pull up a lp in next st [5 lps on hk], yo and pull thru 5 lps. Repeat from * once. The 2nd inc Daisy should end in an eye. *To decrease:* You must dec 2 sts (1 complete Daisy) every time you dec. Follow directions for making Daisy until there are 5 lps on your hk. Insert hk into next st, pull up a lp, insert hk into next st, pull up a lp [7 lps on hk], yo and pull thru all 7 lps.

Variation: To make a Half Daisy st, make a row of sc or hdc after each row of Daisies. You can either make 1 sc or hdc in every st, or you can make 2 sts in each eye and skip the non-eye st. Either method allows you to work the st back and forth in rows.

49

Scallop Edging Stitch

Shrimp Edging Stitch

Picot Edging Stitch

Scallop Edging Stitch

First edge your piece in sc.

*Ch 3, make 1 dc in same st as the slst, skip 2 sts, slst in next st. Repeat from * around piece.

Variations: The scallops can be made fuller by using 2 dc instead of 1. You can also ch 4 instead of 3 or use trs instead of dcs and skip 3 sts rather than 2 before you slst into the next st. Try spacing the scallops farther apart by making 1 or 2 scs between each scallop.

Shrimp Edging Stitch

First edge your piece in sc.

This st is a sc worked from left to right instead of from right to left. Insert your hk under the head of the 1st sc and make 1 sc, *insert hk under head of next st *to the right* of st just completed and make a sc. Repeat from * around piece.

Note: This is difficult to work in rows since the heads of the sts formed are difficult to pick up.

Picot Edging Stitch

First edge your piece in sc.

*1 slst in each of next 2 sts, (1 sc, ch 3, 1 slst) in next st [1 Picot formed]. Repeat from * around piece.

Variations: There are 4 variations of the basic Picot Edging st. The 1st variation is: 1 sc in 1st st, *ch 3, slst in base of sc, skip 1 st, 1 sc in next st. Repeat from *. The 2nd variation is: *1 sc in each of next 3 sts, ch 4, take hk out and insert it into 4th ch from hk, pick up 1st ch from hk and pull thru lp on hk. Repeat from *. The 3rd variation is: 1 sc in 1st st, *ch 3, skip 1 st, 1 sc in next st. Repeat from *. The 4th variation is: 1 sc in each of 1st 3 sts, *ch 4, 1 sc in 2nd ch from hk, ch 1, skip 1 st, 1 sc in each of next 3 sts. Repeat from *.

Three Planters

The here-to-stay plant boom has given rise to a need for more and more decorative pot holders. We think these three are a good representation of the different kinds of planters you can crochet. The size of each planter can be altered according to your needs. Since many of the heavy yarns used for planters are dyed or spray painted, it is best to take the pot out of its holder before watering the plant.

Green Hanging Planter

Materials:
- 4 spools dark green Lily jute *or* any thin jute
- ½ spool Lily jute *or* ½ skein dyed seine twine in each of the following colors: orange, shocking pink, light green, and yellow (see instructions for dyeing seine twine on page 58)
- 10″ plastic hanging planter
- 3 or 4 S-hooks (these can be made from the wire hanger that comes with the plastic planter)

Hooks: K and F

Gauge:
Planter: Rounds 1–4 = 4″ diameter
Harness: 2 sts = 1½″

Finished Size:
Planter = 10½″ across top, 8″ (approximately) high
Harness = 27″
Tassel = 12″

Instructions:
For Rounds 1–15 work 2 strands of dark green jute tog with the K hk.
Foundation chain: Ch 5, join last ch to 1st with slst.
Round 1: [In this and subsequent rnds, the 1st st of the rnd is made in the 1st st of the previous rnd.] Ch 1, 8 sc in center of circle, join last sc to 1st with slst. Ch 1.
Round 2: *(2 sc in next st) 3 times, ch 3, skip 1 sc. Repeat from *, ending with ch 3, slst in 1st sc. Ch 1. [The 2 sps will be used to tie the tassel to the planter.]
Round 3: *(1 sc in next st, 2 sc in next st) 3 times, 3 sc in ch-3 lp. Repeat from *, ending with slst into 1st sc. Ch 1 [24 sts].
Round 4: 1 sc in every st, join with slst to 1st sc. Ch 1.
Round 5: *1 sc in each of next 2 sts, 2 sc in next st. Repeat from *, ending with 2 sc in last st, join with slst to 1st sc. Ch 1.
Round 6: 1 sc in every st, join with slst. Ch 1.
Round 7: *1 sc in each of next 3 sts, 2 sc in next st. Repeat from *, ending with 2 sc in last st, join with slst to 1st sc. Ch 1 [48 sts].
Rounds 8–11: 1 sc in every st, join with slst to 1st sc. Ch 1.
Round 12: *1 sc in each of next 5 sts, 2 sc in next st. Repeat from *, ending with 2 sc in last st, join with slst to 1st st. Ch 1 [54 sts].
Round 13: 1 sc in every st, join with slst to 1st st. Ch 1.
Round 14: *1 sc in each of next 7 sts, 2 sc in next st. Repeat from *, ending with 2 sc in last st, join with slst to 1st st. Ch 1 [60 sts].
Round 15: 1 sc in every st, join with slst to 1st st [60 sts]. End off dark green jute. Change to a *single strand* of jute and use an *F hk.* For the rest of the project you will use 1 strand of jute and the F hk.
Round 16: *1 sc in next st, 2 sc in next st. Repeat from *, ending with 2 sc in last st, *but* complete the last sc with orange, join with a slst to 1st st. Ch 1 with orange [90 sts]. End off green jute.
Round 17: Orange—1 sc in every st, complete last sc with pink, join with slst to 1st st. Ch 1 with pink. End off orange.
Round 18: Pink—repeat Round 17, complete last sc with yellow, join with slst to 1st st. Ch 1 with yellow. End off pink.
Round 19: Yellow—repeat Round 17, complete last sc with dark green, join with slst to

1st st. Ch 1 with dark green. End off the yellow.

Round 20: Dark green—*1 sc in each of next 3 sts, ch 3, skip 3 sc. Repeat from *, ending with ch 3, join with slst to 1st st. End off dark green [15 ch-3 sps].

Round 21: Light green—attach light green in center sc of 3-sc group of previous rnd, *1 sc in center of any 3-sc group, 5 dc in ch-3 sp. Repeat from *, ending with 5 dc in ch-3, slst into 1st st. End off light green.

Round 22: Attach pink in center dc of any 5-dc group, *1 sc in center dc of 5-dc group, 5 dc *over light green rnd* and into center sc of 3-sc group of Round 20. [That is, work the pink 5-dc group in the same st that the light green sc is in—1 Bar st Shell formed.] Repeat from *, ending with 1 Bar st Shell in last 3-sc group, join with slst to 1st st. End off pink [15 Bar st Shells].

Round 23: Attach orange in center st of 1st Bar st Shell, *3 sc in center st of Bar st Shell, 1 sc in next st, skip next st, (yo, work over pink sc and insert hk into center st of light green 5-dc group) 3 times, yo and pull a lp thru 6 lps on hk, yo and pull a lp thru last 2 lps on hk [1 Bar st Pineapple formed], skip 1st st of Bar st Shell, 1 sc in next st. Repeat from *, ending with 1 sc in last st, join with slst to 1st st. End off orange.

Round 24: Attach light green in center st of any 3-sc group of previous rnd, *3 sc in center st of 3-sc group, ch 4, skip next 5 sts. Repeat from *, ending with ch 4, join with slst to 1st st. End off light green.

Round 25: Attach yellow in center st of 3-sc group of previous rnd, *1 sc in center st of next 3-sc group, 7 dc over light green and into top of Bar st Pineapple in Row 23. Repeat from *, ending with 7 dc into last Bar st Pineapple, join with slst to 1st st. Ch 1.

Round 26: Skip 1st st, *1 sc in each of next 2 sts, 3 sc in center dc of 7-dc Shell, 1 sc in each of next 2 sts, insert hk thru last st of 7-dc Shell, next sc, and 1st st of next 7-dc Shell, yo and pull a lp thru all 4 lps on your hk [one 3-st dec]. Repeat from *, ending with insert hk thru last st, ch 1, yo and pull a lp thru all 3 lps on hk, closing them tog. Break off yellow.

Round 27: Working over any 3-st dec group of Round 26, attach dark green into 1-sc of Round 25. *1 sc Bar st into 1-sc of Round 25, skip 1 st. 1 sc in each of next 2 sts. (1 sc, 1 Picot, 1 sc) in center of 3-sc group [top of Shell]. 1 sc in each of next 2 sts, skip 1 st. Repeat from *, ending with skip 1 st, join with slst to 1st st. Break off jute.

Harness: These directions can also be followed to make a harness for the Basket Planter, page 54.

Note: We suggest you use plain plastic hanging planters [with the wire hanger removed] inside your crocheted planters. These are designed with either 3 or 4 small holes in the brim through which the wire hanger is inserted. You will use these holes to attach the harness directly to the plastic planter. In this way the crocheted planter need not support the weight of the soil and plant. The number of straps you need for your harness is determined by the number of holes in the brim of your plastic planter.

Foundation chain: Ch 40.

Row 1: 1 sc in *bottom lp* of 3rd ch from hk and bottom lp of every ch. Ch 1, turn [38 sts].

Row 2: 1 sc in each of next 4 sts only. Ch 36.

Row 3: 1 sc in *bottom lp* of 3rd ch from hk and bottom lp of each of next 33 chs [34 sts], 1 sc in *loop B only* of each of next 4 sc. Ch 1, turn.

Repeat Rows 2 and 3 once for 3 straps and twice for 4 straps. Slst the 1st and last rows of 4-sc tog thru loop A of 1st row and loop B of last row. Break off jute. Tie jute on securely to top side of 1st row of sc, 1 sc into top of harness, ch 5, 1 sc in top side of 3rd row of sc. Ch 1, turn. 1 sc in each of the 5 chs, 1 slst into 1st sc. Break off jute.

ASSEMBLING

Make or buy 3 or 4 S-hooks, depending on how many straps your harness has. You can easily make an S-hook from the wire hanger that came connected to the plastic planter. Break off the wire about 2″ from the bend in the bottom of the wire and bend the top of the wire in the opposite direction to make an S. If the wire is doubled, simply break it in half at the bottom and make an S-hook with each half. You can also take a 2–3″ piece of wire clothes hanger and bend it ½″ from each end to make an S-curve.

Put the plastic planter into the crocheted planter. Insert an S-hook thru several sts on the inside of the planter and *then* thru the hole of the plastic planter. Insert the other end of the S-hook thru the end of 1 strap of the harness. Repeat this procedure to attach each strap.

Tassel: These directions also apply to a tassel for the Basket Planter [below].

Refer to the directions for making tassels on page 37. Wrap 1 strand of jute around a 12″ piece of cardboard approximately 40 times for Lily jute or 25 times for 5-ply jute. Tie the tassel to the planter through the holes in the bottom of the planter.

Basket Planter

Materials:
- 4 balls 5-ply natural jute (approximately ¼″ in diameter)
- 10″ plastic hanging planter
- 3 or 4 S-hooks (these can be made from the wire hanger that comes with the planter)

Hook: K

Gauge:
Round 1 = 1½″

Finished Size:
10½″ across top, 7″ high

Note: This planter can be adjusted to fit any size pot. For instructions on how to adapt it see the section on tubes on page 125.

Instructions:
Foundation chain: Ch 5, join to 1st ch with slst to make circle. Ch 1.
Round 1: [In this and subsequent rnds the 1st st of the rnd is made in the 1st st of the previous rnd.] Work 8 sc over ch into center of circle, join with slst to 1st st. Ch 1 [8 sts].
Round 2: 2 sc in each sc of previous rnd, join with slst to 1st st. Ch 1 [16 sts].
Round 3: *1 sc in next sc, 2 sc in next sc. Repeat from *, ending with 2 sc in last st, join with slst to 1st st. Ch 1 [24 sts].
Round 4: Repeat Round 3 [36 sts].
Round 5: 1 sc in every sc [no inc—36 sts], join with slst to 1st st. Ch 1.

Round 6: *1 sc in each of next 2 sts, 2 sc in next st. Repeat from *, ending with 2 sc in last st, 1 sc in 1st st of Round 6 [48 sts].
Rounds 7–18: Put a marker in the 1st st of Round 6. It is no longer necessary to join each rnd with a slst. Instead spiral the end of 1 rnd into the beg of the next, as is done at the end of Round 6. Using the marker to keep track of the number of rnds, work 12 more rnds making 1 sc in every st [18 rnds total], ending with a sc in the st before the st directly above the marker in Round 6, then slst into the st above the marker. Ch 1.
Round 19: 1 Shrimp st in every sc, join with a slst to 1st st. End off jute.

Follow the directions above and on page 53 to make the harness and tassel.

Two-Plant Planter

Materials:
- 2 balls sisal
- 1 piece ¾″ plywood, 17x5½″
- 1¾″ wooden dowel, 48″ long
- White glue
- Heavy-duty stapler
- 1 can white enamel spray paint

Hook: K

Gauge:
2 sts = 1″, 2 rows = 1″

Finished Size:
6x6x18″

Instructions:
Foundation chain: Ch 11.
Row 1: 1 sc in 2nd ch from hk, *1 sc in next ch. Repeat from *, ending with 1 sc in last ch. Ch 1, turn.
Rows 2–32: 1 sc in 1st st of previous row, *1 sc in next st. Repeat from *, ending with 1 sc in last st. Ch 1, turn.
Row 33: Insert hk from back to front in the sp between the 1st and 2nd sts of previous row, across the post of the 2nd st, and thru to the back between the 2nd and 3rd sts, yo, draw a lp across the post and out to the back between the 1st and 2nd sts, yo, draw thru 2 lps [Post

st]. Insert hk between 2nd and 3rd sts and repeat. Continue to work around post of each st, ending with insert hk between 9th and 10th sts, across the post of the 10th st, yo, draw up a lp, yo and draw thru 2 lps. Ch 1, turn [10 sts made —Rows 32 and 33 form a corner].

Row 34: Repeat Row 2.

Row 35: 1 sc in each of 1st 3 sts of previous row, 1 sc in each loop A of each of next 3 sts, 1 sc in each of next 4 sts. Ch 1, turn.

Note: It will be helpful to mark the 3 sc done in loops A of the previous row with a piece of yarn. The front lps that remain exposed will be used later to attach and crochet the handles of the planter.

Rows 36–40: Repeat Row 2.

Row 41: Repeat Row 35.

Row 42: Repeat Row 2.

Row 43: Repeat Row 33.

Rows 44–75: Repeat Row 2.

Row 76: Repeat Row 33.

Row 77: Repeat Row 2.

Row 78: Repeat Row 35.

Rows 79–83: Repeat Row 2.

Row 84: Repeat Row 35.

Row 85: Repeat Row 2. Break sisal.

Hold the crocheted piece so that the foundation ch lies next to and in front of Row 85. You will be slip-stitching these 2 rows tog to join the beg of the piece to the end of the piece. Attach sisal thru the 1st st of the foundation ch and loop A of the 1st st of Row 85, join with a slst according to the instructions on page 29. Break sisal.

EDGING

Hold the planter so that the sc rows run vertically. Attach sisal in 1 corner of the planter, 3 sc in the attaching st, *1 sc in side of each sc row, 3 sc in the next corner. Repeat from *, ending with 1 slst in 1st edging sc. Break sisal.

Handles: The 1st handle is worked off the 3 exposed front lps of Row 35 of the planter and attached to the 3 exposed front lps of Row 41 of the planter. Similarly, the 2nd handle is worked off the exposed front lps of Row 78 of the planter and attached to the 3 exposed front lps of Row 84 of the planter.

Attach sisal to 1st of 3 exposed front lps of Row 35 of the planter.

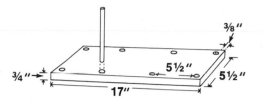

Diagram 67

Row 1: 1 sc in attaching st, 1 sc in each of next 2 sts. Ch 1, turn [3 sts made].

Rows 2–11: 1 sc in 1st st of previous row, 1 sc in each of next 2 sts. Ch 1, turn. Break sisal after Row 11.

Hold Row 11 of the handle next to the 3 exposed front lps of Row 41 of the planter. Attach sisal thru the 1st exposed front lp and the 1st sc of Row 11, slst in the attaching st, slst in each of next 2 sts. Break sisal. Draw any loose ends thru to the inside of the planter. Repeat on opposite side for 2nd handle.

CONSTRUCTING BASE

Sand the piece of plywood lightly. Using a drill with a ⅜″ bit, drill 8 holes in the base, 4 on each long side of the rectangle. Space the holes 5½″ from each other and ⅜″ from the edge of the wood [that is, the center of each hole should be ⅜″ from the edge of the piece of wood]. The holes should be about ⅜″ deep. [See Diagram 67.]

Cut the dowel into eight 6″ pieces and sand them lightly. Put a dab of white glue in each hole and insert a dowel into each. Hold them in place until the glue dries.

ASSEMBLING

Slide the crocheted piece over the dowels so that the bottom edge of the crocheted piece is even with the bottom edge of the wood base. With your crochet hk, pull both ends of a 6″ piece of sisal thru to the inside of the planter so that the ends are on either side of a dowel, about halfway up the dowel. Tie the ends in a secure knot *around* the dowel and bury the loose ends of the knot in the inside st of the planter. Repeat this process of tieing and securing for each dowel. Spray the planter lightly with the spray paint. Hold the can 6″ away from the planter to avoid dripping. Allow the 1st coat to dry thoroughly and then apply a 2nd and perhaps 3rd coat to the planter.

Hammock and Two Pillows

Constructing a hammock is a multi-craft endeavor. Besides crocheting the body of the hammock and its brightly colored pillows, you will prepare and dye the seine twine, make rope, weave the harnesses, and cut and drill holes in the wooden stretchers. Although some of these steps can be shortened or eliminated, most are fun, easy to do, and result in a hammock that is both beautiful and functional.

Hammock

Materials:
- 11 balls #36 seine twine (each approximately 450') *or* #18 or #21 cable cord, dyed as follows: dark blue, 3 balls; fuchsia, 7 balls; gold, 1 ball (see instructions for dyeing seine twine on page 58)
- 3 large cup hooks
- 2 pieces tongue-and-groove oak flooring, ¾ x 2½ x 50"
- Electric drill with bit
- Cloth tape

Hook: N

Gauge:
2 sts = 1", 1 row = ¾" (approximately)

Finished Size:
Hammock = 48x60" (approximately); stress due to the weight of bodies will cause the hammock to stretch to approximately 8'
Harness = 2' (from harness loop to spreaders)

Note: The body of the hammock is made up of 7 panels, crocheted separately and then joined.

Two of the fuchsia seine twine balls will be used to make the harness. Each harness loop requires 10 ropes, each 7–8' in length. We wanted the harness to match the hammock exactly, so we made rope out of the dyed seine twine. However, you can use any strong rope or clothesline, if you prefer, to avoid the extra work.

Instructions:
Panel A: Make 1 panel with the dark blue seine.
Foundation chain: Ch 36.

Row 1: 1 sc in 2nd ch from hk, *1 sc in next ch. Repeat from *, ending with 1 sc in last ch. Ch 1, turn [35 sts].
Row 2: 1 sc in 1st st, *ch 1, skip 1 st, 1 sc in next st. Repeat from *, ending with ch 1, skip next-to-last sc, 1 sc in last st. Ch 1, turn [17 meshes—35 sts].
Row 3: 1 sc in 1st st, *1 sc in ch-1 sp, ch 1, skip next sc. Repeat from *, ending with 1 sc in last ch-1 sp, 1 sc in last st. Ch 1, turn [16 meshes—35 sts].
Row 4: 1 sc in 1st st, *ch 1, skip 1 sc, 1 sc in next ch-1 sp. Repeat from *, ending with 1 sc in last ch-1 sp, skip 1 sc, 1 sc in last sc. Ch 1, turn [17 meshes—35 sts].
Repeat Rows 3–4 until you have completed 80 rows.
Row 81: 1 sc in every st [35 sc]. Break seine twine and tie knot securely.
Panel B: Make 2 panels with the fuchsia seine twine.
Foundation chain: Ch 22.
Row 1: 1 sc in 2nd ch from hk and in every ch [21 sc].
Row 2: Work as Row 2, Panel A [10 meshes].
Rows 3–4: Repeat Rows 3–4, Panel A. You will have alternately 9 meshes and 10 meshes.
Repeat Rows 3–4 until you have completed 80 rows.
Row 81: 1 sc in every st [21 sts]. Break seine twine and tie knot securely.
Panel C: Make 2 panels with the gold seine twine.
Foundation chain: Ch 12.
Row 1: 1 sc in 2nd ch from hk, *1 sc in next ch. Repeat from * to end. Ch 1, turn.
Row 2: Repeat Row 2, Panel A [5 meshes].
Rows 3–4: Repeat Rows 3–4, Panel A. You will have alternately 4 meshes and 5 meshes.

Dyeing Seine Twine

Materials:
- Several balls of seine twine
- 1 package cold-water dye for every 4 to 8 balls of twine, depending upon desired intensity of color
- Water softener (optional)

Instructions:
Before the seine twine can be dyed, it must be made into loose skeins and boiled to remove the sizing. To make a skein, wrap the twine around two straight parallel bars, such as the legs of an up-ended small table, or wrap it around your arm—over your hand and under your bent elbow. If you are using rigid bars, wrap as loosely as possible, or you won't be able to remove the skein from the bars when it is complete. Keep track of the beginning of the ball, and when the skein is made, tie the beginning to the end. Before you remove the skein (or immediately after if you are using your arm), you must tie the skein in several places to keep it from tangling. Thread three or four 8-inch pieces of string or twine in and out of the skein in a figure eight and tie the ends of each piece together. Be sure to make these figure eights quite loose; if they are too tight, they will keep the dye from reaching the twine underneath.

Put the skeins in a large pot and cover them with hot water. It's best to use a pot that is enamel, stainless steel, ceramic, flameproof glass, or pyroceram because some metal pots may react with the sizing in the seine twine, causing your twine to turn dark brown. If you're not sure about your pot, test it out with one skein. You'll know after a few minutes whether or not there is a reaction. Since the twine darkens naturally as it absorbs water, put another skein in water in your sink so you can compare the two.

Simmer the skeins gently for 45 minutes to an hour, changing the water every 20 minutes. If you have water softener, add some each time you change the water. Rinse the skeins and let them cool. Then you are ready to follow the directions on the package of cold-water dye. We found that the most vivid colors could be obtained by dyeing very few skeins per package and by leaving the skeins in the dye bath for twice the length of time suggested on the package.

Repeat Rows 3–4 until you have completed 80 rows.

Row 81: Repeat Row 81, Panel A.

Panel D: Make 2 panels with the fuchsia seine twine.

Foundation chain: Ch 8.

Row 1: 1 sc in 2nd ch from hk, *1 sc in next ch. Repeat from * to end [7 sts]. Ch 1, turn.

Row 2: Repeat Row 2, Panel A [3 meshes].

Rows 3–4: Repeat Rows 3–4, Panel A. You will have alternately 2 meshes and 3 meshes.

Repeat Rows 3–4 until you have completed 80 rows.

Row 81: Repeat Row 81, Panel A.

EDGING PANELS

Edge each one of the panels with its own color seine twine in the following manner: Attach seine twine in the side of the last sc in Row 81. Make 1 sc in the side of the 1st st and in the side of every st until you reach the bottom; make 3 sc in the corner for turning. Working over the foundation ch, make 1 sc in the side of Row 1 and in the side of every st until you reach the top; make 3 sc in the 1st st of Row 81, 1 sc in every sc until last st, 3 sc in last st, and then join to the 1st edging st with a slst. Break the seine twine and then tie securely.

JOINING

Join all of the 7 panels in the following order: D to C to B to A to B to C to D. Place 2 adjoining panels tog, front sides facing down. Attach seine twine of either color thru top side st of both pieces and slst the panel tog as described in the discussion of joining on page 29. Join tog each of the 7 panels.

EDGING HARNESS

With the front side of the hammock facing up, attach fuchsia seine twine in the top right-hand corner. You must space 120 sc across the top edge. The following method may give you a few more or a few less than you need. Adjust it to give you exactly 120 sts.

Row 1: 1 sc in every sc of the 1st panel until last st. 1 dec in last st of panel and 1st st of next panel. Repeat across row. Make sure that you have 120 sts. Ch 1, turn.

Row 2: Insert hk in 1st st and draw up a lp, repeat in 2nd and 3rd sts [3 lps on hk], yo and close all 3 lps tog, ch 3, draw up a lp thru each of the next 3 sts [3 lps on hk], yo and close them all tog. Repeat across top to form 20 ch-3 sps. One rope of the harness will be tied into each sp.

Repeat edging Rows 1 and 2 across other end of hammock.

Harnesses: Refer to the directions for making rope on page 60.

MAKING HARNESS LOOP

Make 10 ropes for both harnesses, each 7–8′ in length.

Put 1 of the cup hooks in the wall at a height you find comfortable to sit in front of and weave ropes that hang from it.

Hang the 10 ropes for the 1st harness over the wall hook so that the ropes hang in 2 equally long bunches on either side of the hook. Tie a 20′ piece of the seine twine [a single strand, not a rope] tightly around the bunch on the left about 4″ below the hook, leaving a 4″ tail of seine twine. Tie *the tail* less tightly around the right-hand bunch, 4″ below the hook, making a ½″ bridge of seine twine between the 2 bunches. [See Diagram 68.]

You are now going to wrap the strand of seine twine around the ropes very tightly, working from point A, around the curve, and then down to point B. Keep the seine twine held taut as you work. After you have wrapped an inch or so of the left-hand bunch, you can remove the ropes from the cup hook and hold the work in your lap.

When you make the curve in the loop, you'll find that you will occasionally have to wrap over the previous turn on the inside of the curve

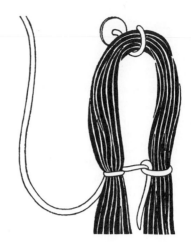

Diagram 68

in order to have each wrapping side by side on the outside of the curve.

You'll find that you must pull down on the right-hand group of ropes as you wrap in order to keep them snugly together in the curve. This is why you tied the right-hand group loosely.

When you have wrapped down to point B, wrap the seine twine tightly around both groups a few times and then wrap between the bunches over the wraps just made [Diagram 69]. Tie and knot the wrapping strand.

WEAVING HARNESS

Put the 2 remaining cup hooks in the wall, 1 on either side of and approximately 1″ from the original hook, so that the 3 hooks are in a somewhat horizontal line. Hang the harness loop on the center hook.

Divide each group of ropes into a front row

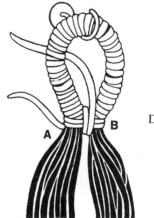

Diagram 69

Making Rope

Place a cup hook in a wall at about waist height. You must be able to stand about 20 feet away from this wall. You'll need a friend to help you make the ropes. If this isn't possible, place a rigid upright bar about 10 feet from the wall and slightly higher than the cup hook; the leg of an up-ended table will do. Insert the threaded end of a second cup hook into a nonelectric hand drill as you would insert a drill bit.

For each rope cut a 40-foot length of twine and tie its ends together. Place the knotted end of the doubled piece over the cup hook on the wall and place the opposite end over the cup hook in the drill. Step back about 20 feet until there is some tension on the twine. Then crank the drill about 250 times or until the twine has enough twists so that it begins to twist back on itself in knots when the tension is eased.

Have a friend grasp the twine at a point halfway between the wall and the drill and pull it laterally, as if it were a bowstring. Keeping the twine taut at all times, walk back to the wall, remove the end of the twine from the drill, and place it over the twine on the wall cup hook. Pinch the two strands together about 4 inches from the point at which your friend is holding them and have your friend let go. The strands will twist together up to the point at which they are pinched. Continue to pinch and release, allowing the strands to twist together a few inches at a time, until you reach the cup hook. Wrap a piece of tape around the strands just below the cup hook so that the rope can't unravel. Remove the rope from the cup hook.

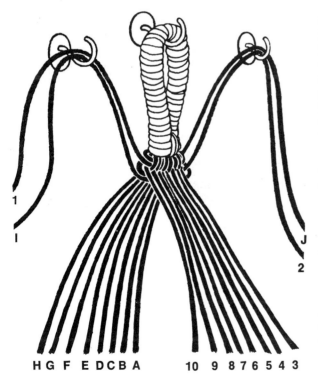

HG F E DCB A   10 9 8 7 6 5 4 3

Diagram 70

of 5 and a back row of 5 (Diagram 70), making a total of 10 ropes in the front and 10 ropes in the back. Temporarily tie off the back row of 10 ropes. Put a piece of cloth tape around each of the 10 ropes in the front row about 3′ down from the harness. These will help you identify which ropes are in the front row and which are in the back row. In your mind number the 10 ropes with the tape in the front row 1 through 10, reading from *right to left*. Untie and mentally label the back row of ropes A to J, also reading from right to left.

You are now going to weave the harness, using your hands in place of a loom. Since the process is most difficult at the beginning, it's a good idea to have a sense of what you're doing before you start. You will move all the front ropes, in order, to the back and all the back ropes, in order, to the front, creating an interlocking pattern of front and back ropes. Next you will pass 1 outside rope from each row between the rows and out the side. Once passed between the rows, the ropes are no longer moved but hang over the 2 side cup hooks. Then you are ready to repeat the 1st step, moving all the ropes now in the front to the

60

back and bringing those in back to the front. [See Diagram 70 for work in progress.]

Use your left hand to separate the ropes that haven't yet been switched. The index finger and the 3rd finger of your right hand manipulate the ropes, and the rest of your right hand keeps the newly switched ropes in their new position. The new back ropes lie against the back of your right hand, and the new front ropes lie against the palm, loosely held in place by your little and ring fingers. You're going to wish you had 3 hands when you begin, but once you get started, you'll find it's not as hard as it seems.

There are two important points to remember while you're working. First, the ropes must stay in the same order in which they begin [that is, Rope 5 must stay between Ropes 6 and 4], so the ropes must always be moved in the same sequence, straight forward or straight back. Once the 1st interlocking is made, you will be able to see the sequence more clearly.

You also must make sure that you always select 1 rope from the front row and 1 rope from the back row to pass between the rows, and as you weave, these ropes must be pushed up tightly into the crotch where the rows cross.

Untie the back group and put your left hand between the front and back groups to keep them apart. With the index finger of your right hand, move Rope 1 [the *right-most* rope in the *front* row] straight back and slide it behind your right hand so that it lies against the back of your hand. Pick up Rope A [the *right-most* rope in the *back* row] and bring it straight forward. Close your little finger and ring finger loosely over it to keep it on your palm.

Now pick up Rope 2 and move it to the back behind your right hand. Pick up Rope B, bring it forward, and hold it in your palm with A. Your left hand will stay more or less stationary, keeping the unused rope in place. Continue moving the ropes until all the ropes with tape [1 thru 10] are in the back and all the ropes without tape [A thru J] are in the front.

Keep the rows separate with your left hand. With your right hand, pick up Rope A [now the *right-most* rope in the *front* row], pass it between the 2 rows to the left, and hang it over the left cup hook. Then pick up Rope 10 [the

left-most rope in the *back* row], pass it between the 2 rows to the right, and hang it over the right cup hook.

Now reweave the remaining 18 ropes. Pick up Rope B [now the right-most rope in the front row] and bring it to the back. Bring Rope 1 [the right-most rope in the back row] forward. Continue until the groups of ropes have been switched again. The row with tape is now in the front again.

Then pass Rope 1 [now the right-most front rope] and Rope J [the left-most back rope] between the groups and hang them over the hooks with the 1st 2 ropes.

Repeat the weaving process until only 2 ropes remain. Remember as you work to tighten the weave so that the ropes on the hooks are continuously pushed upward. Tie the 2 final ropes tog in a single knot.

Your 1st harness is complete. To make the 2nd harness repeat the process using the remaining 10 ropes.

MAKING SPREADERS

Without spreaders, a hammock curls up around its occupant like a cocoon. You must use hardwood to make your spreaders. We found that the most easily available hardwood of the right size was tongue-and-groove oak flooring. This kind of flooring has a ridge down 1 edge and a groove down the other, which we found rather decorative.

Drill 20 holes in each piece of flooring. [Use an electric drill even if you must borrow one. Drilling hardwood like oak is difficult and tiring to do by hand.] Beginning 1¼″ from either end of the board, mark off 20 points, 2½″ apart. The final hole should also be 1¼″ from the end. Use a ⅜″ drill bit to make the holes.

ASSEMBLING

Thread the 20 harness ropes from 1 harness thru the corresponding 20 holes in the spreader. Tie a slip knot in the ropes at each end of the harness, about 4″ from the end of each rope. Hang the harness from a hook. Tie knots in each of the ropes underneath the spreader so that the spreader is perfectly horizontal and is supported equally by all the ropes in the harness. The tails of the center ropes will be longer than the tails of the side ropes. You may want to make these knots slip knots at first, since they may need some adjusting before they are even. However, permanent knots must be tied before the hammock is connected.

With the right side of the hammock facing up, put the tail of each rope thru the corresponding ch-3 lp on the hammock. Tie another knot as near as possible to the knot under the harness.

Repeat with the harness at the other end of the hammock.

When hung, the hammock should be stretched tightly between 2 very solid points 4–5′ above the ground and about 16–18′ apart.

Pillows

Materials:
- 5 balls #36 seine twine (each approximately 450′) *or* #18 or #21 cable cord, dyed to match hammock as follows: main color, 2 balls; color A, less than 1 ball; color B, less than 1 ball; color C, less than 1 ball (see instructions for dyeing seine twine on page 58)
- Fabric backing
- Muslin casing
- Stuffing

Hook: H

Gauge:
3 sts = 1″, 3 rows = 1¼″

Finished Size:
20″ square before stuffing

Note: Directions are given for making 1 side of the pillow. You can either make 2 identical sides and join them, as we did for the blue pillow, or you can cover the 2nd side with fabric, as we did for the orange pillow.

To simplify the directions, color changes are given separately from st directions.

Instructions:
Foundation chain: Ch 2.

Row 1: 3 sc in 2nd ch from hk. Ch 1, turn.

Rows 2–38: 2 sc in 1st st, *1 sc in next st. Repeat from *, ending with 2 sc in last st. Ch 1, turn.

Row 39: 1 sc every st [no inc].

Rows 40–77: 1 dec in 1st 2 sts, *1 sc in next sc. Repeat from *, ending with 1 dec in last 2 sts. Ch 1, turn. [Each of these rows will dec by 2 sts.]

Row 78: Pull up a lp thru each of the 3 remaining sts, yo and close them all tog. Break seine twine.

Color pattern: Foundation ch–Row 15—main color (MC); Row 16—color A; Rows 17–18—color B; Rows 19–21—MC; Row 22—color B; Rows 23–25—color C; Rows 26–27—color B; Rows 28–31—color A; Rows 32–46—MC; Rows 47–50—color A; Rows 51–52—color B; Rows 53–55—color C; Row 56—color B; Rows 57–59—MC; Rows 60–61—color B; Row 62—color A; Rows 63–78—MC.

EDGING

If you plan to make 2 identical sides and join them, you should change the color of the edging seine twine to match the color of the row being edged. Follow the directions for changing yarn in mid-row on page 23. If the pillow will be backed with material, the entire pillow can be edged in the main color. In this case try to make your edging sts as uniform as possible.

Edge according to the directions on page 25.

Block the piece [see page 35] and complete the pillow following the directions for pillows on page 36.

Shell Stitch Tablecloth

Tasseled lampshades, velvet curtains, and silver tea servers bring to mind the rooms of Victorian England. In such a room you might find a tablecloth similar to this one. By using a large hook and working with thin cotton yarn we were able to give the various Shell stitch patterns of the tablecloth an open and luxurious look that is in keeping with other opulent furnishings of the Victorian era.

Materials:
- 10 oz. light blue (color A) UKI or 10 balls light blue Coats & Clark's Speed Cro-Sheen
- 26 oz. dark blue (color B) UKI or 26 balls dark blue Coats & Clark's Speed Cro-Sheen

Hook: I

Gauge:
Rounds 1–3 = 1½″ diameter
Rounds 1–11 = 13″ diameter

Finished Size:
6′ diameter

Instructions:
Foundation chain: Color A—ch 5, join with slst.
Round 1: Ch 2, 7 hdc in ring, join with slst in top of ch-2. Ch 2.
Round 2: 2 hdc in 1st st, *2 hdc in next st. Repeat from *, ending with 2 hdc in last st, join with slst to top of 1st st. Ch 2 [16 sts].
Round 3: Color B—1 dc in 1st st, *(1 dc, ch 1, 1 dc) in next hdc. Repeat from *, ending with (1 dc, ch 1, 1 dc) in last st, join with slst to 1st dc of rnd. Ch 3.
Round 4: (1 dc, ch 1, 1 dc) in 1st ch-1 sp, *(1 dc, ch 1, 1 dc) in next ch-1 sp. Repeat from *, ending with (1 dc, ch 1, 1 dc) in last ch-1 sp. Join with slst to 1st dc of rnd. Ch 3.
Round 5: Repeat Round 4.
Round 6: Color A—3 dc in 1st ch-1 sp [½ Shell], *1 sc in next ch-1 sp, 7 dc in next ch-1 sp. Repeat from *, ending with 3 dc in last ch-1 sp, join with slst to top of ch-3.
Round 7: Color B—1 sc in 1st dc, *7 dc in next sc, 1 sc in center dc of next Shell. Repeat from *, ending with 7 dc in last sc, join with slst to 1st sc.

Round 8: Color A—ch 3, 3 dc in 1st sc, *1 sc in center st of next Shell, 7 dc in next sc. Repeat from *, ending with 3 dc in same sc as 1st 3 dc of rnd, join with slst to 1st dc of rnd [this makes a complete Shell when joined to the beg of the rnd].
Round 9: Color B—repeat Round 7.
Round 10: Color A—repeat Round 8.
Round 11: Color B—1 sc in 1st dc, *ch 6, 1 Pineapple in next sc, ch 6, 1 sc in center dc of next Shell. Repeat from *, ending with 1 Pineapple in last sc, join with slst to 1st sc of rnd.
Round 12: Ch 1, 1 sc in 1st st, *5 dc in next ch-6 sp, 1 sc in next Pineapple st. Repeat from *, ending with 5 dc in last ch-6 sp, join with slst to 1st st.
Round 13: Ch 3, 1 dc in 1st dc, *(1 dc, ch 1, 1 dc) in next dc. Repeat from * to end, join with slst to 1st dc of rnd.
Round 14: Ch 3, 1 dc in 1st dc, *(1 dc, ch 1, 1 dc) in next ch-1 sp. Repeat from * to end, join with slst to top of ch-3.
Round 15: Repeat Round 14.
Round 16: Repeat Round 14, ending with ch 1. *Turn your work* after you join the rnd so that the back of the piece faces you. [The next 9 rnds are joined and turned after each rnd.]
Round 17: Color A—ch 1, *7 sc in 1st ch-1 sp, 1 sc in next ch-1 sp. Repeat from *, ending with slst in 1st sc of rnd. Ch 1, turn.
Round 18: Color B—1 sc in 1st st, (yo, draw up a lp in next dc, yo and thru 2 lps) 3 times [½ Shell], ch 1 for eye of inverted Shell, ch 2, 1 sc in next dc, *ch 2, (yo, draw up a lp in next dc, yo and thru 2 lps) in each of next 3 dc, the sc, and the next 3 dc, yo and thru all 8 lps, ch 1 for eye, ch 2, 1 sc in next dc.* Repeat from * to *, ending with ch 2, repeat from * to * in each of last 3 dc, yo and thru 4 lps [½

Shell], slst in eye of 1st ½ Shell. Ch 2, turn.
Round 19: Color B—3 dc in eye of 1st inverted Shell [this is the same eye in which you made the final slst on the previous rnd], *1 sc in next sc, 7 dc in eye of next Shell. Repeat from *, ending with 1 sc in last sc, 4 dc in eye of 1st inverted Shell [same st as 1st 3 dc of rnd], slst in 1st dc of rnd. Ch 1, turn.

Round 20: Color A—ch 3, 1 sc in 1st dc. Repeat from * to * of Round 18 to end, join with slst to 1st sc. Ch 1, turn.
Round 21: Color A—1 sc in 1st sc, *7 dc in eye of next Shell, 1 sc in next sc. Repeat from *, ending with 7 dc in eye of last Shell, join with slst, ch 2, turn, 1 slst in 1st sc of rnd.
Round 22: Color B—repeat Round 18.

Round 23: Repeat Round 19.
Round 24: Color A—repeat Round 20.
Round 25: 5 dc in eye of 1st Shell, *1 sc in next sc, 9 dc in eye of next Shell. Repeat from *, ending with 4 dc in eye of 1st Shell [same st as 1st 5 dc of rnd], join with slst to 1st dc of rnd.
Round 26: Color B—ch 1, 1 sc in 1st st, *ch 3, Pineapple st in next sc, 1 sc in center dc of next Shell. Repeat from *, ending with 1 sc in center dc of last Shell. Join with slst to 1st sc of rnd.
Round 27: Ch 3, 3 dc in 1st ch-3 sp, *1 dc in next Pineapple, 3 dc in next ch-3 sp, 1 dc in next sc, 3 dc in next ch-3 sp. Repeat from *, ending with 3 dc in last ch-3 sp, slst in top of ch-3.
Round 28: Ch 3, 1 dc in 1st dc, *skip 1 dc, (1 dc, ch 1, 1 dc) *over all 3 lps* of next dc. Repeat from *, ending with (1 dc, ch 1, 1 dc) over all 3 lps of last dc, join with slst in top of ch-3.
Round 29: Ch 3, 1 dc in 1st dc, *(1 dc, ch 1, 1 dc) in next ch-1 sp. Repeat from * to end, join with slst in top of ch-3.
Round 30: Ch 1, 3 sc in 1st dc, *ch 3, (1 dc, ch 1, 1 dc) in next ch-1 sp, ch 3, skip next ch-1 sp, 3 sc in next ch-1 sp. Repeat from *, ending with (1 dc, ch 1, 1 dc) in 3rd ch-1 sp from end of rnd, ch 3, 1 sc in next ch-1 sp, (1 dc, ch 1, 1 dc) in last ch-1 sp, slst in 1st sc.
Round 31: Ch 1, 1 sc in next sc, *ch 3, 7 dc in next ch-3 sp between 2 dc of previous rnd, ch 3, 1 sc in center of next 3-sc group. Repeat from * to end, join with slst in 1st sc of rnd, slst in each of next 3 chs.
Round 32: Ch 1, 1 sc in each dc of 1st Shell, *ch 5, 1 sc in each dc of next Shell. Repeat from *, ending with ch 5, slst in 1st ch of rnd.
Round 33: Ch 1, slst in 1st 3 sc of 1st Shell, 3 sc in next sc [center of 1st Shell], *ch 3, (1 dc, ch 3, 1 dc) in 3rd ch of ch-5, ch 3, 3 sc in center sc of next Shell. Repeat from *, ending with (1 dc, ch 1, 1 dc) in 3rd ch of last ch-5, ch 3, slst in 1st sc of 1st 3-sc group of rnd.
Round 34: Repeat Round 31. [At the end of this rnd and every 3 rnds that you do this pat you will notice that you move over 1 Shell each time you start the pat over again.]

Round 35: Repeat Round 32.
Round 36: Repeat Round 33.
Round 37: Repeat Round 31.
Round 38: Repeat Round 32.
Round 39: Repeat Round 33.
Round 40: Repeat Round 31.
Round 41: Repeat Round 32.
Round 42: Repeat Round 33.
Round 43: Repeat Round 31.
Round 44: Repeat Round 32.
Round 45: Repeat Round 33.
Round 46: Repeat Round 32.
Round 47: Repeat Round 33.
Round 48: Slst in 1st 3 sc of 1st Shell. 1 sc in next sc [center sc of Shell], *ch 5, 1 Popcorn st in 3rd ch of next ch-5 group, ch 5, 1 sc in center sc of next Shell. Repeat from *, ending with 1 Popcorn in 3rd ch of last ch-5 group, slst in 1st sc of rnd.
Round 49: Ch 3, 5 dc under 1st ch-5 group, *1 sc in top of next Popcorn, 5 dc under next ch-5 group. Repeat from *, ending with slst in top of ch-3.
Round 50: Ch 3, 1 dc in 1st dc going over all 3 lps of the dc, *skip 1 dc, (1 dc, ch 1, 1 dc) in next dc [again going over all 3 lps of the dc]. Repeat from *, ending with skip 1 dc, slst in top of ch-3.
Round 51: Repeat Round 14.
Round 52: Repeat Round 14, ending with slst in top of ch-3. Ch 1. *Turn your work* so that the back of the piece faces you. [The next 13 rnds are to be joined and then turned at the end of each rnd.]
Round 53: Color A—repeat Round 17.
Round 54: Color B—repeat Round 18.
Round 55: Repeat Round 19.
Round 56: Color A—repeat Round 20.
Round 57: Repeat Round 21.
Round 58: Color B—repeat Round 18.
Round 59: Repeat Round 19.
Round 60: Color A—repeat Round 20.
Round 61: Repeat Round 21.
Round 62: Color B—repeat Round 18.
Round 63: Repeat Round 19.
Round 64: Color A—repeat Round 20.
Round 65: Repeat Round 21. Break yarn.

Mohair Afghan

Who could resist snuggling under this pastel cloud? Soft, light, and luscious, the effect of this afghan is created by crocheting two identical pieces in single crochet, using a giant hook. The double thickness produces warmth without weight.

Materials:
- 22 skeins Reynolds #1 mohair (each approximately 1⅓ oz.) in the following amounts: light green #20, 4 skeins; medium green #64, 7 skeins; dark green #10, 6 skeins; purple #50, 2 skeins; aqua #14, 2 skeins; yellow #8, 1 skein *or* corresponding amounts of any mohair or mohair-acrylic blend

Note: The amounts given above are enough for 8 panels.

Hook: N

Gauge:
2 sts = 1″, 2 rows = 1″ (approximately)

Finished Size:
Each panel = 15x60″ (approximately). The completed afghan is a double thickness. You will make a front piece and a back piece of equal size, then st them tog. The afghan shown in the photograph on the opposite page is made up of 8 panels—4 in the front piece and 4 in the back piece—and measures approximately 60x60″.

Note: You can make the afghan any size you like. The length can be adjusted simply by changing the length of the foundation ch. The width is determined by the number of panels you make.

Instructions:
Foundation chain: Ch 113 with aqua.
Row 1: 1 sc in 2nd ch from hk, *1 sc in next ch. Repeat from *, ending with 1 sc in last ch [112 sts], complete last st and ch 1 using medium green, turn. [See the instructions for changing yarn at the end of a row on page 23.]
Row 2: 1 sc in 1st st thru loop A only. *1 sc in loop A only of next st. Repeat from *, ending with 1 sc in last st thru loop A. Ch 1, turn.

Repeat Row 2 for pat, changing colors, when indicated, as you did at the end of Row 1.
Rows 3–5: Medium green.
Row 6: Dark green.
Rows 7–8: Purple.
Row 9: Dark green.
Row 10: Aqua.
Rows 11–13: Dark green.
Rows 14–15: Medium green.
Rows 16–17: Light green.
Row 18: Purple.
Rows 19–20: Dark green.
Row 21: Medium green.
Row 22: Dark green.
Rows 23–25: Medium green.
Row 26: Light green.
Row 27: Medium green.
Rows 28–29: Light green.
Row 30: Yellow.

You have completed 1 panel. For the 2nd panel repeat the directions in *reverse order,* beg with Row 30 and ending with Row 1. The 3rd panel begins with Row 1 and ends with Row 30. Continue to alternate the panels until the afghan is the width you desire. Repeat from the beg for the back piece.

The pieces do not need edging. Place the front and back pieces tog, with the front sides facing each other. [The pieces have no specific front and back sides; whichever side of each looks the neatest can be the front.] Using medium green, join the tops of the pieces with loose sc sts. The afghan stretches so much that you will need to inc every so often, or the joining will be too tight. Repeat on the bottom. Turn the afghan inside out; using aqua, join the sides with sc thru 2 inside lps only.

Carefully and lightly block the top and bottom seams only, following the instructions for blocking on page 35.

Tahki Floor Pillow

Both the stitch and texture of our giant floor pillow reflect the growing popularity of the woven look in contemporary home decoration. The beautiful natural yarns used for years by weavers are well suited for crochet as well. Here we've used a combination of Tahki handspun sheepswool and Reynolds Lopi in light gray, medium gray, dark brown, and off white to achieve an earthy, rustic mood that's perfect for the casual look of today.

Materials:
- 14 skeins Reynolds Lopi in the following amounts: light gray #7356, 4 skeins; medium gray, #7357, 3 skeins; dark brown #7352, 2 skeins; off white #7354, 3 skeins *or* corresponding amounts of any bulky weight yarn
- 3 balls Tahki multicolored handspun sheepswool *or* any bulky weight yarn
- Muslin casing
- Stuffing

Hook: N

Gauge:
3 sts = 1¾", 3 rows = 1¾"

Finished Size:
26x58" (1 side only: 26" square)
   Note: The materials listed above are sufficient to cover an overstuffed 30" floor pillow on 2 sides. If you plan to cover only 1 side, you will need approximately half the listed quantity of each color.
   This pillow can be made any size you wish simply by adjusting the foundation ch. The pillow is worked in 1 direction only, from right to left. Cut the yarn at the end of each row and reattach it in the 1st st of the previous row so that you never work with the back of the piece facing you.
   Always use 2 strands of Lopi worked tog.

Instructions:
Foundation chain: Medium gray Lopi—ch 101 [ch 51 for 1 side only].
Row 1: 1 hdc in 2nd ch from hk, *1 hdc in next ch. Repeat from *, ending with 1 hdc in last ch [100 sts].

Row 2: Light gray Lopi—1 hdc Post st around post of 1st st from back to front, *1 hdc Post st around post of next st from back to front. Repeat from *, ending with 1 hdc Post st around last post [100 sts].
Rows 3–4: Multicolored Tahki—repeat Row 2.
Row 5: Dark brown Lopi—repeat Row 2.
Row 6: Multicolored Tahki—repeat Row 2.
Row 7: Dark brown Lopi—repeat Row 2.
Row 8: Multicolored Tahki—repeat Row 2.
Row 9: Medium gray Lopi—repeat Row 2.
Row 10: Light gray Lopi—1 hdc in *loop A and post loop* of 1st st, *1 hdc in back and bottom lps of next st. Repeat from *, ending with 1 hdc in loop A and post lp of last st.
Rows 11–12: Medium gray Lopi—repeat Row 10.
Row 13: Multicolored Tahki—repeat Row 2.
Row 14: Light gray Lopi—repeat Row 2.
Row 15: Multicolored Tahki—repeat Row 2.
Row 16: Off-white Lopi—repeat Row 2.
Row 17: Multicolored Tahki—1 hdc in 1st st, *1 hdc in next st. Repeat from *, ending with 1 hdc in last st.
Row 18: Multicolored Tahki—repeat Row 2.
Row 19: Light gray Lopi—repeat Row 2.
Row 20: Multicolored Tahki—repeat Row 2.
Rows 21–22: Light gray Lopi—repeat Row 2.
Row 23: Multicolored Tahki—repeat Row 10.
Row 24: Multicolored Tahki—repeat Row 2.
Row 25: Dark brown Lopi—repeat Row 2.
Row 26: Light gray Lopi—repeat Row 10.
Row 27: Multicolored Tahki—repeat Row 2.
Row 28: Medium gray Lopi—repeat Row 2.
Row 29: Light gray Lopi—repeat Row 2.
Row 30: Multicolored Tahki—repeat Row 2.
Row 31: Dark brown Lopi—repeat Row 2.

Row 32: Multicolored Tahki—repeat Row 2.
Row 33: Light gray Lopi—repeat Row 10.
Row 34: Multicolored Tahki—repeat Row 2.
Row 35: Off-white Lopi—repeat Row 2.
Row 36: Multicolored Tahki—repeat Row 2.
Row 37: Off-white Lopi—repeat Row 2.
Row 38: Multicolored Tahki—repeat Row 10.
Row 39: Multicolored Tahki—repeat Row 2.
Row 40: Light gray Lopi—repeat Row 2.
Row 41: Off-white Lopi—repeat Row 10.
Row 42: Multicolored Tahki—repeat Row 2.
Row 43: Medium gray Lopi—repeat Row 2.
Row 44: Multicolored Tahki—repeat Row 2.

Row 45: Light gray Lopi—repeat Row 2.
Row 46: Medium gray Lopi—repeat Row 10.

Break yarn and weave tails into back side. If you are making 1 side only, edge piece in hdc, using medium gray Lopi. If piece is to cover 2 sides, edge side of foundation ch only. Fold the piece in half to make a square, with the back side facing out. Sc the top and bottom tog using Tahki. Turn inside out so that front side faces out. Insert a stuffed muslin casing [see page 36] and join the edges of the 2 open sides with sc worked thru the 2 inside lps of each st only, using medium gray.

Braided Rug

Early American settlers covered the floors of their homes with braided rugs coiled from rags and scraps of fabric. The same method can be applied to crocheted strips of yarn coiled and sewn into an interesting rug for contemporary American homes. Try using various balls and skeins of yarn left over from other projects—a variety of color and texture adds to the effect.

Materials:
- 24 skeins Paternayan knitting yarn (each 4 oz.) in the following amounts: dark rust (color A) #815, 8 skeins; off white (color B) #030, 8 skeins; burnt orange (color C) #863, 8 skeins *or* corresponding amounts of any worsted weight yarn

Hook: H

Gauge:
3 sts = 1″

Note: If you have lots of leftover skeins of yarn lying around the house from projects long completed, abandoned, or forgotten, this braided rug might be the perfect opportunity to use them up.

Different types, colors, and textures of yarn often look terrific when they are worked together. They work especially well when they are repeated several times in motifs such as those featured in this rug. Nubby novelty yarns, shiny rayon ribbons, soft, fluffy mohairs, and variegated acrylics can be worked successfully with knitting worsteds, linen, and plain thread.

When combining yarns to make your strips, the only important factor to keep in mind is that the st gauge [in this project it is 3 sts to the inch] for all strips must be the same or the coiled motifs will not be the proper uniform sizes and will not fit together correctly. It's a good idea to make a practice swatch with the combination of yarns you have chosen before starting your coils. This will ensure that the groupings you have chosen will give you 3 sts to the inch.

Finished Size:
3x5′ (approximately)

Instructions:
The chart below gives most of the information needed to make this rug. All circle motifs are crocheted in the same way. The only difference in motifs is size, which is determined by the number of chs you make to start a motif. The numbers on the left side of the chart give the number of chs you need to start each of the motifs. The letters on the top tell you the different combinations of yarns to use in the motifs. There are always 2 letters for each box because each motif is made by working 2 strands of yarn tog.

Number of Motifs

	AA	BB	CC	AB	AC	BC
#1—ch 360	2	4	4	7	4	8
#2—ch 250	5	4	4	3	2	4
#3—ch 180	4	7	6	2	3	3
#4—ch 120	5	5	3	2	1	4
#5—ch 55	6	5	5	3	2	5

Look first at the left side of the chart. Motif 1 is the largest. Reading from left to right, you see that you need 2 Motif 1's worked with 2 strands of color A, 4 Motif 1's made with 2 strands of color B, 4 Motif 1's worked with 2 strands of color C, 7 Motif 1's worked with 1 strand of color A and 1 strand of color B, 4 Motif 1's worked with 1 strand of color A and 1 strand of color C, 8 Motif 1's worked with 1 strand of color B and 1 strand of color C. You will therefore make a total of 29 Motif 1's. Read the chart in the same way for Motifs 2–5. Later on, refer to Diagram 71 for assembly instructions.

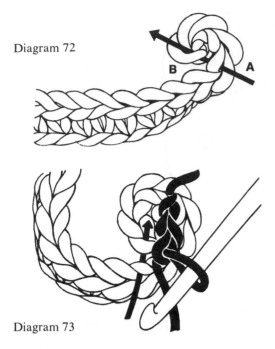

Diagram 72

Diagram 73

The directions below are for a Motif 1 [the largest]. To do the other 4 sizes just substitute the proper number of chs for the foundation ch as given in the chart and then repeat Row 1.
Foundation chain: Ch 360.
Row 1: Insert hk into the *bottom* lp of the 2nd ch from hk and make 1 sc, *1 sc in bottom lp of next ch. Repeat from *, ending with 1 slst in each of the last 3 chs. Break yarn.

You now have a strip of crocheted yarn with a neat edge on both the top and bottom. The top edge has neat sc heads and the bottom looks very much the same because you picked up the foundation ch from the bottom strand. This strip will be coiled and tacked in place to form the motif.

Start your coil from the end that does *not* have the slst. The sc heads should be on top. Coil the braid so that the 6th st from the end [A in Diagram 72] lies in front of the 2nd st from the end [B in Diagram 72]. Insert your hk thru the *back lp* of this 6th st and the *front lp* of the 2nd st [Diagram 72]. Pull a strand of yarn thru and tie a knot. Insert your hk thru these same sts once again and pull up a lp. Insert your hk into the back of the 7th st and the front of the 3rd st and make a sc. Next pick

up the back of the 8th st and the front of the 4th st and make a sc. These scs are called *tacking scs* and will be utilized a little later on in forming the coil. Now you have started your coil. Pin the coil ahead 4 or 5 sts. Look at these sts. Sometimes the heads of 2 front sts will have to be attached to the head of the same back st [Diagram 73].

When you reach the 12th st, insert your hk into the back lp of the 12th st and the *tacking sc of the previous rnd* and make a sc. From now on you will make each new tacking sc by inserting your hk into the back lp of the front coil st and the closest tacking sc of the previous rnd. The important thing to remember is that the coils should not be so loose that they gap on the front side or so tight that they begin to cup abruptly.

Pinning ahead will help you keep the right tension. Continue tacking the coil until all the sts are attached, including the last 3 slsts.

Note: Due to the nature of the yarn there may be a slight cupping. A mild steam pressing will eliminate this.

ASSEMBLING MOTIFS

When you have finished all the motifs, place them back side up on the floor in accordance with the pat in Diagram 71. You will have to join the motifs on the floor, leaving them in place. Your motifs should touch the motifs adjoining them in such a way that at least 3 tacking scs of 1 motif meet 3 opposing tacking scs of an adjoining motif. Join these opposing pairs of sts, following the directions for edge-to-edge joining on page 29. Join all motifs to each other wherever they meet.

EDGING

You will edge only *outside* motifs. Attach the edging yarn [2 strands of color A worked tog] thru the outside lp only of any outside motif. Make 1 sc in the attaching st. Make scs around the outside of the motif until you reach the next outside motif. Then pick up the closest outside st of the next outside motif and continue around the new motif. When you come back to the attaching st, slst in the lst sc and break the yarn.

Note: Put strips of carpet tape on the back of the rug to prevent skidding.

Window Shade Trim

Not only shades, but drapes, curtains, bedspreads, bolsters, place mats, napkins, and lampshades can be enhanced by crochet trim. Just blanket stitch around the edge of the fabric, spacing the stitches so that the number of blanket stitches per inch approximates the number of crochet stitches you will be making per inch. Then crochet into each blanket stitch just as though it were a crochet stitch.

Materials:
- 4 balls DMC #5 Pearl Cotton (each 53 yds.) in the following amounts: light peach #754, 1 ball; medium peach #353, 2 balls; dark peach #352, 1 ball *or* corresponding amounts of any thin cotton or linen
- Window shade cut to desired size *or* fabric and iron-on interfacing to make shade (see instructions for measurements)
- Shade roller, wood slat, and shade pull (remove an old shade from its roller, remove slat and pull from shade, discard shade)

Note: The amounts of yarn given are for a 26″ shade.

Hook: 00 steel

Gauge:
4 sts = 1″, Rows 1 and 2 = 1″

Finished Size:
3½″ from shade to bottom of trim (width is adjustable—see instructions for trim)

Instructions:
Shade: If you are making your shade, cut fabric 1″ wider than you want the window shade to be [= ½″ hem on each side] and 4″ longer [= ½″ hem on top and bottom, plus 3″ for pocket to hold wood slat at bottom]. Make a ½″ hem all around the fabric, using a backstitch if you are sewing by hand [see page 38], or set the st regulator on your machine to 10 sts to the inch. Cut the interfacing ¼″ smaller than the measurements of the fabric after hemming. Pin or loosely baste the interfacing to the back of the fabric. Make sure that the adhering side of the interfacing [the rough side] lies against the back of the fabric. Place a thin piece of cloth over the interfacing and press

with your iron on a medium-low setting, or follow the directions for the interfacing you are using. Do *not* iron over the pins—as you reach them, remove them before pressing. Remove the basting sts after pressing.

A window shade must be weighted at the bottom so that it hangs evenly. This is done by inserting a wood slat in a pocket at the bottom of the shade. To make this pocket, turn up the bottom of the shade to the back, making a 1½″ hem. Machine sew or backstitch this hem as close to the original hem as possible, then place the bottom of the shade front side down on the ironing board, cover the back with the thin cloth, and press lightly.

Trim: With dressmaker's chalk, make a mark every ¼″ across the bottom of the shade on the back. Thread a needle with light peach and make 1 blanket st [see page 38] every ¼″, using the marks as guidelines. You will crochet into the lp of each blanket st as if it were a crochet st. Count the number of lps you have across the bottom of the shade. This is the number of sts you have. You should have approximately 4 sts to the inch.

The shade trim pat is designed to be worked over a multiple of 6 times an odd number of sts, plus 1. For example, 6 × 13 = 78 + 1 = 79; 6 × 15 = 90 + 1 = 91; 6 × 17 = 102 + 1 = 103; 6 × 19 = 114 + 1 = 115. You can work the shade trim pat on 79 sts, 91, 103, 115, or any other product of 6 times an odd number plus 1. It is unlikely, of course, that you have the exact number of sts required to work the pat. If you are within 1 st of a correct pat number, inc or dec 1 st on the 1st row. [To inc 1 st on a Shell st pat, skip 1 st rather than 2 after any Shell before making the sc; to dec 1 st, skip 3 sts rather than 2.] If you have 2 or

3 sts *too few* for a correct pat number [e.g., the pat number is 103 sts, and you have 100], inc on the 1st row so that you have the exact number required. If you have 2 to 7 sts *too many,* divide the extra sts by 2. Half the extra sts will go on either end of the shade. If you have an odd number of extra sts, inc 1 st on the 1st row and divide the rest of the extra sts between the 2 ends of the shade. The instructions are written as if you have extra sts on each side of your pat. If you have the exact number of sts required, simply ignore the instructions for extra sts at the beg and end of each row. Always work with the front of the shade facing you.

Row 1: Attach light peach in 1st extra st. 1 sc in each extra st, 1 sc in 1st pat st, *skip 2 sts, one 5-dc Shell st in next st, skip 2 sts, 1 sc in next st. Repeat from *, ending with 1 sc in last st of pat, 1 sc in each extra st. Break yarn.

Row 2: Reattach light peach in 1st extra st. 1 sc in each extra st, 1 sc in each of 1st 3 pat sts, *(1 hdc, 1 dc, 1 hdc) in center st of Shell st, 1 sc in next st, (insert hk in next st and draw up a lp) 3 times, yo and pull thru all 3 lps [one 3-st dec made], 1 sc in next st. Repeat from *, ending with (1 hdc, 1 dc, 1 hdc) in center of last Shell, 1 sc in each of last 3 pat sts, 1 sc in each extra st. Break yarn.

Row 3: Attach medium peach in 1st extra st. 1 sc in loop A of each extra st, 1 sc in loop A of each of 1st 4 pat sts, *(1 sc, 1 Pineapple st, 1 sc) over all lps of center dc of previous row, 1 sc in loop A of next st, ch 3, skip 3 sts, 1 sc in loop A of next st. Repeat from *, ending with (1 sc, 1 Pineapple, 1 sc) over all lps of last center dc, 1 sc in loop A of each of last 4 pat sts, 1 sc in loop A of each extra st. Break yarn.

Row 4: Work in loop A only. Attach light peach in *side* of 1st extra st of 1st row. 1 sc in side of each row [= 3 sc], 3 sc in corner st, 1 sc in each extra st and in each of 1st 5 pat sts, *1 sc in Pineapple st, 7 tr in ch-3 sp. Repeat from *, ending with 1 sc in last Pineapple, 1 sc in each of last 5 pat sts and in each extra st, 3 sc in corner, 1 sc in side of each row. Break yarn.

Row 5: Attach medium peach in center st of 3-sc corner. 1 sc in each extra st and in each of 1st 9 pat sts, *(1 sc, 1 Pineapple st, 1 sc) in center st of 7-tr Shell, 1 sc in each of next 2 sts, ch 3, skip 3 sts, 1 sc in each of next 2 sts. Repeat from *, ending with (1 sc, 1 Pineapple, 1 sc) in center st of last 7-tr Shell, 1 sc in each of last 9 pat sts and in each extra st. Break yarn.

Row 6: Attach medium peach in top of 1st Pineapple st. *1 sc in Pineapple, ch 5, 1 sc in ch-3 sp, ch 5, 1 sc in next Pincapple, 1 sc in each of next 2 sts, 5 sc in next ch-3 sp, 1 sc in each of next 2 sts. Repeat from *, ending with 1 sc in next-to-last Pineapple, ch 5, 1 sc in last ch-3 sp, ch 5, 1 sc in last Pineapple. Break yarn.

Row 7: Attach medium peach in 1st sc of Row 6 above 1st Pineapple st. *1 sc in sc above Pineapple, 5 dc in 1st ch-5 sp, 5 tr in sc, 5 dc in next ch-5 sp, 1 sc in sc above next Pineapple, one 3-st dec, 1 sc in each of next 4 sts, one 3-st dec. Repeat from *, ending with 1 sc in sc above last Pineapple. Break yarn.

Row 8: Work in loop A only. Attach dark peach in 1st st of Row 4. 1 sc in each of side sts of Row 4, 3 sc in 1st st of Row 5 [corner st], 1 sc in each extra st and each pat st until center st of 5-tr Shell, *(1 sc, ch 3, 1 sc) in center st of 5-tr Shell, 1 sc in each of next 7 sts, one 3-st dec over next 3 sts, 1 sc in next st, ch 3, 1 sc in next st, one 3-st dec over next 3 sts, 1 sc in each of next 7 sts. Repeat from *, ending with 1 sc in each of last pat sts and in each extra st, 3 sc in last st of Row 5, 1 sc in each of side sts of Row 4. Break yarn.

Row 9: Work in loop A only. Attach medium peach in 1st st of Row 8. 1 sc in each side st, 3 sc in corner st, 1 sc in each extra st, 1 sc in each pat st until ch-3 sp above 1st Pineapple st of Row 7, *(1 sc, 1 Pineapple, 1 sc) in ch-3 sp above Pineapple, 1 sc in each of next 7 sts, one 3-st dec over next 3 sts. 1 Pineapple in ch-3 sp, one 3-st dec over next 3 sts, 1 sc in each of next 7 sts. Repeat from *, ending with (1 sc, 1 Pineapple, 1 sc) in ch-3 sp above last Pineapple, 1 sc in each of last pat sts and in each of last extra sts, 3 sc in corner, 1 sc in each of last side sts. Break yarn.

Tack 1st and last side sts of Row 9 to shade.

Shade pull: This pat can be worked on a dough-nut-shaped shade pull ring of any size.

Round 1: Tie light peach around ring. *Insert hk thru hole in center, yo, pull up a lp to top of ring, and complete sc. Repeat from * until ring is completely covered [push sts tog to get a thick covering]. Join to 1st sc with slst and break yarn. Count the number of sts you have made and put a marker at either end of what will be the 18 sts on the *bottom* of the shade pull.

Round 2: Attach medium peach in 1st st of bottom 18 sts. 1 sc in 1st st, skip 2 sts, 5 dc in next st, skip 2 sts, 1 sc in next st, skip 2 sts, 7 tr in next st, skip 2 sts, 1 sc in next st, skip 2 sts, 5 dc in next st, skip 2 sts, 1 sc in each remaining st, join to 1st sc with slst. Break yarn.

Round 3: Work in loop A only. Attach dark peach in 1st st of **Round 2.** 1 sc in each st until center st of 7-tr Shell, (1 sc, ch 3, 1 sc) in cen-ter st, 1 sc in each remaining st, join with slst to 1st st. Break **yarn.**

Round 4: Work in loop A only. Attach medium peach in st over center st of 1st 6-dc Shell. You should have 8 sts before the ch-3 sp, in-cluding the attaching st. 1 Pineapple st in at-taching st, 1 sc in each of next 7 sts, (1 sc, 1 Pineapple, 1 sc) in ch-3 sp, 1 sc in each of next 7 sts, 1 Pineapple in next st, 1 sc in each of remaining sts, join to 1st st with slst. Break yarn.

The chain attaching the ring to the trim can be any length desired. Attach medium peach in top center st of ring. 1 Pineapple st in at-taching st, ch desired number, 1 slst thru cen-ter Pineapple of center pat of trim, 1 sc in each ch, slst to top of Pineapple. Break yarn.

ASSEMBLING

Block trim and shade pull [see page 35]. Attach shade to roller with staple gun. Insert slat in pocket of shade. Roll up and hang.

Using Other Materials

As exemplified by the Window Shade Trim, crochet can be used as a trim for fabric. The beginning crochet stitches are worked off evenly spaced blanket stitches that have been made on the fabric. Substitute fur, needlepoint canvas, or leather for fabric and you've literally tripled your crochet possibilities. For that mat-ter, virtually any material can be used with crochet trim as long as there is a way to join the two. Blanket stitches will work well for soft leathers and needlepoint canvas; for less flexi-ble materials, such as stiff leather, you will have to punch holes.

Regardless of which material you use, your first step must be to determine the gauge of your crochet. Make a practice swatch. The number of crochet stitches per inch must be as close as possible to the number of blanket stitches or holes per inch to be made. Some-times it will not be possible to fit enough holes or blanket stitches on your material. In that case, try making half as many, putting 2 cro-chet stitches in each one. For needlepoint can-vas, turn under the edge of the canvas and make blanket stitches along the doubled edge. Soft leather, such as suede or chamois, can be treated the same way.

For stiff leather you will have to punch holes. Rotary punches, which can make holes of many different sizes, are available in hobby and leather supply stores. Experiment on a practice piece of leather first. Decide how far apart to make the holes, how far away from the edge they should be (¼ " is a good distance generally), and what size punch to use. The hook you used to make your practice crochet swatch should be able to fit through the hole, enabling you to crochet directly into it. When you're ready to start on the good piece of leather, turn it over to the back side, measure, and mark spots for holes with a felt-tipped pen. Measure carefully—once a hole is made it must be used.

For fur, punch holes as you did for leather, or sew a running stitch around the piece on the back side and work off the stitches.

Mohair Baby Blanket

The most enjoyable way we know to practice new stitches is to make a stitch sampler. The interplay of stitches creates texture as well as a seemingly complex design. Our stitch sampler baby blanket is easy to make, and combines the practicality of machine-washable acrylic with the formality of a fine heirloom. For a more vivid effect, try alternating several colors as you alternate the stitches.

Materials:
- 4 balls white Unger Fluffy *or* any mohair acrylic blend
- 4 balls white Reynolds Pearlette or Unger Nanette *or* any sport weight acrylic

Hook: K

Gauge:
Round 1 = 10″ long, 1″ wide

Finished Size:
30x39″

Note: When you make the corners for this project, it is important to remember that the head of a dc is to the *right* of its post. [See Diagram 34, page 18.] This means that the 2nd skipped st of a corner appears to be part of the ch-1 sp. Always work the sts of a corner *over all lps* into the ch-1 sp, even when the directions for the row tell you to work in loop A of the sts only.

Instructions:
Foundation chain: Fluffy—ch 32.
Round 1: 1 hdc in 2nd ch from hk, **1 hdc in next ch.** Repeat from ** to ** until last ch, 3 hdc in last ch. Do *not* turn. Working down other side of ch, repeat from ** to **, ending with 2 hdc in ch that has 1st hdc, join to 1st hdc with slst [29 sts on each side, plus 3 sts in each end = 64 sts].
Round 2: Work in loop A only. Ch 2 [= 1 hdc], 1 hdc in 1st st, ch 1, 2 more hdc in 1st st, skip next st, **1 hdc in each of next 27 sts, skip next st, (2 hdc, ch 1, 2 hdc) in next st, 1 hdc in next st,** (2 hdc, ch 1, 2 hdc) in next st, skip next st. Repeat from ** to **, ending with 1 hdc in last st, join to top ch of ch-2 with slst.
Round 3: Work in loop A only. Ch 2, **skip next st, (2 hdc, ch 1, 2 hdc) in ch-1 sp, skip next st [= 1 corner], 1 hdc in each of next 29 sts, 1 corner,** 1 hdc in next st. Repeat from ** to **, ending with last corner, join to top ch of ch-2 with slst.
Round 4: Work in loop A only. Ch 2, 1 hdc in next st, **1 corner, 1 hdc in each of next 31 sts, 1 corner,** 1 hdc in each of next 5 sts. Repeat from ** to **, ending with last corner, 1 hdc in each of last 3 sts, join to top ch of ch-2 with slst.
Round 5: Work in loop A only. Ch 2, 1 hdc in each of next 2 sts, **1 corner, 1 hdc in each of next 33 sts, 1 corner,** 1 hdc in each of next 7 sts. Repeat from ** to **, ending with last corner, 1 hdc in each of last 4 sts, join to top ch of ch-2 with slst.
Round 6: Work in loop A only. Slst in next st, ch 3, skip next st, 1 hdc in next st, **1 corner, (1 hdc in next st, ch 1, skip 1 st) 16 times, 1 hdc in next st, 1 corner,** (1 hdc in next st, ch 1, skip 1 st) 4 times, 1 hdc in next st. Repeat from ** to **, ending with last corner, (1 hdc in next st, ch 1, skip 1 st) 3 times, join to 2nd ch of ch-3 with slst.
Round 7: Ch 1, 2 hdc in ch-1 sp, 1 hdc in next st, **1 corner, 1 hdc in each of next 2 sts, 2 hdc in each of next 16 ch-1 sps, 1 hdc in next st, 1 corner,** 1 hdc in each of next 2 sts, 2 hdc in each of next 4 sps, 1 hdc in next st. Repeat from ** to **, ending with last corner, 1 hdc in each of next 2 sts, 2 hdc in each of next 3 sps, complete final hdc and join to 1st hdc with slst using Pearlette [37 sts on long sides, 11 sts on short sides, *not* including corners].
Round 8: Work in loop A only. Ch 1, 1 sc in each of 1st 4 sts, **1 corner, 1 sc in each of next 39 sts, 1 corner,** 1 sc in each of next 13

sts. Repeat from ** to **, ending with last corner, 1 sc in each of next 9 sts, join to 1st sc with slst.

Round 9: 1 sc in 1st st, (1 Hazelnut st in next st, 1 sc in next st) 2 times, **1 corner, (1 sc in next st, 1 Hazelnut in next st) 20 times, 1 sc in last st, 1 corner,** (1 sc in next st, 1 Hazelnut in next st) 7 times, 1 sc in next st. Repeat from ** to **, ending with last corner, (1 sc in next st, 1 Hazelnut in next st) 5 times, join to 1st sc with slst, change to Fluffy. [On rnds that end with a Hazelnut, change yarn after the joining so that the Hazelnut is pulled tight.]

Round 10: Ch 1, 1 sc in each of 1st 6 sts, **1 corner, 1 sc in each of next 43 sts, 1 corner,** 1 sc in each of next 17 sts. Repeat from ** to **, ending with last corner, 1 sc in each of last 11 sts, complete last st with Pearlette, join to 1st sc with slst.

Round 11: Work in loop A only. Ch 1, 1 sc in each of 1st 7 sts, **1 corner, 1 sc in each of next 45 sts, 1 corner,** 1 sc in each of next 19 sts. Repeat from ** to **, ending with last corner, 1 sc in each of last 12 sts, join to 1st sc with slst.

Round 12: Ch 1, 1 Hazelnut st in 1st st, (1 sc in next st, 1 Hazelnut in next st) 3 times, 1 sc in next st, **1 corner, (1 sc in next st, 1 Hazelnut in next st) 23 times, 1 sc in next st, 1 corner,** (1 sc in next st, 1 Hazelnut in next st) 10 times, 1 sc in next st. Repeat from ** to **, ending with last corner, (1 sc in next st, 1 Hazelnut in next st) 5 times, 1 sc in last st, complete this st and join with slst to 1st Hazelnut with Fluffy.

Round 13: Ch 1, 1 sc in each of 1st 9 sts, **1 corner, 1 sc in each of next 49 sts, 1 corner,** 1 sc in each of next 23 sts. Repeat from ** to **, ending with last corner, 1 sc in each of last 15 sts, join to 1st sc with slst.

Round 14: Work in loop A only. Ch 3 [=1 dc], 1 dc in last st of previous rnd, (skip next st, 1 dc in next st, 1 dc in skipped st) 3 times [= 3 Crossed dc], **1 corner (1 Crossed dc over next 2 sts) 25 times, 1 dc in next st, 1 corner,** (1 Crossed dc over next 2 sts) 12 times, 1 dc in next st. Repeat from ** to **, ending with last corner, (1 Crossed dc over next 2 sts) 7 times, join to top ch of ch-3.

Round 15: Ch 3, 1 dc over all lps of dc of previous rnd, (skip next st, 2 dc over all lps of next st) 5 times [= 5 V-dc worked into Crossed dc of previous rnd], **1 corner, 1 dc in next st, (1 V-dc in Crossed dc of previous rnd) 25 times, skip next st, 2 dc in next st, 1 corner,** 1 dc in next st, (1 V-dc in Crossed dc of previous rnd) 12 times, skip 1 st, 2 dc in next st. Repeat from ** to **, ending with last corner, 1 dc in next st, (1 V-dc in next Crossed dc) 7 times, complete last dc and join with Pearlette.

Round 16: Ch 1, 1 sc in each of 1st 12 sts, **1 corner, 1 sc in each of next 55 sts, 1 corner,** 1 sc in each of next 29 sts. Repeat from ** to **, ending with last corner, 1 sc in each of last 17 sts, join to 1st sc with slst.

Round 17: Ch 1, 1 sc in 1st st, (1 Hazelnut st in next st, 1 sc in next st) 6 times, **1 corner, (1 sc in next st, 1 Hazelnut in next st) 28 times, 1 sc in next st, 1 corner,** (1 sc in next st, 1 Hazelnut in next st) 15 times. Repeat from ** to **, ending with last corner, (1 sc in next st, 1 Hazelnut in next st) 9 times, join to 1st sc with slst using Fluffy.

Round 18: Ch 1, 1 sc in each of 1st 14 sts, **1 corner, 1 sc in each of next 59 sts, 1 corner,** 1 sc in each of next 33 sts. Repeat from ** to

**, ending with last corner, 1 sc in each of last 19 sts, join to 1st sc with slst.

Round 19: Work in loop A only. Ch 1, 1 sc in each of 1st 15 sts, **1 corner, 1 sc in each of next 61 sts, 1 corner,** 1 sc in each of next 35 sts. Repeat from ** to **, ending with last corner, 1 sc in each of last 20 sts, join to 1st sc with slst.

Round 20: Work in loop A only. Ch 3 [= 1 dc], 1 dc in each of next 2 sts, bring hk in front of sts and complete Judith st in last st of previous rnd, (1 Judith over next 4 sts) 3 times, 1 dc in next st, **1 corner, (1 Judith over next 4 sts) 15 times, skip 1 st, 1 dc in each of next 2 sts, bring hk in front and complete Judith in skipped st [= one 3-st Judith], 1 corner,** (1 Judith over next 4 sts) 9 times, 1 dc in next st. Repeat from ** to **, ending with last corner, (1 Judith over next 4 sts) 5 times, join to top ch of ch-3 with slst.

Round 21: Ch 1, 1 sc in each of 1st 17 sts, **1 corner, 1 sc in each of next 65 sts, 1 corner,** 1 sc in each of next 39 sts. Repeat from ** to **, ending with last corner, 1 sc in each of last 22 sts, join to 1st sc with slst.

Round 22: Work in loop A only. Ch 1, 1 sc in each of 1st 18 sts, **1 corner, 1 sc in each of next 67 sts, 1 corner,** 1 sc in each of next 41 sts. Repeat from ** to **, ending with last corner, 1 sc in each of next 23 sts, join to 1st sc with slst.

Round 23: Work in loop A only. Slst into next st, ch 3, 1 dc in each of next 2 sts, complete Judith st in 1st st of rnd, (1 Judith over next 4 sts) 3 times, one 3-st Judith over next 3 sts, **1 corner, (1 Judith over next 4 sts) 17 times, 1 dc in next st, 1 corner,** (1 Judith over next 4 sts) 10 times, one 3-st Judith over next 3 sts. Repeat from ** to **, ending with last corner, (1 Judith over next 4 sts) 6 times, join with slst to top ch of ch-3.

Round 24: Ch 1, 1 sc in each of 1st 19 sts, **1 corner, 1 sc in each of next 71 sts, 1 corner,** 1 sc in each of next 45 sts. Repeat from ** to **, ending with last corner, 1 sc in each of last 24 sts, join to 1st sc with slst.

Round 25: Work in loop A only. Ch 1, 1 sc in each of 1st 20 sts, **1 corner, 1 sc in each of next 73 sts, 1 corner,** 1 sc in each of next

47 sts. Repeat from ** to **, ending with last corner, 1 sc in each of last 25 sts, join to 1st sc with slst.

Round 26: Work in loop A only. Slst into next st, ch 3, 1 dc in each of next 2 sts, complete Judith in 1st st of rnd, (1 Judith over next 4 sts) 4 times, 1 dc in next st, **1 corner, (1 Judith over next 4 sts) 18 times, one 3-st Judith over next 3 sts, 1 corner,** (1 Judith over next 4 sts) 12 times, 1 dc in next st. Repeat from ** to **, ending with last corner, (1 Judith over next 4 sts) 7 times, join to top ch of ch-3 with slst.

Round 27: Ch 1, 1 sc in each of 1st 22 sts, **1 corner, 1 sc in each of next 77 sts, 1 corner,** 1 sc in each of next 51 sts. Repeat from ** to **, ending with last corner, 1 sc in each of last 29 sts, complete last st and join with slst to 1st sc with Pearlette.

Round 28: Work in loop A only. Ch 1, 1 sc in each of 1st 23 sts, **1 corner, 1 sc in each of next 79 sts, 1 corner,** 1 sc in each of next 53 sts. Repeat from ** to **, ending with last corner, 1 sc in each of last 30 sts, join to 1st sc with slst.

Round 29: Ch 1, 1 Hazelnut st in 1st st, (1 sc in next st, 1 Hazelnut in next st) 11 times, 1 sc in next st, **1 corner, (1 sc in next st, 1 Hazelnut in next st) 40 times, 1 sc in next st, 1 corner,** (1 sc in next st, 1 Hazelnut in next st) 27 times, 1 sc in next sc. Repeat from ** to **, ending with last corner, (1 sc in next st, 1 Hazelnut in next st) 15 times, 1 sc in last st, complete last st and join with slst to Hazelnut with Fluffy.

Round 30: Ch 1, 1 sc in each of 1st 25 sts, **1 corner, 1 sc in each of next 83 sts, 1 corner,** 1 sc in each of next 57 sts. Repeat from ** to **, ending with last corner, 1 sc in each of next 32 sts, join with slst to 1st sc with Pearlette.

Round 31: Work in loop A only. Ch 1, 1 sc in each of 1st 26 sts, **1 corner, 1 sc in each of next 85 sts, 1 corner,** 1 sc in each of next

59 sts. Repeat from ** to **, ending with last corner, 1 sc in each of last 33 sts, join to 1st sc with slst.

Round 32: Ch 1, 1 sc in 1st st, (1 Hazelnut st in next st, 1 sc in next st) 13 times, **1 corner, (1 sc in next st, 1 Hazelnut in next st) 43 times, 1 sc in next st, 1 corner,** (1 sc in next st, 1 Hazelnut in next st) 30 times, 1 sc in next st. Repeat from ** to **, ending with last corner, (1 sc in next st, 1 Hazelnut in next st) 17 times, join with slst to ch-1 with Fluffy.

Round 33: Ch 1, 1 sc in each of 1st 28 sts, **1 corner, 1 sc in each of next 89 sts, 1 corner,** 1 sc in each of next 63 sts. Repeat from ** to **, ending with last corner, 1 sc in each of last 35 sts, complete last st and join with slst to 1st sc with Pearlette.

Round 34: Work in loop A only. Ch 1, 1 sc in each of 1st 29 sts, **1 corner, 1 sc in each of next 91 sts, 1 corner,** 1 sc in each of next 65 sts. Repeat from ** to **, ending with last corner, 1 sc in each of last 36 sts, join to 1st sc with slst.

Round 35: Ch 1, 1 Hazelnut st in 1st st, (1 sc in next st, 1 Hazelnut in next st) 15 times, **1 corner, (1 sc in next st, 1 Hazelnut in next st) 46 times, 1 sc in next st, 1 corner,** (1 sc in next st, 1 Hazelnut in next st) 33 times, 1 sc in next st. Repeat from ** to **, ending with last corner, (1 sc in next st, 1 Hazelnut in next st) 17 times, 1 sc in last st, complete last st and join with slst to 1st sc with Fluffy.

Round 36: Ch 1, 1 sc in each of 1st 31 sts, **1 corner, 1 sc in each of next 95 sts, 1 corner,** 1 sc in each of next 69 sts. Repeat from ** to **, ending with last corner, 1 sc in each of last 31 sts, join to 1st sc with slst.

Round 37: Work in loop A only. Ch 1, 1 sc in each of 1st 32 sts, **1 corner, 1 sc in each of next 97 sts, 1 corner,** 1 sc in each of next 71 sts. Repeat from ** to **, ending with last corner, 1 sc in each of last 39 sts, join to 1st sc with slst, break yarn.

Block the blanket [see page 35].

Chapter 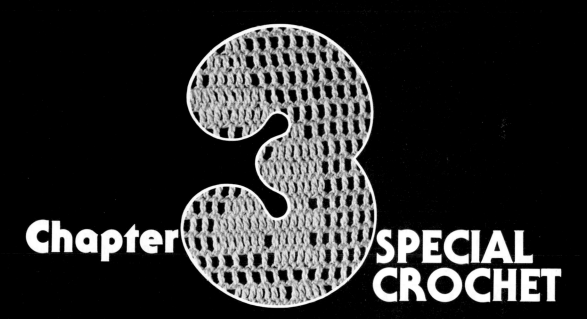 **3** SPECIAL CROCHET

As lovely and interesting as stitchery can be, it is only one of many forms crochet can take. In this chapter we will explore some of the other possibilities of crochet—Tapestry stitch, Filet, Afghan, and Woven crochet. Nowhere is the versatility of crochet more apparent than in these special styles. Filet crochet, the technique used to make the Filet Curtain shown on page 107, resembles exquisite lace. Tapestry stitch on the other hand looks like cross-stitch needlepoint or jacquard knitting, as exemplified in the Animal Headboard on page 99 and the Japanese Director's Chairs shown on page 92. With Woven crochet you can produce a fabric that appears to have been created on a loom, while Afghan crochet allows you to create unusual textures and stitches. See the Woven Crochet Pillow on page 111 and the Afghan Crochet Pillows on page 119 for examples.

Tapestry Stitch (Single Crochet)

for working the swatch back and forth in single crochet and double crochet so that you can see the relationship between the directions and the graph. Remember to give yarn a tug each time you change colors.

Single-Crochet Swatch

Foundation chain: Ch 10 with color C.

Row 1: 1 sc in 2nd ch from hk, *1 sc in next ch. Repeat from *, ending with 1 sc in last ch, complete last sc with color A. Ch 1 with A, turn [9 sts].

Row 2: 1 sc in 1st st, *1 sc in next st. Repeat from *, ending with 1 sc in last st. Ch 1, turn.

Row 3: [The tapestry pat begins on this row. Make sure that you read this line of the graph from right to left, as the arrow indicates.] 1 sc in each of the 1st 4 sts, complete 4th st with color B. Carrying A behind the piece and crocheting over it, work 1 sc with B in each of the next 3 sts. Complete the 3rd st with A, drop B. 1 sc with A in each of the last 2 sts, complete final st with C. Ch 1, turn.

Row 4: [This row is worked with the back facing you, so the graph is read from left to right. Drop each color after it's used and pick it up again when you need it. Remember that after a color is used, it must be brought forward

to hang against the back side before it is dropped.] 1 sc with C in 1st st, complete this st with A, 1 sc with A in each of the next 2 sts, complete 2nd st with B. 1 sc with B in each of the next 4 sts, complete 4th st with A. 1 sc with A in each of the last 2 sts, complete last sc with B. Ch 1, turn.

Row 5: 1 sc with B in each of the 1st 4 sts, complete 4th st with A. 1 sc with A in each of the next 2 sts, complete 2nd st with C. 1 sc with C in each of the last 3 sts. Ch 1, turn.

Row 6: Repeat Row 4, ending with 1 sc with A in each of the last 2 sts. Ch 1, turn. Break off C.

Row 7: Repeat Row 3. Break off B.

Row 8: Repeat Row 2. Break off A.

Row 9: Reattach C. Repeat Row 1. Break yarn.

Double-Crochet Swatch

Each square on the graph equals 2 dc, so begin with enough chs to make 18 sts.

Foundation chain: Ch 20 with color C.

Row 1: 1 dc in 4th ch from hk [3 chs = 1 dc], *1 dc in next ch. Repeat from *, ending with 1 dc in last ch, complete last dc with color A. Ch 3 with A [= 1st dc of next row], turn.

Row 2: Skip 1st st, *1 dc in next st. Repeat from *, ending with 1 dc in top of ch-3. Ch 3, turn.

Row 3: Skip 1st st, 1 dc in each of next 7 sts [8 dc = 4 squares of graph], complete 7th dc with color B. 1 dc with B in each of the next 6 sts, complete 6th st with A. 1 dc with A in each of the last 4 sts, complete final st with C. Ch 3, turn.

Row 4: Skip 1st st, 1 dc with C in next st, complete this st with A, 1 dc with A in each of the next 4 sts, complete 4th st with B. 1 dc with B in each of the next 8 sts, complete 8th st with A. 1 dc with A in each of the next 4 sts, complete final st with B. Ch 3, turn.

Row 5: Skip 1st st, 1 dc with B in each of the next 7 sts, complete 7th st with A, 1 dc with A in each of the next 4 sts, complete 4th st with C. 1 sc with C in each of the last 6 sts. Ch 3 and turn.

Now repeat Rows 1–4 of the graph in reverse order, as you did in the sc swatch.

Filet Crochet

With unimaginably small hooks and the thinnest thread, crocheters of past centuries created delicate, lacelike, very beautiful designs in filet crochet. In this traditional style of crochet, blocks of double crochet stitches form a design on a background of open-work chain meshes. The piece is worked in one color only and depends on the contrasting light (open mesh) and dark (solid mesh) areas to create the effect. To be fully appreciated traditional filet crochet—picture lace, as it has been called—must be displayed against a window with light coming through it or against a contrasting background (see the photograph of the Filet Curtain on page 107).

Like Tapestry stitch, filet crochet is most easily made from a graph (see Diagram 75). Each square on the graph represents a specific number of stitches, usually 2 or 3. We find the 2-stitch variation the simplest to follow and shall use it consistently in our projects. In this variation each square on the graph equals 2 stitches, as in double crochet Tapestry stitch. One open mesh (☐) = 1 dc, ch 1, skip 1 st; 1 solid mesh (☒) = 1 dc in each of next 2 sts. The graph is read from the bottom up, so Row 1 of the practice swatch is at the bottom of the graph. Odd-numbered rows are read from right to left (←); even-numbered rows are read from left to right (→). Each row begins with 3 chs [= 1st dc of solid mesh] or

4 chs [= 1 dc, ch 1 of open mesh] and ends with a solitary double crochet—a post that completes the last mesh. When you work a double crochet into a chain-1 space, don't try to insert your hook in the chain itself. Instead work over all the loops into the space.

Filet Crochet Swatch

Foundation chain: Ch 13.
Row 1: 1 dc in 5th ch from hk [5 chs = 1 dc, ch 1, skip 1 ch-1 open mesh], ch 1, skip 1 ch, *1 dc in next ch, ch 1, skip 1 ch [1 open mesh]. Repeat from *, ending with 1 dc in last ch. Turn [6 dc and 5 ch-1 sps = 5 open meshes + 1 post].
Row 2: [Read graph from left to right.] Ch 4, skip 1st st and 1st ch-1 sp. 1 dc in next dc, ch 1, skip next ch [2 open meshes], (1 dc in next dc, 1 dc in next ch-1 sp) 2 times [2 solid meshes], 1 dc in next st, ch 1, skip top ch of ch-5, 1 dc in next ch of ch-5. Turn. [Because the open mesh that follows any solid mesh begins with a dc, every block of solid mesh will appear to have 1 st more than it actually has, so the 2-mesh block on this row appears to have 5 sts.]
Row 3: Ch 4, skip 1st st and 1st ch, 1 dc in next dc, ch 1, skip next dc, 1 dc in each of next 3 dc, 1 dc in next ch, 1 dc in next dc, ch 1, skip top ch of ch-4, 1 dc in 3rd ch of ch-4. Turn.
Row 4: Ch 3, 1 dc in next ch-1 sp, 1 dc in each dc and each ch-1 sp of the row, ending with 1 dc in top ch of ch-4, 1 dc in 3rd ch of ch-4. Turn [11 dc].
Row 5: Ch 4, skip 1st 2 dc, 1 dc in next st, ch 1, skip next dc, 1 dc in each of next 5 dc, ch 1, skip next dc, 1 dc in top ch of ch-3. Turn.
Row 6: Ch 4, skip 1st st and 1st ch-1, 1 dc in next dc, ch 1, skip next dc, 1 dc in each of next 3 dc, 1 dc in ch-1 sp, 1 dc in next dc, ch 1, skip top ch of ch-4, 1 dc in 3rd ch of ch-4. Turn.
Row 7: Ch 4, skip 1st st and 1st ch-1 sp, 1 dc in next dc, (ch 1, skip next dc, 1 dc in next dc) 2 times, ch 1, skip next ch-1, 1 dc in next dc, ch 1, skip top ch of ch-4, 1 dc in 3rd ch. Break yarn.

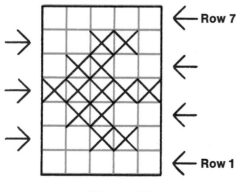

Diagram 75

Afghan Crochet

Afghan-stitch, or Tunisian, crochet is an almost forgotten art. When we first approached it, we thought of it as a functional but rather limited technique for making afghans. As we experimented, however, we found that it was a wonderfully easy way to produce all kinds of striking fabrics. Afghan crochet is more constraining than other techniques since it can only be worked in rows and is more easily worked without increases or decreases. But home decoration frequently requires square or rectangular fabrics of unusual textures—pillows, rugs, patchwork, pot holders, even slipcovers. Afghan crochet is a simple and elegant solution to these design problems.

You will need a special hook. Its head looks like that of a regular crochet hook, but its shaft is much longer and has a uniform diameter, and it has a knob on its end like that of a knitting needle. The difference between the regular crochet hook and the afghan hook reflects the difference in technique. In afghan crochet you will pick up all the stitches, then work them off the hook one at a time. The shaft of the hook must be long and uniform to hold stitches as they are picked up; the knob keeps the stitches on the hook.

One row of afghan crochet is made up of 2 rows of work. First you will work from right to left, pulling up a loop through each stitch and leaving it on your hook. This is called *the first half of a row* in the directions. Then without turning your work, you will work the stitches off your hook 1 or 2 at a time—*the second half of the row.* Try a few rows of the basic stitch, and you'll see how it works. Then you'll be ready for the variations, including Tapestry stitch, in the afghan crochet pillow in this chapter (page 120).

If possible, make increases and decreases at the ends of your piece so that they don't interfere with the pattern. Both are made on the first half of a row. To decrease, insert your hook through the vertical bar of each of the next 2 stitches, yarn over, draw up a loop. To increase, insert your hook into chain between the next 2 stitches, yarn over, and draw up a loop.

Diagram 76

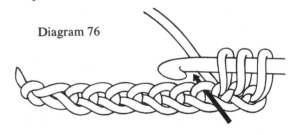

Afghan Crochet Swatch

Foundation chain: Ch 10. [In afghan crochet your foundation ch should be *exactly* the number of sts you want your piece to have.]

Row 1 [1st half]: [Lp on hk = 1 st.] Insert hk in 2nd ch from hk and pull up a lp [2 lps on hk]. *Insert hk in next ch, pull up a lp [3 lps on hk]. See Diagram 76. Repeat from * adding more and more lps to your hk, ending with insert hk in last ch, pull up a lp [10 lps on hk]. *Do not turn work.*

Row 1 [2nd half]: Yo and draw lp thru 1st lp on hk. See Diagram 77. [Except for a few unusual pats, the 1st st of the 2nd half is made

Afghan Crochet

thru only 1 lp.] *Yo, draw thru next 2 lps. Repeat from *, ending with yo, draw thru last 2 lps [1 lp left on hk = 1st lp of next row]. *Do not turn work.*

Diagram 77

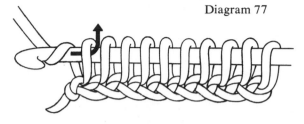

Diagram 78

Diagram 79

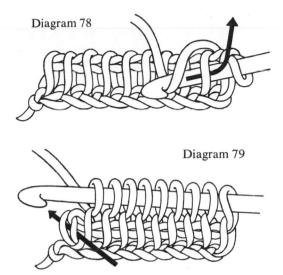

Row 2 [1st half]: Skip 1st st, *insert hk under vertical bar of next st, yo, draw up a lp. See Diagram 78. Repeat from *, ending with insert hk under 2 outside vertical bars of last st, draw up a lp [10 lps on hk]. Always go thru the 2 outside vertical bars on the last st for a trim selvage (edge), as shown in Diagram 79.
Row 2 [2nd half]: Repeat Row 1, 2nd half. To

continue the piece repeat both halves of Row 2. After you have completed the piece, work a row of sc into the final row.

Woven Crochet

Woven crochet is a simple technique that closely resembles weaving. Begin by crocheting a grid of stitches—single crochet, half double crochet, or double crochet for a tight weave; filet crochet for an open weave; or even fancy stitches such as Hazelnuts or Pineapples. Then thread a tapestry needle with one or more strands of yarn and weave through the rows of the grid in horizontal or vertical lines.

Crocheting the Grid

Crochet a practice grid with either a tight or open grid. For a tight grid, chain any desired number of stitches and work rows of single crochet or double crochet stitches back and forth until the grid is the desired size.

For an open grid, chain any desired number of stitches and, following the directions for filet crochet in this chapter (page 87), work rows of double crochet filet crochet meshes until the grid is the desired size.

Weaving Horizontal Rows

All rows are started on the right-hand side of the grid. At the completion of each row of weaving, cut your yarn. (When the project is completed, the yarn ends can be woven into the back of the piece or tied together and left to hang as fringe.)

Insert the yarn-threaded tapestry needle from front to back in the space between the first and second stitches of Row 1 of the grid and out from back to front between the second and third stitches of the same row. Continue weaving the yarn over and under the posts of each stitch of Row 1 of the grid. Remove the needle and cut the yarn on the right-hand side. Row 2 of the grid is woven in the same way as Row 1, except that you work over and under the posts in the opposite direction to the weaving in Row 1. Insert the needle from back to front in the space between the first and second stitches of Row 2 of the grid and out from

Woven Crochet (Horizontal Weave)

front to back between the second and third stitches of the same row. Weave over and under the posts of each stitch of Row 2. Continue weaving each row, going over and under the posts in alternate directions on each row. (See the swatch in the photograph at the top of this page for an example of horizontal weaving.)

Weaving Vertical Rows

Begin the first line of weaving by inserting the needle in the space between the first and second stitches of Row 1 of the grid from front to back and out from back to front in the space between the first and second stitches of Row 2. Continue weaving in and out between the first and second stitches of each row. The second line of weaving is worked in the same way, except that you go over and under in the opposite direction. Insert the needle from back to front in the space between the second and third stitches of Row 1 of the grid and out from front to back between the second and

third stitches of Row 2. Continue weaving between the second and third stitches of each row of the grid. Weave each row in this way, alternating the direction in which you go over and under the stitches. (See the swatch in the photograph below for an example of vertical weaving.)

Double Weaving

You can work a double, or even triple, weave in each row, horizontally or vertically. To do so work 1 line of weaving as described above. Then go back and work another line of weaving in the same spaces as the first line of weaving, but alternate the direction in which you go over and under the stitches. That is, if you started the first line by inserting the needle from the front to back of the grid, begin the second line by inserting the needle from the back to front.

If you are weaving several strands through each row, don't be concerned if the unwoven part of the piece ruffles; it will flatten out.

Woven Crochet (Vertical Weave)

Japanese Director's Chairs

A walk through the Brooklyn Museum resulted in the design on these. The character on one chair was part of a family crest on a fifteenth-century Japanese warrior's coat. The character on the other was delicately imprinted on a small painting at the same exhibit. We think these contemporary director's chairs adapt beautifully to the elegant Oriental designs we've chosen.

Materials:
- 3 spools Berga Ullman (16/2) Linen (each 1500 yds.) in the following amounts: gray #557, 1 spool; white #3, 1 spool *or* any comparable linen or crochet cotton
- 2 chrome director's chair frames
- 1½ yds. medium-weight dark gray canvas
- 2 yds. fusible web
- Dressmaker's pins
- Sewing machine
- Iron

Hook: #2 steel

Gauge:
7 sts = 1", 8 rows = 1"

Note: It is possible that your gauge will vary 1 st more or less per inch. If that occurs, you can add or eliminate sts from the right and left sides of the piece, because the hook you are using is quite small.

Finished Size:
4 backs (2 per chair) = 20x8" each
2 seats (1 per chair) = 24x14" each

Note: All seams for this project are sewn by machine. We do not recommend handstitching since it does not produce a strong enough seam to hold the weight of a person sitting.

The graphs [see Diagram 80] for this project are designed specifically for the chrome director's chairs available in many stores. If your chairs are a different size, you will have to alter the graphs to suit your needs. The width of the backs and seats can be shortened or lengthened by simply chaining fewer or more sts than specified. Be sure to add or subtract the same number of sts to or from the left side as you do to or from the right side so that the pat letter stays centered on the graph. To lengthen the seat or back add a row or rows of blank boxes [gray sts] after Row 5 and after Row 60. Again, be sure to add as many rows to the bottom of the piece as you do to the top to keep the design balanced. Any alterations in size should be applied to the canvas and web lining when you assemble the pieces.

Instructions:
Seats: The borders are done in sc Tapestry st as described on page 86. Since they are only 3 rows wide, we have given row-by-row directions for them instead of including them on a graph. All rows in between the borders are worked in regular rows of sc in gray. All sts are designated gray [G] or white [W].
Foundation chain: Ch 169.
Row 1: [Front] Insert hk into 2nd ch from hk and make 1 sc, *1 sc in next ch, repeat from * ending with 1 sc in last ch. Ch 1, turn.
Row 2: [Back] 1 [G] sc in 1st st, *1 [W] sc in each of next 3 sts, 1 [G] sc in next st, repeat from * ending with 1 [W] sc in each of last 3 sts. Ch 1, turn.
Row 3: 1 [G] sc in 1st st, *1 [W] sc in next st, 1 [G] sc in next st, repeat from * ending with 1 [W] sc in last st. Ch 1, turn.
Row 4: Repeat Row 2.
Row 5: Gray—1 sc in 1st st, *1 sc in next st, repeat from * ending with 1 sc in last st. Ch 1, turn.
Rows 6–108: Gray—repeat Row 5.
Row 109: Repeat Row 2.
Row 110: Repeat Row 3.
Row 111: Repeat Row 2.
Row 112: Repeat Row 5. Break yarn.
Back #1: The borders for the chair backs are also done in sc Tapestry st and are given in row-by-row directions.

Foundation chain: Ch 141 [G].

Row 1: [Front] Insert hk into 2nd ch from hk and make 1 sc, *1 sc in next ch, repeat from * ending with 1 sc in last ch. Ch 1, turn.

Row 2: [Back] 1 [G] sc in 1st st, *1 [W] sc in each of next 3 sts, 1 [G] sc in next st, repeat from * ending with 1 [W] sc in each of last 3 sts. Ch 1, turn.

Row 3: 1 [G] sc in 1st st, *1 [W] sc in next st, 1 [G] sc in next st, repeat from * ending with 1 [W] sc in last st. Ch 1, turn.

Row 4: Repeat Row 2.

Row 5: Gray—1 sc in 1st st, *1 sc in next st, repeat from * ending with 1 sc in last st. Ch 1, turn.

Note: Refer to the 1st graph for Row 6. Since Row 6 is worked looking at the back of the piece, the 1st row of the graph is read from left to right. The graph refers to only the center 37 sts of the piece. When working even rows make 1 [G] sc in each of the 1st 52 sts and then refer to the graph for the next 37 sts. Complete the row, making 1 [G] sc in each of the last 51 sts of the piece. When working odd rows, begin reading the graph [from right to left] after you have made 1 [G] sc in each of the 1st 51 sts of the piece; refer to the graph for the next 37 sts. Then complete the piece making 1 [G] sc in each of the last 52 sts of the piece. As an example, here is Row 6:

Row 6: [Including Row 1 of the graph] 1 [G] sc in 1st st, 1 [G] sc in each of next 51 sts, [now begin to read the graph] 1 [G] sc in next st, 1 [W] sc in each of next 6 sts, 1 [G] sc in each of next 30 sts [37 sts worked from the graph] 1 [G] sc in each of the next 51 sts. Ch 1, turn.

Rows 7–59: Continue to work in this way until the Japanese character is completed.

Row 60: Gray—1 sc in 1st st, *1 sc in next st, repeat from * ending with 1 sc in last st. Ch 1, turn.

Row 61: [Back] 1 [G] sc in 1st st, *1 [W] sc in each of next 3 sts, 1 [G] sc in next st, repeat from * ending with 1 [W] sc in each of last 3 sts. Ch 1, turn.

Row 62: 1 [G] sc in 1st st, *1 [W] sc in next st, 1 [G] sc in next st, repeat from * ending with 1 [W] sc in last st. Ch 1, turn.

Row 63: Repeat Row 61.

Row 64: Repeat Row 60.

Make another Back #1.

Back #2:

Foundation chain–Row 1: Repeat Foundation chain–Row 1 of Back #1.

Row 2: [Back] 1 [G] sc in 1st st, *1 [W] sc in each of next 3 sts, 1 [G] sc in next st, repeat from * ending with 1 [W] sc in each of last 3 sts. Ch 1, turn.

Row 3: 1 [G] sc in 1st st, *1 [W] sc in next st, 1 [G] sc in next st, repeat from * ending with 1 [W] sc in last st. Ch 1, turn.

Row 4: Repeat Row 2.

Row 5: Gray—1 sc in 1st st, *1 sc in next st, repeat from * ending with 1 sc in last st. Ch 1, turn.

Note: For Row 6 of 2nd back, refer to the center 36 sts of graph, and read from Row 1 of 2nd graph. Begin to read 2nd graph after working 1 [G] sc in each of the 1st 52 sts of the piece. Refer to the graph for the next 36 sts, and then make 1 [G] sc in each of the last 52 sts. Work Rows 6–59 in this manner.

Rows 60–64: Repeat Rows 60–64 of Back #1.

Make another Back #2.

BLOCKING

Block each piece according to the directions on page 35. Each seat should measure 24x14″ and each back should measure 20x8″. If it is short, you can stretch it to the correct measurement when blocking.

MAKING SEATS

For each seat, cut your canvas into a rectangle measuring 15½ x26″. Fold the top and bottom edges 1″ to 1 side [this becomes the *back* side of your work]. Press the folds with an iron. Set your sewing machine for 10 sts to the inch and thread with 1 strand of dark gray linen. Sew 2 rows of stitching ¼″ apart over each fold. Fold each short side over 1″ to the back side of the canvas. Press these sides and sew in the same manner as you did the top and bottom folds. Your canvas piece will now measure 13½ x24″. Cut the fusible web to measure slightly larger than the piece of canvas just completed. Lay the piece of web over the back side of the canvas and make basting sts [by hand] along all the edges. Trim off all excess

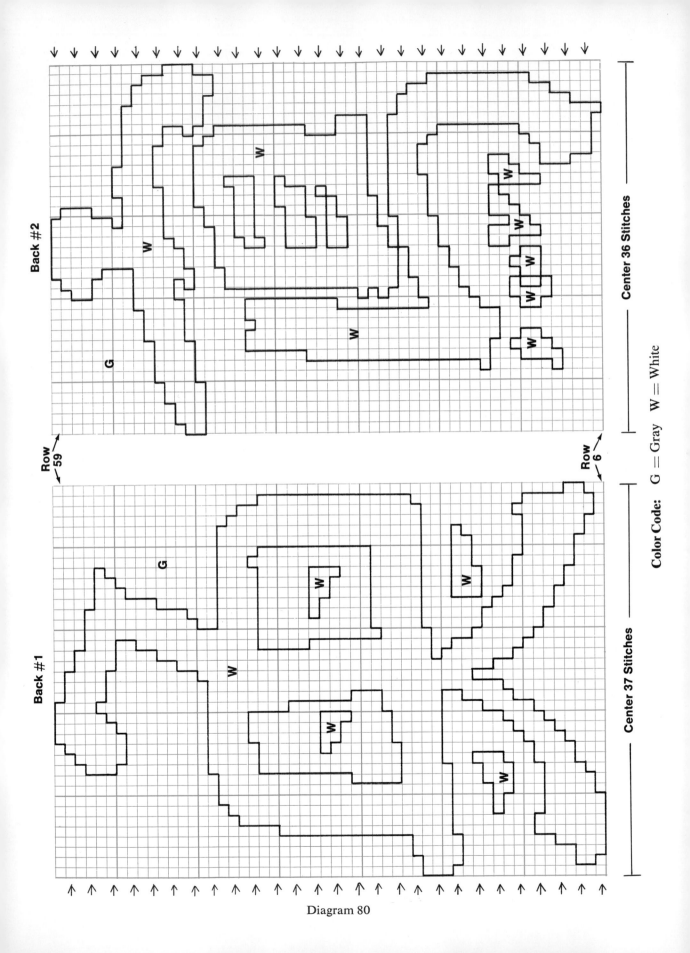

Back #2

W

W

W

W

W

W

W

W

W

G

Center 36 Stitches

Row 59

Row 6

Back #1

G

W

W

W

W

W

Center 37 Stitches

Color Code: G = Gray W = White

Diagram 80

web. Lay the crocheted seat on top of the piece of canvas so that the front side of each piece faces out. The top and bottom of the crocheted seat will extend ½″ beyond the canvas; the sides should match the edges of the canvas evenly. Holding the crocheted edges tog, baste around all edges. [There is no need to turn in the crocheted edges since they are even and cannot unravel.] Turn the seat over to the canvas side and sew a seam on your machine ⅛″ in from each edge. Sew a 2nd one ⅛″ in from the 1st seam. Take out your basting sts. Pin the seat to any blocking board with dressmaker's pins and stretch the fabric gently so that the canvas lies smooth. With a warm iron, press the canvas side to fuse the web to the canvas. [Be sure to read the web directions, as they may vary from brand to brand.] Allow the piece to set and then fold each side 3″ to the canvas side and pin. Remove the small pin at each end of the seat rods on one of the chair frames and remove the rods. Slide the seat onto the rods to check the fit—the seat should be quite taut. Adjust the pinned folds until the seat is stretched as tight as possible. Set the st gauge on your machine for 8 sts to the inch and adjust the setting to heavy fabrics. Sew on the canvas side. Sew 2 rows ¼″ apart over each fold, starting ⅛″ in from the edge. Slide the seat over the rods and insert the rods back into the chair frame.

MAKING BACKS

For each chair's back, lay the 2 pieces of crochet worked from the 1st graph on top of each other so that the back of each piece faces out. Following the directions for joining pieces on page 29, slst the left-hand edges tog. Your crocheted piece should now measure 40x8″. Cut your canvas into a rectangle measuring 9x42″. Lay the short sides of the canvas on top of each other and st them tog 1″ from the edge: Set the machine 10 sts to the inch. Sew over the 1st row several times to secure the seam. Press the seam open and zig-zag [if possible; if not, a straight line of sewing will do] over the seam allowance ½″ from the original seam. Fold the top and bottom edges 1″ to the back side, press, and sew 2 seams ¼″ apart on each fold. Your canvas will now be a tube measuring 7x40″. Cut a rectangular piece of web slightly larger than the piece of canvas just completed. The short edges of the web will overlap the canvas piece about ½″. Baste [by hand] the web to the canvas around the edges and then cut away the excess web. Lay the crocheted back over the canvas so that the front side of each faces out. You may have to pull the crocheted fabric a little to make it fit. Pin the pieces tog. The crocheted piece should extend ½″ beyond the canvas on the top and bottom. Baste the pieces tog. From the canvas side, machine st a seam ⅛″ in from the top edge. Make another seam ⅛″ from the first. Repeat along the bottom edge. Take the basting threads out. With the canvas side out and working 8″ to 9″ at a time, pin sections of the tube to a blocking board and gently stretch the fabric evenly until the canvas is smooth. Press the pieces on the canvas side with a warm iron to fuse the web to the canvas and allow to set. Lay the crocheted piece flat so that the canvas faces in and the crocheted fabric is outside. The pat letter should be centered, and the short seams should be at the right and left edges. Starting 1¾″ from the upper right-hand corner and working along the top, slst the front of the crocheted piece to the back of the crocheted piece, stopping 1¾″ from the upper left-hand corner. Turn the piece upside down and repeat along the bottom of the piece. Turn the piece right side up. With a piece of masking tape, mark a straight line 1¾″ from the upper right-hand corner to a point 1¾″ from the lower right-hand corner. Repeat on the left-hand side. Set the machine to 8 sts to the inch and adjust it for heavy fabric. Sew a seam along each of the tape lines. Sew once more over these seams for added security. Slip the back over the upright frame of the chair.

Repeat this procedure for the 2nd back.

Boat-Shaped Basket

The bright colors and geometric pattern of this basket are reminiscent of American Indian design. Through the use of the Tapestry-stitch technique we are able to add a dimension to crochet normally reserved for weaving and basketry. For another idea, work a Tapestry-stitch pattern into the sides of a circular crocheted basket, making it large enough to hold your favorite plant.

Materials:
- 7 spools Lily jute *or* any thin jute in the following amounts: white, 3 spools; orange, 1 spool; pink, 1 spool; blue, 1 spool; red-orange, 1 spool
- Trussing needle
- White glue
- Small paintbrush

Hook: G

Gauge:
4 sts = 1″
Inside of basket: 4 rows = 1″
Bottom and sides of basket: 3 rows = 1″

Finished Size:
8″ wide x 12″ long x 3″ high (approximately)

Instructions:
Tapestry-stitch piece: Work this with white, orange, pink, blue, and red-orange.
Foundation chain: Ch 2.
   Note: Rows 1–13 of the graph [Diagram 81] are read by working Tapestry st back and forth as explained on pages 84–86. You inc in the 1st and last sts of each of these rows, using the appropriate color. At the end of Row 13 you should have 25 sts.
Rows 1–13: Inc 1 st in 1st st, *1 sc in next st, repeat from * ending with 1 inc in last st. Ch 1, turn.
   Note: Rows 14 to the end are worked in only one direction, from left to right, and the graph is read accordingly. Follow the directions for working Tapestry st in one direction on page 85.
Rows 14–48: 1 sc in 1st st of previous row, *1 sc in next st. Repeat from *, ending with 1 sc in last st. Ch 1, turn. Weave loose yarn tails

Color Code:

B = Blue   R = Red-orange
O = Orange   W = White
P = Pink

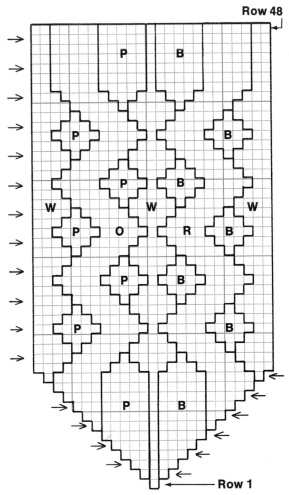

Diagram 81

into the back side of the piece, following the directions for weaving in loose yarn tails on page 24. Edge the piece, following the directions for edging on page 25.

Bottom piece: Work this with the white jute.
Foundation chain: Ch 21.
Row 1: Insert hk into 2nd ch from hk and make 1 sc, *1 sc in next ch. Repeat from *, ending with 1 sc in last ch. Ch 1, turn.
Rows 2–38: 1 sc in 1st st of previous row, *1 sc in next st. Repeat from *, ending with 1 sc in last st. Ch 1, turn.
Rows 39–48: 1 sc dec, *1 sc in next st. Repeat from *, ending with 1 sc dec [2 decs per row]. Ch 1, turn. Break the jute. Edge the piece, following the directions for edging on page 25.

Place the Tapestry-st piece face up on top of this piece so that points and edges meet. Thread a trussing needle with a long strand of white jute and sew the 2 pieces tog along all the edges, following the directions for sewing crocheted pieces tog on page 29.

Side pieces: Work these with the white jute. Hold the crocheted base so that the Tapestry-st design faces you and the pointed end is on the left-hand side.
Row 1: Attach the jute in the side of the 1st row in the upper right-hand corner. Make a sc in the same st, 1 sc in the side of each of the next 8 rows. Ch 1, turn [9 sts].
Rows 2–30: 1 sc in 1st st of previous row, *1 sc in next st. Repeat from *, ending with 1 sc in last st. Ch 1, turn.
Row 31: 1 sc in 1st st of previous row, *1 sc in next st. Repeat from *, ending with 1 sc dec. Ch 1, turn [8 sts].
Row 32: 1 sc dec, *1 sc in next st. Repeat from *, ending with 1 sc in last st. Ch 1, turn [7 sts].
Row 33: Repeat Row 31 [6 sts].
Row 34: Repeat Row 32 [5 sts].
Row 35: Repeat Row 31 [4 sts].
Row 36: Repeat Row 32 [3 sts].
Row 37: Repeat Row 31 [2 sts].
Row 38: Repeat Row 32 [1 st]. Break the jute.

Turn the base piece so that the bottom is facing you and the pointed end is on the left-hand side. Repeat Rows 1–38 of the side piece. Break the jute.

Hold the basket so that the design is facing you and the point is on the left-hand side. Starting at the side of the 10th row from the right, match the top side piece to the upper edge of the basket. The pointed end of the side piece should meet the pointed tip of the base. Thread the trussing needle with white jute and sew the side piece to the upper edge of the base. Turn the piece upside down and repeat on the opposite edge. Edge the top rim [both the sides and the back edge] of the basket with white jute.

Hold the basket so that the pointed end is on top and the design is facing you. Starting at the tip, attach the white jute thru the 1st pair of opposing sts of each side piece. Join the next 4 pairs of opposing sts with a slst, following the directions for joining with a slst on page 29. Break the jute and pull the loose end thru to the inside of the basket and weave it in.

Your basket will probably be a little misshapen from the pulling and sewing of the side pieces. The next step should help stiffen the sides and bring the basket back into shape. Stuff the basket with newspaper, shaping the sides as you add paper. Mix 2 tablespoons white glue with ½ cup water. Brush the outside of the basket [the side pieces only] with this wash, using a small paintbrush. Allow it to dry thoroughly and repeat 2 more times. Remove the newspaper when the basket is dry. Brush the inside of the side pieces with the wash, allow it to dry, and repeat 2 more times. Weave in any loose jute tails.

Animal Headboard

Elephants, lions, giraffes, and macaws coexist in this lively jungle scene. If you divide the graph into thirds, you can crochet panels with pairs of animals in each section. The panels could then be used to make shutters or other window treatments, or could be framed individually to make pictures, transforming a child's bedroom into a well-coordinated fantasy spot he or she is sure to enjoy.

Materials:
- 52 oz. Borgs i Lund Cows Hair (Nöthaisgain) in the following amounts: light green #67, 24 oz.; medium green #14, 4 oz.; dark green #63, 4 oz.; lavender #109, 4 oz.; purple #38, 4 oz.; gold #87, 4 oz.; dark brown #58, 4 oz.; light yellow #8, 4 oz.; dark yellow #86, 4 oz. *or* corresponding amounts of any bulky or worsted weight yarn
- 4 strands of Paternayan Tapestry yarn in each of the following colors: dark blue #343, light blue #353, coral #822, and black #050 *or* corresponding amounts of any bulky or worsted weight yarn
- Heavy-duty stapler
- Staples
- 1 piece of 1″ thick foam rubber, 28x40″
- ¼″ plywood, 24x36″

Hook: G

Color Code:

A and ▱ = Medium green   C and ◪ = Dark blue   F = Lavender

B and ◐ = Dark green   D and ◉ = Light yellow   G = Light blue

               E and ◎ = Dark yellow   H = Coral

Diagram 82

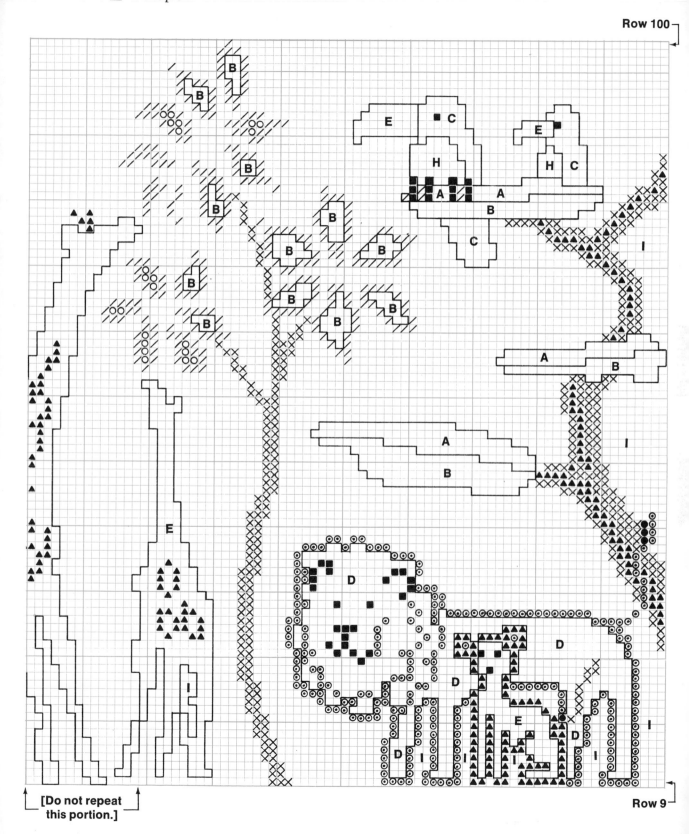

I = Light green   ⊠ = Dark brown

▲ = Gold   ■ = Black

△ = Purple

Gauge:
4 sts = 1″, 4 rows = 1″
The gauge will vary slightly if you use a bulky or worsted yarn in place of the Cows Hair.

Finished Size:
Headboard = 24x36″

Instructions:
Foundation chain: Light green—ch 144.
Rows 1–8: Insert hk into 2nd ch from hk and make 1 sc, *1 sc in next ch, repeat from * ending with 1 sc in last ch. Ch 1, turn.

Note: These 8 rows will form a 2″ bottom edge of the headboard and will be secured to the back of a plywood base.

Rows 9–100: The graph [see Diagram 82] is worked following directions for working Tapestry st back and forth [pages 84–86]. Each row of the graph has 144 sts. The background color is carried along as you work. All others are dropped after they are used and picked up again on subsequent rows. Because of the many different colors being used in this panorama [see photograph on page 99], we strongly recommend that you use a plastic yarn bobbin for each color. The bobbins will help to keep the different yarns accessible and will limit the amount of messy tangling that often results when you are juggling lots of different skeins. Odd-numbered rows are worked from right to left, even-numbered rows are worked from left to right. Row 9 begins at the lower right-hand corner of the graph.

Rows 101–108: Light green—1 sc in 1st st, *1 sc in next st, repeat from * ending with 1 sc in last st.

BLOCKING
Each piece should be blocked according to the directions for blocking on page 35. If your piece is small, stretch it to the correct finished size, pin it in place, and block.

EDGING
You will need to edge only the sides of the headboard, since the top and bottom edging were worked into the body of the headboard. Turn the headboard so that the right-hand side is on top.

Row 1: Attach the background color to the side of the 1st st of the 1st row of the graph, 1 sc in same st, *1 sc in side of next row. Repeat from *, ending with 1 sc in side of last row of graph. Ch 1, turn.

Row 2: 1 sc in 1st st of previous row, *1 sc in side of next st. Repeat from *, ending with 1 sc in last st of previous row. Ch 1, turn.

Rows 3–8: Repeat Row 2. Break yarn.

Turn the headboard so that the left-hand side is on top.

Row 1: Attach the background color to the side of the 1st st of the last row of the graph, 1 sc in same st, *1 sc in side of next row. Repeat from *, ending with 1 sc in side of last st of 1st row of graph. Ch 1, turn.

Rows 2–8: Repeat Rows 2–8 of right-hand edging. Break yarn.

ASSEMBLING
Place the foam rubber piece on a flat surface and put the plywood base on top of it so that the edges of the foam extend beyond the base 2″ on each side. Fold the top edge over the base and staple into place. Fold the bottom edge of the foam rubber over the base, pulling it so that it is taut. Staple the edge to the front of the base. Repeat this on the right- and left-hand edges. Place the crocheted piece back side up on a flat surface and lay the padded plywood base over it so that the foam is on top of the back side of the crocheting and the wood faces out. The edges of the crocheted piece should extend 2″ beyond the plywood base on each side. Repeat the same procedure used for attaching the foam rubber pad to the base to attach the crocheted piece to the base.

Filet Shower Curtain

Filet designs are traditionally produced by alternating solid and open meshes. This filet shower curtain, however, is made entirely of open mesh. The undulating sweeps of green are created by varying the height of the stitches within each row.

Materials:
- 1 oz. dark green #28 UKI mercerized cotton *or* 2 balls green Speed Cro-Sheen
- 8 oz. sea green #60 UKI mercerized cotton *or* 8 balls sea green Speed Cro-Sheen
- 2 oz. light green #57 UKI mercerized cotton *or* 2 balls light green Speed Cro-Sheen
- Waterproof shower curtain liner
- 27 small shower curtain hooks

Note: These materials are for 1 panel. Tub showers will require 3 or 4 panels, while stall showers will need 1 or 2.

Hook: J

Gauge:
1st row: 1 mesh = 1″, 1 tr row = 1½″

Note: The combination of an open-work st pat and large hk produces a loose fabric that changes shape as more weight is added. The result is a gauge in which the sts get narrower and the rows elongate as the shower curtain grows longer and the fringe is added. The gauge for the 1st row, therefore, does not reflect the gauge of the finished piece.

Finished Size:
Each panel, 24x80″ (approximately)

Instructions:
Foundation chain: Ch 115 with sea green.
Row 1: 1 dc in 6th ch from hk [5 chs = 1 dc, ch 1, skip 1 ch = 1 dc mesh], ch 1, skip 1 ch, *1 dc in next ch, ch 1, skip 1 ch [1 dc mesh]. Repeat from *, ending with 1 dc in last ch. Turn. [Counting the initial 5 chs as 1 dc, ch 1, you should have 55 dc and 54 ch-1 sps, forming 5 meshes and 1 post (the final dc).]
Row 2: Ch 5, skip 1st st and 1st ch [= 1 tr, ch 1, skip 1 ch = 1 tr mesh], *1 tr in next st, ch 1, skip ch-1 sp [= 1 tr mesh]. Repeat from *, ending with skip last ch-1 sp, 1 tr in last st. Turn.

Note: You have now learned to make a tr mesh and a dc mesh. The only other st pat in this project is a sc mesh: [1 sc in next st, ch 1, skip next ch-1 sp] = 1 sc mesh.

In the next and many subsequent rows, the height of the sts changes irregularly, making the use of repeat *s impossible and standard directions difficult to read. We have simplified the directions as follows:

Each row begins with standard crochet directions for the 1st mesh. Directions for working across the row are abbreviated. For example, in Row 3, 4 dc M(esh) = (1 dc in next st, ch 1, skip next ch-1 sp) 4 times; 8 tr M = (1 tr in next st, ch 1, skip next ch-1 sp) 8 times, and so on. It's important to remember that sts are always made in the *sts* of the previous row, never into the ch-1 sps, creating a design of sts above sts and chs above chs.

Each row ends with a single st, a post that completes the last mesh. Counting the initial chs as the 1st mesh, each row has 55 sts and 54 chs, which form 54 meshes and a final post. The panel is worked back and forth and should be turned at the end of each row even when the color changes.

Row 3: Ch 4, skip 1st st and 1st ch-1 [= 1 dc M(esh)], 4 dc M, 8 tr M, 5 dc M, 5 tr M, 3 dc M, 3 sc M, 2 dc M, 3 tr M, 5 dc M, 5 sc M, 2 dc M, 4 tr M, 2 dc M, 2 sc M, ending with 1 sc in last st. Turn [55 sts + 54 chs = 54 meshes + 1 post].
Row 4: Ch 4, skip 1st st and 1st ch [= 1 dc M], 53 dc M, ending with 1 dc in last st. Turn [54 M + 1 post].
Row 5: Repeat Row 4 [all dc M].
Row 6: Ch 3, skip 1st st and 1st ch-1 sp [= 1 sc M], 14 sc M, 1 dc M, 9 tr M, 4 dc M, 9 tr M, 1 dc M, 5 sc M, 1 dc M, 9 tr M, ending with 1 tr in last st. Turn [54 M + 1 post].
Row 7: Ch 5, skip 1st st and 1st ch-1 sp [= 1 tr

M], 53 tr M, ending with 1 tr in last st. Turn.

Row 8: Repeat Row 4 [all dc M]. Complete last st of row with light green yarn according to the directions on page 23. Break sea green, turn.

Row 9: Ch 5, skip 1st st and 1st ch-1 sp, 10 tr M, 4 dc M, 7 sc M, 6 dc M, 10 tr M, 4 dc M, 12 sc M, ending with 1 sc in last st. Turn.

Row 10: Ch 3, skip 1st st and 1st ch-1 sp, 9 sc M, 3 dc M, 16 tr M, 7 dc M, 7 sc M, 3 dc M, 8 tr M, ending with 1 tr in last st. Change to sea green, turn.

Row 11: Repeat Row 7 [all tr M].

Row 12: Repeat Row 4 [all dc M].

Row 13: Ch 3, skip 1st st and 1st ch-1 sp, 8 sc M, 2 dc M, 8 tr M, 2 dc M, 13 sc M, 4 dc M, 16 tr M, ending with 1 tr in last st. Turn.

Row 14: Ch 5, skip 1st st and 1st ch-1 sp, 12 tr M, 2 dc M, 11 sc M, 1 dc M, 2 tr M, 3 dc M, 5 sc M, 1 dc M, 5 tr M, 7 dc M, 4 sc M, ending with 1 sc. Change to dark green, turn.

Row 15: Repeat Row 7 [all tr M].

Rows 16–18: Repeat Row 4 [all dc M].

Row 19: Ch 3, skip 1st sc and 1st ch-1 sp, 10 sc M, 1 dc M, 15 tr M, 12 dc M, 5 tr M, 4 dc M, 6 sc M, ending with 1 sc in last st. Turn.

Row 20: Ch 4, skip 1st st and 1st ch-1 sp, 7 dc M, 16 tr M, 5 dc M, 16 tr M, 5 dc M, 4 sc M, ending with 1 sc in last st. Turn.

Row 21: Repeat Row 7 [all tr M].

Row 22: Repeat Row 4 [all dc M]. Change to light green, turn.

Row 23: Ch 3, skip 1st st and 1st ch-1 sp, 4 sc M, 5 dc M, 20 tr M, 4 dc M, 5 sc M, 4 dc M, 11 tr M, ending with 1 tr in last st. Turn.

Row 24: Repeat Row 7 [all tr M].

Row 25: Ch 3, skip 1st st and 1st ch-1 sp, 6 sc M, 5 dc M, 23 tr M, 6 dc M, 6 sc M, 3 dc M, 4 tr M, ending with 1 tr. Change to sea green, turn.

Rows 26–27: Repeat Row 4 [all dc M].

Rows 28–30: Repeat Row 7 [all tr M].

Row 31: Ch 5, skip 1st st and 1st ch-1 sp, 6 tr M, 5 dc M, 9 sc M, 5 dc M, 5 tr M, 4 dc M, 19 tr M, ending with 1 tr in last st. Turn.

Row 32: Ch 5, skip 1st st and 1st ch-1 sp, 6 tr M, 8 dc M, 18 sc M, 9 dc M, 3 sc M, 5 dc M, 4 tr M, ending with 1 tr in last st. Turn.

Row 33: Repeat Row 7 [all tr M].

Row 34: Ch 4, skip 1st st and 1st ch-1 sp, 4 dc M, 11 tr M, 4 dc M, 12 sc M, 18 dc M, 4 tr M, 1 tr in last st. Turn.

Row 35: Ch 5, skip 1st st and 1st ch-1 sp, 4 tr M, 31 dc M, 18 tr M, ending with 1 tr in last st. Turn.

Row 36: Repeat Row 7 [all tr M].

Row 37: Ch 5, skip 1st st and 1st ch-1 sp, 15 tr M, 4 dc M, 18 sc M, 3 dc M, 13 tr M, ending with 1 tr in last st. Turn.

Rows 38–40: Repeat Row 4 [all dc M]. Change to light green, turn.

Row 41: Ch 5, skip 1st st and 1st ch-1 sp, 17 tr M, 6 dc M, 8 sc M, 8 dc M, 14 tr M, ending with 1 tr in last st. Turn.

Row 42: Repeat Row 4 [all dc M].

Row 43: Ch 5, skip 1st st and 1st ch-1 sp, 11 tr M, 4 dc M, 12 sc M, 6 dc M, 20 tr M, ending with 1 tr in last st. Turn.

Rows 44–46: Repeat Row 7 [all tr M]. Change to dark green, turn.

Row 47: Ch 3, skip 1st st and 1st ch-1 sp, 15 sc M, 8 dc M, 12 tr M, 4 dc M, 14 sc M, ending with 1 sc in last st. Turn.

Row 48: Repeat Row 4 [all dc M].

Row 49: Ch 4, skip 1st st and 1st ch-1 sp, 14 dc M, 19 tr M, 5 dc M, 15 sc M, ending with 1 sc. Turn.

Row 50: Repeat Row 4 [all dc M]. Change to sea green, turn.

Row 51: Ch 3, skip 1st st and 1st ch-1 sp, 17 sc M, 2 dc M, 12 tr M, 6 dc M, 14 sc M, 2 dc M, ending with 1 dc. Turn.

Row 52: Repeat Row 4 [all dc M].

Row 53: Repeat Row 7 [all tr M].

Row 54: Ch 4, skip 1st st and 1st ch-1 sp, 4 dc M, 4 sc M, 2 dc M, 5 sc M, 8 dc M, 8 tr M, 18 dc M, 4 tr M, ending with 1 tr in last st. Turn.

Row 55: Ch 4, skip 1st st and 1st ch-1 sp, 26 dc M, 1 tr M, 15 dc M, 2 sc M, 9 dc M, ending with 1 dc in last st. Turn.

Row 56: Repeat Row 4 [all dc M].

Row 57: Repeat Row 7 [all tr M]. Break yarn.

Fringe: Follow directions for making fringe on page 37, wrapping sea green yarn around an 8″ piece of cardboard. Divide the yarn into groups of about 10 strands. Attach 2 groups of yarn in the 1st mesh of the bottom row and 1 group in the 2nd mesh. Continue to alternate in this manner across the bottom row.

Filet Curtain

Fragile and elegant, this curtain seems to belong to an earlier century when time, patience, and craftsmanship produced lacy heirlooms of great beauty and delicacy. To simplify the creation of your own personal heirloom, copy the design onto larger graph paper before you begin; you'll find it easier to read. Then, as you work, cover the completed rows of the graph with a blank piece of paper.

Materials:
• 8 skeins ecru Bucilla Wondersheen for each curtain *or* any thin cotton

Hooks: #5 steel
       #2 steel

Gauge:
4 meshes = 1", 4 rows = 1¼"

Finished Size:
Side panel, 10x48"
Center panel, 20x48"
(This does not include the edging; top and bottom edgings will add approximately 1" to overall length.)

    Note: Each curtain is composed of 3 panels, which are made separately, then edged and joined.

    Each square of the graph [Diagram 83] equals 2 sts. 1 open mesh □ = 1 dc, ch 1, skip 1 st. 1 solid mesh ⊠ = 1 dc in each of next 2 sts. Refer to page 87 for a more detailed explanation of filet crochet.

Instructions:
Side panels: Use the #5 hk.
Foundation chain: Ch 85.
Row 1: 1 dc in 5th ch from hk, ch 1, skip next st, *1 dc in next st, ch 1, skip next st. Repeat from * [40 meshes], ending with 1 dc in last ch. Ch 4, turn.
Row 2: Skip 1st dc and ch-1 of previous row, 1 dc in next dc, ch 1, skip ch-1 sp, *1 dc in next dc, ch 1, skip ch-1 sp. Repeat from *, ending with 1 dc in 3rd ch of ch-4.
Row 3: You are ready now to begin the 3rd row of the graph for the side panels. It is read from right to left. Continue to follow the graph until you complete it.

Rows 158–161: Repeat Row 2. Break yarn. Repeat to make a 2nd side panel.
Center panel: Use the #5 hk.
Foundation chain: Ch 149.
Rows 1–2: Follow directions for Rows 1–2 of side panels. [Each row should have 72 meshes + 1 post.]
Row 3: Follow graph for center panel, beginning with the 3rd row. Continue to follow the graph until you complete it.
Rows 158–161: Repeat Row 2. Break yarn.
EDGING LEFT PANEL
Change to the #2 hk. With the panel facing the same way as the graph [that is, with the leaves at the bottom pointing left], attach yarn in the side of the 1st dc in the upper left-hand corner.
Row 1: Ch 2 [= 1 sc], 1 sc in side of 1st dc, **2 sc in side of next dc.** Repeat from ** to ** until corner. 4 sc in corner. 1 sc in each ch-1 sp of 1st row, 4 sc in next corner. Repeat from ** to **, ending with 2 sc in side of last dc in upper right-hand corner. Ch 1, turn. [Do *not* work across top of panel.]
Row 2: 1 sc in each of 1st 8 sts, **(1 sc in loop A of next st) 5 times, ch 3, skip 3 sts.** Repeat from ** to ** until corner, ending with (1 sc in loop A of next st) 5 times. Corner: (Ch 3, skip 1 st, 1 sc in next st) 3 times. Repeat from ** to ** across bottom, ending with (1 sc in back lp of next st) 5 times. Repeat corner. Repeat from ** to **, ending with (1 sc in back of next st) 5 times, 1 sc in each of last 8 sts. Ch 2, turn.
Row 3: 1 dc in each of 1st 8 sts, **ch 3, skip next 5 sc, (1 sc, 1 hdc, 3 dc, 1 hdc, 1 sc) in ch-3 sp of previous row [1 Pointed Shell formed].** Repeat from ** to ** until corner, ending with ch 3, skip 5 sc. Corner: (3 hdc, 1 dc) in 1st

Center Panel

Side Panel

Row 161

Row 3

Diagram 83

corner lp, 7 dc in center lp, (1 dc, 3 hdc) in 3rd corner lp. Repeat from ** to ** across bottom. Repeat corner. Repeat from ** to **, ending with ch 3, skip 5 dc, 1 dc in each of last 8 sts. Ch 2, turn.

Row 4: 1 dc in each of 1st 8 sts, **ch 2, 1 hdc in ch-3 lp, ch 2, skip 1st st of Pointed Shell, (1 sc in next st) 2 times, (1 sc, ch 3, 1 sc) in center st, (1 sc in next st) 2 times, skip last st of Pointed Shell.** Repeat from ** to ** until corner, ending with ch 2, 1 hdc in ch-3 lp, ch 2. Corner: (Skip 1 st, 1 sc in next st, ch 3) 3 times, (1 sc, 1 Pineapple st, 1 sc) in center of 7-dc group, (ch-3, skip 1 st, 1 sc in next st) 3 times, skip last sc of corner. Repeat from ** to ** across bottom, ending with ch 2, 1 hdc in ch-3 lp, ch 2. Repeat corner. Repeat from ** to **, ending with ch 2, 1 hdc in ch-3 lp, ch 2, 1 dc in each of last 8 sts. Break yarn.

EDGING RIGHT PANEL

Reverse this panel so that the leaves at the bottom point to the right. Then work as for the left panel.

EDGING CENTER PANEL

Work as you did for the side panels until you come to Row 4. This row joins the side and center panels. Begin with the center and left panels. Make sure that the front side of both panels is facing up.

Row 4: 1 dc in each of the 1st 8 sts, ch 1, 1 sc in last of the 8 dc on the left panel, ch 1, 1 slst in last of 8 dc on center panel. **Ch 2, 1 hdc in ch-3 lp, ch 2, skip 1st st of Pointed Shell, (1 sc in next st) 2 times, (1 sc, ch 1, 1 sc in center ch-3 of corresponding Pointed Shell on left panel, ch 1, 1 sc) in center st, (1 sc in next st) 2 times, skip last st of Pointed Shell.** Repeat from ** to ** until corner, ending with (1 sc in next st) 2 times, skip last st of Pointed Shell. Work corners and bottom as in Row 4 of side panel. Repeat from ** to **, attaching right panel, ending with ch 2, 1 hdc in ch-3 lp, ch 2, 1 dc in 1st of 8 dc, ch 1, 1 sc in corresponding dc on right panel, ch 1, slst in same dc on center panel, 1 dc in each of last 7 dc. Break yarn.

Block the curtain according to the directions on page 35.

Creating Designs

Why not create your own filet crochet or tapestry-stitch designs? First crochet a small swatch with the yarn you want to use, in order to find out what gauge (that is, how many stitches per inch and how many rows per inch) you get. Make sure that you use the same stitch technique to make the swatch that you plan to use for the project, since both tapestry stitch and filet crochet produce a different gauge than you would get with back and forth rows of single crochet. Next you must relate this gauge to the graph paper from which you will draw your design. As you learned in the sections in this chapter about filet crochet and tapestry stitch, each square on the graph paper represents a certain number of stitches: For single crochet tapestry stitch, each square = 1 stitch; for double crochet tapestry stitch, each square = 2 stitches; for filet crochet, each square = 1 mesh or 2 stitches (see graphs on pages 84 and

87). Keep in mind that the more intricate your design, the more squares you will need to represent it accurately. If your yarn is thick, you will not get very many stitches per inch and your finished project may be unmanageably large. An easy way to make sure you know the finished size of the project is to use graph paper that has the same number of squares per inch as your gauge gives you. For example, if you are working in filet crochet and your gauge is 6 meshes per inch, buy graph paper that has 6 squares per inch. Draw your design onto a piece of paper and then trace it onto the graph paper or draw your design directly onto the graph paper. When you are satisfied with the design make an X in each square that is incorporated in any part of the design. If freehand drawing is not one of your strengths, just try filling in the boxes of the graph until you get a design that pleases you.

Woven Crochet Pillow

Unspun sheepswool, called tops or roving, is just one of the surprises waiting for you at the weaving stores in your area. This wool, already cleaned and carded, is ready to be handspun and dyed—perhaps with natural dyes made from common plants and vegetables. Treat roving gently; since it is unspun it can be pulled apart.

Materials:
- 2 skeins white #7351 Reynolds Lopi *or* any bulky weight
- 2 balls white #01 Reynolds mohair *or* any mohair blend
- 2 skeins white #1 Plymouth Apollo *or* 1 skein Henry's Attic Periwinkle
- ¼ lb. roving or tops (undyed, unspun sheepswool) in lengths of at least 70″
- Muslin casing
- Stuffing
- Blunt yarn needle with large eye (or large trussing needle)

Hook: H

Gauge:
10 sts = 3″, 3 rows = 1″

Finished Size:
Before weaving: 13x40″ (= 2 sides of pillow, worked as 1 piece)
After weaving: 14x35″

Instructions:
Foundation chain: Ch 44 with Apollo.
Row 1: 1 sc in 2nd ch from hk, *1 sc in next ch. Repeat from *, ending with 1 sc in last ch [43 sc].
Row 2: Ch 3 [= 1 sc, ch 1], skip 1st and 2nd sc, *1 sc in next st, ch 1, skip next sc. Repeat from *, ending with 1 sc in next st, ch 1, skip next-to-last st, 1 sc in last sc. [Counting the initial 3 chs as 1 sc, ch 1, you should have 22 sc and 21 ch-1 sps, forming 21 meshes and 1 post.] Turn.
Row 3: Ch 3, skip 1st sc and 1st ch-1 sp, *1 sc in next st, ch 1, skip next ch-1 sp. Repeat from *, ending with 1 sc in next st, ch 1, skip 3rd ch of ch-3, 1 sc in 2nd ch of ch-3. Turn [21 meshes and 1 post].

Repeat Row 3 for pat, changing yarn according to the directions for changing yarn at the end of a row on page 23 in the following sequence:
Rows 4–8: Apollo.
Rows 9–10: Lopi.
Rows 11–13: Apollo.
Rows 14–17: Mohair.
Rows 18–19: Lopi.
Rows 20–23: Apollo.
Rows 24–30: Lopi.
Rows 31–42: Mohair.
Rows 43–51: Apollo.
Rows 52–55: Lopi.
Rows 56–59: Apollo.

Now repeat Rows 1–59 in *reverse order,* beginning with Row 59 and ending with Row 1. You should end up with 118 rows. Make sure that all the yarn tails are tied securely tog and bring them all to whichever side you designate as the back side of your piece.

With the front side facing you, edge the piece in sc, changing yarn so that the edging yarn always matches the yarn of the piece. Carry the unused yarn behind your work and crochet over it [as well as over yarn tails as you come to them], as described in the sections on hiding yarn tails [pages 23–24] and on Tapestry st [pages 84–86]. Don't worry if the edges look bulky—once the piece is woven, it won't be noticeable. Block the piece according to the directions on page 35.

WEAVING

Always work with the front of the piece facing you. Turn the piece so that the 1st ch-1 sp of the 2nd row [1st row is all sc] is in the upper right-hand corner. The row of ch-1 sps that is now across the top of the piece is the *first mesh;* you will weave the 1st 3 rows of weaving in and out of this mesh. [See the directions for

vertical weaving on page 90. Each mesh may hold 1, 2, or 3 rows of weaving.]

The sc sts appear as a row of sideways V's underneath each mesh. You will weave thru these as well—each V-row will have 1 row of weaving.

Each row of weaving may have 1 or more strands of yarn. The chart below tells you how many strands of a yarn to use for 1 row and how long each strand should be. The lengths given are approximate and depend on how tightly you weave. The strands for each row should be long enough to leave about 10″ of yarn *at each end* for fringe. Cut the yarn for each row as you go along; that way you can adjust the length to suit your hand.

yarn	strands	length
Lopi	2	60″
Mohair	4	60″
Apollo	2	60″
Roving	1	70″

If 2 strands of yarn, each 60″ long, are called for, you will find it easier to cut 1 strand of 120″, thread it thru the yarn needle so that it is double, work the row, then cut the end to free the needle. For 4 strands cut two 120″ strands, thread them both thru the needle, double them, and work in the same way.

Always weave from right to left. A row of weaving may begin in 2 ways—you can insert the needle from the *back* of your piece *to the front* between the edging row and Row 1, or you can insert it from the *front to the back* in the same place. In either case you then continue to weave in and out as described in the section on vertical weaving on page 90. Be sure to leave a 10″ tail of yarn at the beginning.

Since roving is unspun, it must be treated gently. Don't try to weave it using a needle, as you do the other yarns. Instead, carefully divide it into strands of approximately 1″ in diameter [the strands should be as thick as possible but should pass without difficulty thru the mesh]. Then weave it in and out with your fingers, pulling it completely thru one mesh be-

fore inserting it into the next. Weave loosely; this produces the bumpy effect you can see in the photograph of the pillow.

You will find as you work that the unwoven part of your piece will buckle. This is caused by the tightness of the woven fabric compared to that of the regular crochet. Weave as loosely as possible, but don't be too concerned with the buckling. It will disappear when the entire piece has been woven.

Mesh 1: Work with Lopi.

Row 1—Insert needle from back to front.

Row 2—Insert needle from front to back.

Row 3—Insert needle from back to front.

V-Row 1—Insert needle from front to back.

Mesh 2: Roving; insert needle from back to front.

V-Row 2—Lopi; insert needle from back to front.

Mesh 3: Roving; insert needle from front to back.

V-Row 3—Lopi; insert needle from front to back.

Mesh 4: Roving; insert needle from back to front.

V-Row 4—Lopi; insert needle from back to front.

Mesh 5: Work with Apollo.

Row 1—Insert needle from front to back.

Row 2—Insert needle from back to front.

V-Row 5—Insert needle from front to back.

Mesh 6: Work with Apollo and then Mohair.

Row 1—Apollo; insert needle from back to front.

Row 2—Apollo; insert needle from front to back.

V-Row 6—Mohair; insert needle from back to front.

Mesh 7: Work with Apollo and then Mohair.

Row 1—Apollo; insert needle from front to back.

Row 2—Apollo; insert needle from back to front.

V-Row 7—Mohair; insert needle from front to back.

Mesh 8: Roving; insert needle from back to front.

V-Row 8—Mohair; insert needle from front to back.

Mesh 9: Roving; insert needle from front to back.

V-Row 9—Mohair; insert needle from back to front.

Mesh 10: Work with Lopi.

Row 1—Insert needle from front to back.

Row 2—Insert needle from back to front.

V-Row 10—Insert needle from front to back.

Mesh 11: Work with Lopi and then Mohair.

Row 1—Lopi; insert needle from back to front.

Row 2—Lopi; insert needle from front to back.

V-Row 11—Mohair; insert needle from back to front.

Mesh 12: Work with Apollo and then Mohair.

Row 1—Apollo; insert needle from front to back.

Row 2—Apollo; insert needle from back to front.

V-Row 12—Mohair; insert needle from front to back.

Mesh 13: Work with Apollo and then Mohair.

Row 1—Apollo; insert needle from back to front.

Row 2—Apollo; insert needle from front to back.

V-Row 13—Mohair; insert needle from back to front.

Mesh 14: Work with Apollo and then Mohair.

Row 1—Apollo; insert needle from front to back.

Row 2—Apollo; insert needle from back to front.

V-Row 14—Mohair; insert needle from front to back.

Mesh 15: Roving; insert needle from back to front.

V-Row 15—Lopi; insert needle from back to front.

Mesh 16: Roving; insert needle from front to back.

V-Row 16—Lopi; insert needle from front to back.

Mesh 17: Roving; insert needle from back to front.

V-Row 17—Lopi; insert needle from back to front.

Mesh 18: Roving; insert needle from front to back.

V-Row 18—Lopi; insert needle from front to back.

Mesh 19: Roving; insert needle from back to front.

V-Row 19—Lopi; insert needle from back to front.

Mesh 20: Work with Lopi and then Mohair.

Row 1—Lopi; insert needle from front to back.

Row 2—Lopi; insert needle from back to front.

V-Row 20—Mohair; insert needle from back to front.

Mesh 21: Work with Lopi.

Row 1—Insert needle from front to back.

Row 2—Insert needle from back to front.

Row 3—Insert needle from front to back.

Fold the pillow over so that all the fringe is at one end and the front side is facing out. Join the sides with a slst thru the 2 inside lps, using Lopi. [See the directions for joining crocheted pieces on page 29.] Make a muslin pillow according to the directions on page 36. After the pillow is stuffed, pull all the fringe thru to the front side of the pillow. Join the fringed edges with slst.

Floral Coverlet

The impressionistic sprays of flowers arranged in alternating diamond motifs on our coverlet appear to be done in needlepoint, but are in fact good illustrations of the versatility of Tapestry stitch. If Tapestry stitch is new to you, you'll find that the first motif or two will go slowly. Don't be discouraged, though. Once you've gotten used to changing yarn every few stitches, your speed will increase.

Materials:
- 40 skeins Borgs i Lund Frostagarn (each 3.6 oz.) in the following amounts: white #201, 30 skeins; light green #310, 2 skeins; dark green #232, 2 skeins; lavender #296, 2 skeins; pink #295, 1 skein; dark apricot #207, 2 skeins; apricot #321, 1 skein *or* corresponding amounts of any medium-bulky yarn
- Lining for completed coverlet

Note: Amounts given are for the coverlet as shown in the photograph; each motif requires approximately 2.7 oz. of white yarn and small amounts of the other colors.

Hook: J

Gauge:
3 sts = 1″, 3 rows = 1″

Finished Size:
Each motif = 12x20″ after edged and blocked.

The coverlet as shown is 60x80″. The size can be adjusted by increasing or decreasing the number of motifs.

Instructions:
Work motifs in back and forth Tapestry st, following the instructions on pages 84–86. Follow the directions below and the graphs in Diagram 84 on pages 116 and 117. Carry only the white yarn. All other colors should be rolled into small balls or onto bobbins, dropped after use, and picked up again when needed in the same place.

Note: Since the foundation ch is **Row 1** on each graph, to avoid confusion, it is called Row 1 in the directions below.

Motifs A and B: Make 20 of Motif A and 12 of Motif B.

Row 1: Ch 2.
Row 2: 3 sc in 2nd ch. Ch 1, turn [3 sts].
Rows 3–30: 1 sc in 1st st, 2 sc in next st, 1 sc in each remaining st, ending with 1 sc in last st. Ch 1, turn. [Diamond will inc 1 st each row; Row 30 should have 31 sts.]
Row 31: 1 sc in 1st st and in every st, ending with 1 sc in last st. Ch 1, turn [31 sts].
Rows 32–60: 1 sc in 1st st, 1 dec over next 2 sts, 1 sc in each remaining st, ending with 1 sc in last st. Ch 1, turn. [Diamond will dec 1 st each row; Row 60 should have 3 sts.]
Row 61: (Insert hk in st, pull up a lp) 3 times, yo and draw thru all 3 lps. Break yarn.
Motif C: Make 8, following directions for Rows 1–31, Motifs A and B.
Motif D: Make 6.
Row 1: Ch 2.
Row 2: 2 sc in 2nd ch from hk. Ch 1, turn.
Row 3: 1 sc in each sc. Ch 1, turn [2 sts].
Row 4: 1 sc in 1st sc, 2 sc in next sc. Ch 1, turn [3 sts].
Row 5: Repeat Row 3 [3 sts].
Row 6: 1 sc in 1st st, 2 sc in next st, 1 sc in each remaining st, ending with 1 sc in last st. Ch 1, turn [4 sts].
Rows 7–30: Repeat Rows 5 and 6. [Motif will inc 1 st every even-numbered row. Row 30 should have 16 sts.]
Row 31: 1 sc in 1st st and every sc, ending with 1 sc in last st. Ch 1, turn.
Row 32: 1 sc in 1st st, 1 dec over next 2 sts, 1 sc in each remaining st, ending with 1 sc in last st. Ch 1, turn [15 sts].
Row 33: 1 sc in 1st st and in every st, ending with 1 sc in last st. Ch 1, turn [15 sts].
Rows 34–60: Repeat Rows 32 and 33. [Motif will dec 1 st every even-numbered row.]
Row 61: (Insert hk thru st, pull up lp) 2 times,

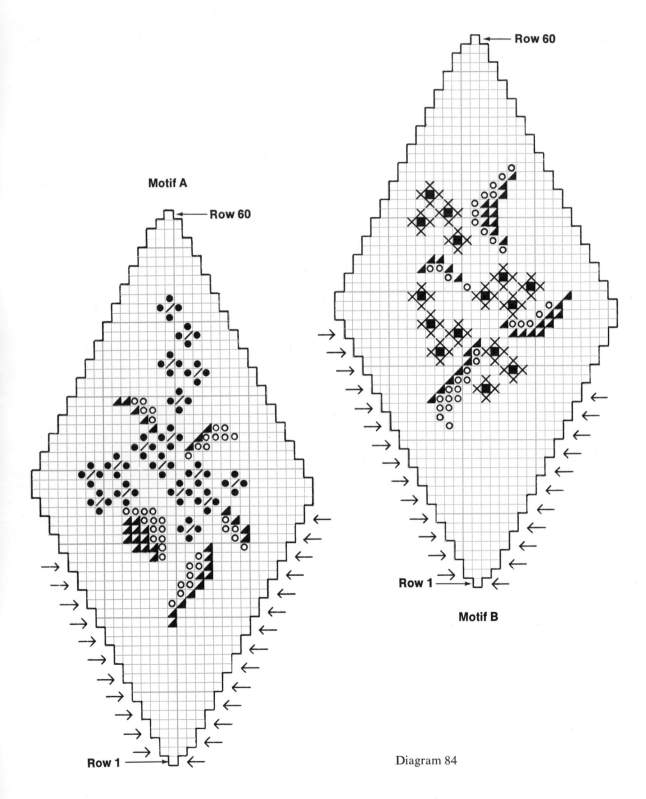

Motif A

Row 60

Row 1

Row 60

Row 1

Motif B

Diagram 84

116

yo and draw thru both lps. Break the yarn.

Edge each motif with white, following directions for edging on page 25. Make 3 sc in each corner [sides of Row 31 are corners].

Block the motifs according to the directions on page 35. Join the motifs with a slst thru the 2 inside lps only, following the directions on page 29, *except* join center sc of each corner thru both lps. Make 2 joining sts in each center st, 1 in the adjacent motif of the other pat, then another in the center st of the motif of the same pat directly opposite.

After all motifs have been joined, make 1 Pineapple st in any corner st of an A or B motif which is on the outside edge of the coverlet. Edge the coverlet in Shrimp st [page 50]. You may want to reinforce the joining of the corners on the back side of the coverlet.

Line the coverlet according to the directions on page 36.

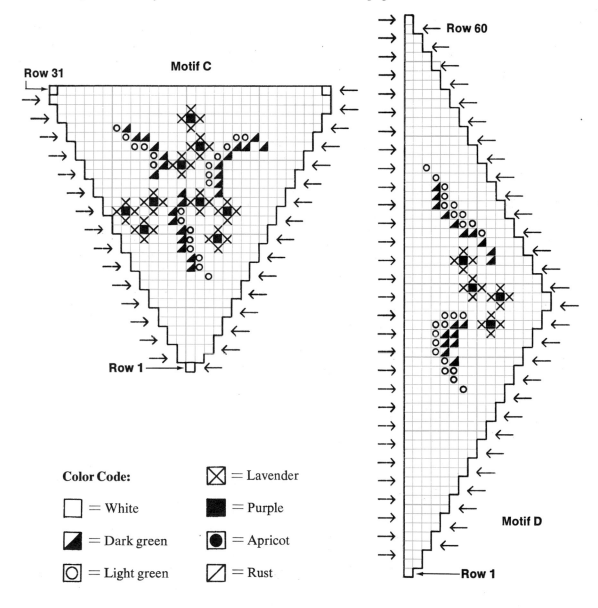

Color Code:

☐ = White

◧ = Dark green

⊙ = Light green

⊠ = Lavender

■ = Purple

⊙ = Apricot

◪ = Rust

117

Afghan Crochet Pillows

These pillows are only two of a variety of stitch patterns that can be worked in Afghan crochet. For the Victorian Striped Pillow a feeling of motion is created through the use of high and low stitches. Although you can work many Afghan crochet stitches in tapestry pattern, we chose the stockinette stitch for the Tapestry-Stitch Pillow because of the tight, knitlike fabric it creates. Even though both pillows have the same colors, note how the designs complement each other.

Materials:

- 3 skeins Berga Ullman Mohairgarn in the following amounts: light blue #3275, 1 skein; purple #2555, 1 skein; navy #3013, 1 skein
- Backing fabric
- Muslin casing
- Stuffing

Note: These materials are for 1 crocheted side of both pillows.

Hook: F

Gauge:

Victorian Striped Pillow: 6 sts = 1", 5 rows = 1"

Tapestry-Stitch Pillow: 6 sts = 1", 6 rows = 1"

Finished Size:

Victorian Striped Pillow: 16½" square (approximate size)

Tapestry-Stitch Pillow: 9x20"

Victorian Striped Pillow

Instructions:

The st pat used for this pillow varies a little from the basic Afghan crochet st described in this chapter. Always insert your hk thru the top bar of the st as usual, but make the sts as follows:

bs [basic stitch]: Insert hk under the bar, yo and pull up a lp [a basic Afghan st].

ss [slip stitch]: Insert hk under bar of the st. The bar becomes the lp on your hk.

hcd [half closed double crochet]: Yo, insert hk thru bar, yo and pull a lp thru the bar, yo and pull a lp thru the 1st 2 lps on your hk.

To change colors [at the end of the 2nd half of a row]: Pull the new color yarn thru the last 2 lps of the previous row. Since the last lp on your hk will become the 1st st of the new row, you will then be ready to start your next row with the new color.

Foundation chain: Ch 100 with light blue.

Row 1 [1st half]: Insert hk into the 2nd ch from hk and make 1 bs, *1 bs in next ch. Repeat from *, ending with 1 bs in last ch.

Row 1 [2nd half]: Yo, pull a lp thru the 1st lp on hk, *yo and pull a lp thru the next 2 lps. Repeat from *, ending with pull a lp thru the last 2 lps on hk.

Row 2 [1st half]: Purple—skip 1st bar, 1 bs in next bar, *1 ss in each of next 2 bars, 1 bs in each of next 2 bars, 1 hcd in each of next 4 bars, 1 bs in each of next 2 bars. Repeat from *, ending with 1 hcd in each of last 4 bars.

Row 2 [2nd half]: Repeat Row 1, 2nd half.

Row 3: Light blue—repeat Row 1.

Row 4: [1st half]: Purple—skip 1st bar, 1 bs in next bar, *1 hcd in each of next 4 bars, 1 bs in each of next 2 bars, 1 ss in each of next 2 bars, 1 bs in each of next 2 bars. Repeat from *, ending with 1 ss in each of last 2 bars.

Row 4 [2nd half]: Repeat Row 1, 2nd half.

Row 5: Navy—repeat Row 1.

Row 6: Purple—repeat Row 2.

Row 7: Navy—repeat Row 1.

Row 8: Purple—repeat Row 2.

Repeat Rows 1–8 seven times; then repeat Rows 1–3 once.

Block the pillow to the correct size [if necessary], following the direction for blocking on page 35.

Complete the pillow, following the directions on pages 36–37.

Tapestry-Stitch Pillow

Instructions:

The Afghan st used in this pillow is worked by inserting your hk from front to back thru the 2 vertical bars of the st, yo and pull up a lp onto your hk. The st resembles a Knitted Stockinette st.

The graph for this project [Diagram 85] is read in the same way as any Tapestry-st graph [see page 84]. Since each row of Afghan crochet consists of 2 parts—picking up sts and then working them off—each line of the graph is read from left to right. One line of the graph is equivalent to the 2 halves of each row of Afghan crochet. We will give written directions for the 1st 2 rows of the graph.

Foundation chain: Ch 54 with light blue.

Row 1 [1st half]: Skip 1st ch, insert hk into 2nd ch from hk, yo and pull up a lp, repeat in each of next 15 chs, drop light blue, with purple pull up a lp in each of the next 20 chs, drop purple, with light blue pull up a lp in each of the last 17 chs.

Row 1 [2nd half]: Work off 1st 16 lps with light blue, drop light blue, with purple work off next 20 sts, drop purple, work off last 18 sts with light blue.

Row 2 [1st half]: Skip 1st bar, pull up a lp in each of the next 15 sts with light blue, drop light blue, with purple pick up each of the next 20 sts, drop purple, pick up the next 2 sts with navy, drop navy, pick up the last 16 sts with light blue.

Row 2 [2nd half]: Work the 1st 15 sts off with light blue, drop light blue, work the next 2 sts off with navy, drop navy, work the next 20 sts off with purple, drop purple, work the last 17 sts off with light blue.

Continue working each row of the graph. To change colors when working the 2nd half of each row, remember to pull up a lp of the new color when you have 1 lp of the old color still left on the hk; then draw the new color thru the last lp of the old color and the 1st lp of the new color.

When you have finished the last row of the graph, break the yarn.

Block the piece to the correct size [if necessary] following the directions for blocking on page 35.

Complete the pillow following the directions on pages 36–37.

Color Code: B = Blue
L = Lilac P = Purple

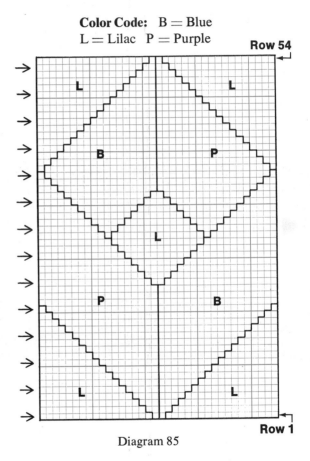

Diagram 85

120

Chapter 4

CROCHET SHAPES

Circles and squares, rectangles and ovals, hexagons and triangles—all of these geometric shapes can become the elements of beautiful designs. Whether they are worked by themselves or combined with other crochet techniques, these simple shapes will broaden your crochet experience. By following step-by-step directions, you will learn how to crochet all the basic shapes. You can then apply these techniques to make any simple shape. The projects in this chapter are designed to give a wide range of ideas for using shape techniques to decorate your home. Circles are rugs, three-dimensional tubes are canister covers, diamonds form bargello-like pillows. Shapes can be worked in simple single crochet stitches such as the decorative pockets of the Wall Organizer (page 157), or in more complicated stitch patterns like those in the Circular Tablecloth (page 146).

Circles

Before beginning this discussion of circles, read the section on working in rounds on pages 27–28, which tells you how to start and complete the first 2 rounds.

To make a circle you will form a small foundation chain into a ring, work several stitches into the ring, and then crochet consecutive rounds of stitches until the circle is the desired size. To keep the circle flat it is necessary to increase in a regular pattern: Too few increases will cause the edge of the circle to cup, too many increases will ruffle the edges, irregularly spaced increases will distort the shape. Therefore it is a good idea to count the stitches at the completion of each round. A mistake of 1 or 2 stitches in the early rounds will multiply itself on subsequent rounds, causing the finished circle to be misshapen.

Joined Rounds Circles

Foundation chain: Ch 5, insert hk into 5th ch from hk and make a slst, joining the ring.
Round 1: Ch 1, work 8 sc over the ch into the ring, join the last sc to the 1st sc with a slst.
Note: Learn to recognize the 1st st of each rnd. It is easy to accidentally pick up the ch-1 or the slst of the previous rnd. Look at Diagram 57 on page 28. Point A is the 1st st of the rnd. This is the st in which you join the last st to the 1st st. It is also the same st in which you make the 1st st of the next rnd.
Round 2: Ch 1, 2 sc in 1st st of previous rnd, *2 sc in next st. Repeat from *, ending with 2 sc in last st, join with slst to 1st sc of this rnd [16 sts].
Round 3: Ch 1, 1 sc in 1st st of previous rnd, *2 sc in next st, 1 sc in next st. Repeat from *, ending with 2 sc in last st, join with slst to 1st sc of this rnd [24 sts].
When you have 24 sts in your circle, begin to apply the general rule for increasing any circle. The rule establishes the regular pat of increasing necessary to keep your circle uniform and flat. Divide the circle into 12 equal parts. In this case, 24 sts divided by 12 is 2.

On Round 4 you will inc every 2nd st, making 12 incs in this rnd.
Round 4: Ch 1, 1 sc in 1st st of previous rnd, *2 sc in next st, 1 sc in next st. Repeat from *, ending with 2 sc in last st, join with slst to 1st sc of this rnd [36 sts].
Round 5: This is a non-inc rnd. Ch 1, 1 sc in 1st st of previous rnd, *1 sc in next st. Repeat from *, ending with 1 sc in last st, join with slst to 1st sc of this rnd.
Round 6: 36 divided by 12 is 3, so you will inc in every 3rd st. Ch 1, 1 sc in 1st st of previous rnd, 1 sc in next st, *2 sc in next st, 1 sc in each of next 2 sts. Repeat from *, ending with 2 sc in last st, join with slst to 1st sc of this rnd [48 sts].
Round 7: This is a non-inc rnd. Repeat Round 5.
Round 8: 48 divided by 12 is 4, so you will inc in every 4th st. Ch 1, 1 sc in 1st st of previous rnd, 1 sc in each of next 2 sts, *2 sc in next st, 1 sc in each of next 3 sts. Repeat from *, ending with 2 sc in last st, join with slst to 1st sc of this rnd [60 sts].
Continue working rnds in this way, increasing on even rnds, not increasing on odd rnds, until the circle has reached the desired size.

Spiraled Rounds Circles

You can avoid the seam caused by joining each round by spiraling your circle. However, you must keep track of your rounds so that you can increase properly. Use a small piece of contrasting yarn as a marker to remind you where one round begins and another ends.

Work a circle in the same way as the Joined Rounds Circles above until you have 24 stitches. Instead of making a slip stitch at the end of Round 3 to join the last stitch to the 1st, work a single crochet in the 1st stitch of Round 3. This stitch becomes the 1st stitch of Round 4. Pull your marker yarn through this stitch and tie a loose knot. Apply the general rule for increasing circles. (24 divided by 12 equals 2—therefore you increase every 2nd st.) When you reach the stitch with the marker, you have completed the round. Continue working rounds, moving the marker up on each round and following the rule for increasing circles. When you are ready to end the circle, make 1 or 2 slip stitches in the last few stitches of the last round and then join the last stitch to the 1st stitch of the last round with a slip stitch and break the yarn.

Double Crochet Circles

Increasing on circles using double crochet or higher stitches is a little different. Since a double crochet is twice as high as a single crochet, 1 double crochet round equals 2 single crochet rounds. Therefore you must increase on every double crochet round.

Foundation chain: Ch 6, insert hk into 6th ch from hk and make a slst, joining the ring.

Round 1: Ch 3 [ch-3 at beg of each dc rnd counts as 1st dc of rnd], work 11 dc in the ring and join with a slst to top of ch 3 [12 sts].

Round 2: Ch 3, 1 dc in same st [top of ch-3], *2 dc in next st. Repeat from *, ending with 1 dc in last st, join with slst to top of ch-3 [24 sts].

Round 3: Apply the general rule—24 sts divided by 12 is 2, so you will inc every 2 sts. Ch 3, *2 dc in next st, 1 dc in next st. Repeat from *, ending with 1 dc in last st, join with slst to top of ch-3 [36 sts].

Round 4: 36 divided by 12 is 3. Ch 3, 1 dc in next st, *2 dc in next st, 1 dc in each of next 2 sts. Repeat from *, ending with 1 dc in last st, join with slst to top of ch-3 [48 sts].

Round 5: 48 divided by 12 is 4. Ch 3, 1 dc in each of next 2 sts, *2 dc in next st, 1 dc in each of next 3 sts. Repeat from *, ending with 2 dc in last st, join with slst to top ch of ch-3 [60 sts].

Continue increasing on each rnd until the circle is the desired size. It is easy to see the incs in each rnd. Each 2-st inc forms a V. On each subsequent rnd work 2 sts in the 2nd st of the inc group of the previous rnd.

Note: Twelve incs per rnd will work well for most circles made with dc or higher sts. If your circle ruffles, indicating too many incs, work a non-inc rnd in between inc rnds, or try making fewer than 12 incs in each rnd.

Squares

There are two ways to make a basic square: One way is to work row-by-row, another is to work in rounds.

Squares Made in Rows

The simplest method for making a square is to work a piece that is as high as it is long.

Foundation chain: Make a ch slightly longer than the desired length of the square.

Note: If you have too many chs after you complete the 1st row, untie slip knot, undo unnecessary chs, and pull knot closed.

Row 1: Insert hk into 2nd ch from hk and make a st, *1 st in next ch. Repeat from *, ending with 1 st in last ch.

Measure this row and continue working rows of sts until the piece is as high as it is long.

Edge your piece according to the directions for edging on page 25.

Squares Made in Rounds

The next and most common method of making a square is to work it from the center. Begin by making a circle, and then work a 3-stitch increase at each of 4 points spaced equally around the circle. These 4 increases will form the "corners" of the square.

Foundation chain: Ch 4, insert hk into 4th ch from hk and make a slst.

Round 1: Ch 1, work 8 sc in ring. Join last st to the 1st st of rnd with a slst.

Round 2: Ch 1, 1 sc in 1st st of previous rnd, 3 sc in next st, (1 sc in next st, 3 sc in next st) 3 times. Join with slst to 1st st of this rnd.

123

Round 3: Ch 1, 1 sc in 1st st of previous rnd, 1 sc in next st, 3 sc in next st, (1 sc in each of next 3 sts, 3 sc in next st) 3 times, ending with 1 sc in last st, join last st to 1st st of this rnd with a slst.

Work each rnd by making 1 sc in each st until you reach the 3-sc group. Make 1 sc in the 1st st of this group, 3 sc in the center st of this group, and 1 sc in the 3rd st of this group. Proceed in this manner in each of the inc groups of each rnd.

Note: Most dc squares start with 12 sts worked into the ring on Round 1 as opposed to only 4 sts for sc. On Round 2 you would make a 3-st inc group every 3rd st to form your 4 corners. On subsequent rnds you work the same inc pat in each corner as you did for sc squares.

Hexagons

A hexagon is a shape with 6 equal sides. It is formed very much like a square; however, the increases are 2-stitch groups instead of 3-stitch groups, and they are made at 6 points on the circle to form 6 corners instead of at 4 points.

Foundation chain: Ch 5, insert hk into 5th ch from hk and make a slst to form a ring.

Round 1: [The number of sts worked in the ring must be divisible by 6.] Ch 1, work 12 sc in the ring, join the last st to the 1st st of this rnd with a slst.

Round 2: Ch 1, 1 sc in 1st st of previous rnd, 2 sc in next st, (1 sc in next st, 2 sc in next st) 5 times, join last st to 1st st with a slst. [The 2-sc inc groups will form the 6 corners.]

Round 3: Ch 1, 1 sc in 1st st of previous rnd, 1 sc in next st, 2 sc in next st. Continue to make 1 sc in each st, working 2 sts in the 2nd st of each 2-sc group. Join each rnd with a slst. Begin each new rnd with a ch 1, 1 sc in 1st st of the previous rnd.

Note: Apply inc pat to any even-sided figure. As an example, for a 10-sided shape [decagon] the number of sts worked into the ring on Round 1 must be divisible by 10, so the smallest number of sts possible would be 20. Twenty divided by 10 is 2, so you will make your 2-st inc in every 2nd st on Round 2. On subsequent rnds make a 2-st inc in the 2nd st of the inc groups of the previous rnd.

Semicircles

A semicircle is worked like a circle, with half the stitches. Instead of joining rounds, chain and turn each row.

Foundation chain: Ch 4, join ring with a slst.

Row 1: Ch 1, work 4 sc over ch into the ring. Ch 1, turn [4 sts].

Row 2: 2 sc in 1st st of previous row, *2 sc in next st. Repeat from *, ending with 2 sc in last st. Ch 1, turn [8 sts].

Row 3: 1 sc in 1st st of previous row, *2 sc in next st, 1 sc in next st. Repeat from *, ending with 2 sc in last st. Ch 1, turn [12 sts].

Note: At this point you can apply a general rule for increasing semicircles. The semicircle is divided into 4 equal parts, to be increased once in each part. In this case, 12 divided by 4 equals 3. On the next row you will inc in every 3rd st.

Row 4: 1 sc in each of 1st 2 sts of the previous row, *2 sc in next st, 1 sc in each of next 2 sts. Repeat from *, ending with 2 sc in last st. Ch 1, turn [4 incs—16 sts].

Row 5: 1 sc in 1st st of previous row, *1 sc in next st. Repeat from *, ending with 1 sc in last st. Ch 1, turn.

Row 6: 16 divided by 4 equals 4, so you will

need to inc in every 4th st. 1 sc in each of 1st 3 sts of previous row, *2 sc in next st, 1 sc in each of next 3 sts. Repeat from *, ending with 2 sc in last st. Ch 1, turn [20 sts].

Row 7: Repeat Row 5 [a non-inc row].

Row 8: 20 divided by 4 is 5, so you will inc in every 5th st. 1 sc in each of 1st 4 sts of the previous row, *2 sc in next st, 1 sc in each of the next 4 sts. Repeat from *, ending with 2 sc in last st. Ch 1, turn [24 sts].

Continue increasing on even-numbered rows and not odd-numbered rows until the semicircle is the desired size. Dc semicircles should be increased on each row.

Tubes

If you were to stop increasing your circle, the edge would begin to turn up. As you kept adding rounds, you would form a tube closed at one end—a most useful shape. Two of the planters on page 51 and the wastepaper basket cover on page 144 are made this way, as are the canisters on page 137.

To determine when to stop increasing your circle so that the subsequent tube will fit a desired shape, make a chain that fits snugly around the widest part of the piece to be covered (remember that a chain has no give). Write the number of chain stitches on a piece of paper and rip out the chain. If you crochet a circle until it has the same number of stitches as the chain you just made and then stop increasing, the tube subsequently formed will fit your piece perfectly. Determine the multiple of 12 that is closest to, but smaller than, the number of needed chain stitches. For example, if your chain was 52 stitches, the number of stitches closest to 52 that is a multiple of 12 is 48 stitches. Make a circle using the general increasing rule until there are 48 stitches. That leaves 4 more stitches to add to your circle. Divide 48 by 4 (the number of additional stitches needed), and you see that you need to make an increase every 12th stitch on the next increase round. You now have 52 stitches in the circle. Continue to work without increasing, and the circle will become a tube that fits the shape you need exactly.

You can control the shape of your tube by the manner in which you stop increasing the circle. When you stop increasing completely, the sides of the circle come up abruptly. However, if you want a more gradual curve to your tube, make fewer increases per round than you would for a flat circle—4 to 8 increases per round.

Open-Ended Tubes

Chain the desired number of stitches. Remember that chains have no give so if your tube must fit over something, so must your foundation chain. Instead of working over the chain and into a ring as you did for circles, you will be working into each stitch of the foundation chain. When working this way, it is easy for the chain to become twisted—something you should try to avoid. After inadvertently twisting countless chains, we feel it is easier to work the 1st round as a row. In other words, do not join the last stitch to the 1st stitch of the foundation chain with a slip stitch. Instead, simply work the 1st row of stitches making 1 stitch in each chain. (The 1st chain in which to insert your hook will depend on the stitch you are making.) When the row is completed, straighten the piece and bring the 2 ends together so that the last stitch of the row is next to the 1st stitch of the row. Insert your hook into the 1st stitch of the row, yarn over, and pull a loop through the 1st stitch of the row and the loop on your hook. The piece is joined. Chain up and work 1 stitch in each stitch of the previous round, joining or spiraling each round as you work.

Note: If you increase enough on the 2nd round, you can make a flat circle with a large hole in the middle instead of a tube.

Triangles

There are 2 ways to do triangles. They can be started at the tip and then increased or they can be started at the base and then decreased. Note too that if you were to put 2 triangles together, base to base, you would end up with a diamond; turn 2 triangles tip to tip and you'll end up with a spool shape (see below). All triangles and shapes formed from triangles should be edged according to the directions for edging on page 25.

Working Triangles from the Tip

Row 1: Ch 2.
Row 2: Work 3 sc in the 2nd ch from the hk. Ch 1, turn.
Row 3: 1 sc in 1st st of previous row, 2 sc in next st, 1 sc in each remaining st of the row. Ch 1, turn.
Row 4: 1 sc in 1st st of previous row, 2 sc in next st, 1 sc in each remaining st of row. Ch 1, turn.

Repeat Row 4, working until the triangle is the desired size.

Working Triangles from the Base

Foundation chain: Ch the desired length of the base of the triangle.
Row 1: Insert hk into 2nd ch from hk and make a sc, work a complete row of sc. Ch 1, turn.
Row 2: 1 sc in 1st st of previous row, 1 sc dec over next 2 sts, 1 sc in each remaining st of row. Ch 1, turn.
Row 3: 1 sc in 1st st of previous row, 1 sc dec over next 2 sts, 1 sc in each remaining st of row. Ch 1, turn.

Repeat Row 3, decreasing 1 st over the 2nd and 3rd sts of each row, until you have 1 st left. Break the yarn.

Note: You can make triangles of different shapes and sizes by changing the method of increasing or decreasing. If you want your triangle to be more obtuse [shorter and wider], make your incs or decs at *both* the beg and end of each row. An acute triangle [taller and thinner] can be made by working your incs or decs *every other row* or even several rows apart.

Diamonds

Start a triangle at the tip and work until the base is as wide as you want the center of the diamond to be. Now decrease the triangle as you would a triangle worked from the base until you have 1 stitch left. Break the yarn.

It is important that you decrease the top part of the diamond the same way you increased the bottom. If you increased 1 stitch in each row on the bottom, decrease 1 stitch per row on the upper half.

Spool Shapes

Start a triangle from the base and decrease as you would for any triangle until you have 3 stitches left. Begin to increase as you would for a triangle worked from the tip until the base has the same number of stitches as the opposite base. You must increase the upper half the same number of stitches per row as you decreased the lower half.

You can alter the shape and size of diamonds in the same manner as for triangles.

Rectangles and Ovals

The simplest way to make a rectangle is to work rows of stitches back and forth until the piece is the desired length and height. However, most rectangles and all ovals are worked from the center out. They are started by working down a foundation chain, around the tip of the chain, and back up the chain. The first and last stitches are joined, and then consecutive rounds are worked with 4 increase points for rectangles and 6 increase points, 3 at each end, for ovals.

After many unsuccessful attempts to make rectangles and ovals from existing formulas, we discovered an important relationship between the size of the ovals or rectangles we made and the size of the original foundation chain. Before you begin to make either of these shapes, decide what size you want the finished rectangle or oval to be. Determine the difference in size between the length and the width of the shape you want. That is the length you will need to make your foundation chain. For example, if the rectangle is to measure 7x10″, the chain should measure 3″.

Rectangles

Foundation chain: Ch the desired number of sts, insert hk into 2nd ch from hk and make 1 sc.

Round 1: Make 1 sc in each ch. When you reach the last ch, work 3 sc in it and then work your way back up the bottom of the ch, working 1 sc in each bottom strand. When you reach the last ch [actually the bottom of the ch in which you worked the 1st st], work 3 sc in this st and join to the 1st st with a slst.

Round 2: Ch 1, 1 sc in 1st st of previous rnd. Make 1 sc in each st. When you reach the 3-sc group, work 3 sc in the 1st st of the group, 1 sc in the 2nd st, and 3 sc in the 3rd st. Continue to make 1 sc in each st, working the same incs in the 3-sc group at the opposite end. You can either join the rnds or spiral them [see pages 27–28]. You will have made 4 inc groups.

Round 3: Make 1 sc in each st, working 3 sc in the center st of each of the four 3-sc inc groups.

Repeat Round 3 until the rectangle is the desired size.

Ovals

The foundation chain and Round 1 of ovals are the same as those for rectangles.

Round 2: Ch 1, 1 sc in 1st st of previous rnd. Make 1 sc in each st. When you reach the 3-sc group, work 2 sc in each st of the group, continue making 1 sc in each st, repeating this inc pat in the 3-sc group at the opposite end. You can either join the rnds or spiral them [see pages 27–28].

Round 3: Make 1 sc in each st, working 2 sc in the 2nd st of each 2-sc group of the previous rnd. Make 1 sc in each of the next sts, repeating this inc pat in the 2-sc groups at the opposite end.

Repeat Round 3 until the oval is as large as you want it to be.

Crocheted Bargello Pillows

Geometric motifs are an important part of crochet design, but all such motifs needn't look like granny squares. These pillows were inspired by the geometric beauty of bargello, the popular needlepoint technique that depends upon subtle color changes and repetitive designs for its effect. The Peacock's Eye is done with a simple single crochet, while the Diamond pillow is a little more difficult.

Peacock's Eye Pillow

Materials:
- 18 oz. uncut Paterna Persian yarn in the following amounts: rose #223 (color A), 2 oz.; rose #250 (color B), 2 oz.; rose #289 (color C), 2 oz.; rose #254 (color D), 2 oz.; rose #256 (color E), 2 oz.; grcen #540 (color F), 2 oz.; green #553 (color G), 2 oz.; green #590 (color H), 2 oz.; green #593 (color I), 2 oz. *or* corresponding amounts of any Persian, tapestry, or worsted yarn
- Backing
- Muslin casing
- Stuffing

Hook: F

Gauge:
4 sts = 1", 5 rows = 1"

Finished Size:
Each motif is a 4" square with a 5½" diagonal (after blocking). The size of the finished pillow will depend on the number of motifs you make:

36 motifs = 24" side, 33" diagonal
25 motifs = 20" side, 27½" diagonal
16 motifs = 16" side, 22" diagonal

Note: You will be using several shades of 1 color. The shades of each color are designated by letter and are listed above in order from darkest to lightest. In order words, rose #223 (color A) is darker than rose #250 (color B). Remember that these numbers apply only to Paterna Persian yarn.

The materials listed above are for 1 crocheted side of each pillow. If you want to crochet both sides, double the materials.

Instructions:
Foundation chain: Ch 4 with color F.

Row 1: 1 sc in 2nd ch from hk, *1 sc in next ch. Repeat from *, ending with 1 sc in last st. Ch 1, turn [3 sts].

Row 2: 1 sc in 1st st, *1 sc in next st. Repeat from *, ending with 1 sc in last st. Ch 1, turn [3 sts].

Row 3: Repeat Row 2, ending with 1 sc in last st. Ch 1. Do *not* turn work.

EDGING

Make 2 sc in *side* of last sc in row, *1 sc in side of next st, 3 sc in corner. Repeat from * around square, ending with 1 sc in 2nd st of Row 3, 1 sc in 3rd st of Row 3, join to 1st sc of edging with slst. Break yarn.

Now work across only 2 sides of the square, from the center st of the 3-sc group in 1 corner to the center st of the 3-sc group in the corner diagonally across from it. Rows are always worked in 1 direction, from right to left. Cut the yarn at the end of each row and reattach the new yarn on the right in the 1st st of the previous row. Hide yarn tails by crocheting over them, as described on page 24.

Row 4: Attach color G in center st of 3-sc corner group. 1 sc in same st, (1 sc in next st) 3 times, 3 sc in center st of corner group [= 3 sc in corner st], (1 sc in next st) 4 times. Break yarn [11 sts].

Row 5: Attach color H in 1st st of Row 4. 1 sc in same st, (1 sc in next st) 4 times, 3 sc in corner st, (1 sc in next st) 5 times. Break yarn [13 sts].

Row 6: Attach color I in 1st st of Row 5. 1 sc in same st, (1 sc in next st) 5 times, 3 sc in corner st, (1 sc in next st) 6 times. Break yarn [15 sts].

Turn the square upside down so that the

dark green (color F) corner is on top. The final st of Row 6 is now in the right-hand corner. You will attach the new yarn in the *side* of this st and work from right to left from this corner to the color F corner to the left-hand corner. Make the last st of Row 7 in the side of the 1st st of Row 6. Rows 7–15 are worked *back and forth* across these 2 sides of the piece only.

Row 7: Attach color A in the side of the last st of Row 6. 1 sc in same st, (1 sc in side of next st) 2 times, (1 sc in next st) 4 times [7 sts made before color F corner st], 3 sc in corner st, (1 sc in next st) 4 times, (1 sc in side of next st) 3 times [7 sts made after corner st]. Ch 1, turn [17 sts].

Row 8: 1 sc in 1st st, (1 sc in next st) 7 times, 3 sc in corner st, (1 sc in next st) 8 times. Break yarn [19 sts].

Row 9: Turn piece over so that front side faces you. Attach color B in last st of Row 8. 1 sc in same st, (1 sc in next st) 8 times, 3 sc in corner, (1 sc in next st) 9 times. Ch 1, turn [21 sts].

Row 10: 1 sc in 1st st, (1 sc in next st) 9 times, 3 sc in corner, (1 sc in next st) 10 times. Break yarn [23 sts].

Row 11: Turn piece over. Attach color C in last st of Row 10. 1 sc in same st, (1 sc in next st) 10 times, 3 sc in corner, (1 sc in next st) 11 times. Ch 1, turn [25 sts].

Row 12: 1 sc in 1st st, (1 sc in next st) 11 times, 3 sc in corner st, (1 sc in next st) 12 times. Break yarn [27 sts].

Row 13: Turn piece over. Attach color D in last st of Row 12. 1 sc in same st, (1 sc in next st) 12 times, 3 sc in corner, (1 sc in next st) 13 times. Ch 1, turn [29 sts].

Row 14: 1 sc in 1st st, (1 sc in next st) 13 times, 3 sc in corner st, (1 sc in next st) 14 times. Break yarn [31 sts].

Row 15: Turn piece over. Attach color E in last st of Row 14. 1 sc in same st, (1 sc in next st) 14 times, 3 sc in corner, (1 sc in next st) 15 times. Break yarn [33 sts].

You have made 1 motif. Repeat the directions until you have made the number of motifs you need. Block each motif, following the directions on page 35.

You will join the motifs according to the directions for overlapping joining on page 30 so the motifs do not need to be edged. Look at the photograph of the pillow on page 129. You can see that the motifs are joined so that they all point in the same direction—the green corner should be at the bottom, pointing down, as it was while you worked Rows 7–15. Begin with the motif that will be the top [all-pink] corner of your pillow. Place the top right side of a 2nd motif over the bottom left side of the 1st motif and sew it in place. Repeat, covering the bottom right side of the 1st motif with a 3rd motif. The next row will have 3 motifs, which will overlap the bottom sides of the 2nd and 3rd motifs. Continue in this manner until you have completed the center row of your pillow, then dec the number of motifs in each row, ending with 1 motif at the bottom. All motifs should overlap the motifs of the previous row.

When the pillow is finished, lightly reblock it. Following the directions on page 36, complete the pillow.

Diamond Bargello Pillow

Materials:
- 18 oz. uncut Paterna Persian yarn in the following amounts: blue #311 (color J), 4 oz.; blue #314 (color K), 3 oz.; blue #380 (color L), 2 oz.; blue #381 (color M), 2 oz.; blue #382 (color N), 2 oz.; green #553 (color O), 2 oz.; green #590 (color P), 2 oz.; ivory #015 (color Q), 1 oz. *or* corresponding amounts of any Persian, tapestry, or worsted yarn
- Backing
- Muslin casing
- Stuffing

Hook: F

Gauge:
5 sts = 1″; after Round 2, long diagonal = 2½″ (approximately)

Finished Size:
Each motif is 12½″ across the long diagonal, 9″ across the short diagonal, and 8″ (approxi-

mately) at each side. The size of the finished pillow (after blocking and before stuffing) is 38″ across the long diagonal, 27″ across the short diagonal, and 24″ at each side.

Note: Refer to note on page 128.

The motifs are worked in a combination of sc and sc Tapestry st. For instructions on working Tapestry st in rnds using 2 colors, see page 85.

See instructions for changing yarn at the end of joined rnds on page 28.

Instructions:

Motif A: Worked with all 8 colors.

Foundation chain: Ch 6 with color P.

Round 1: 3 sc in 2nd ch from hk, 1 sc in next ch, 3 hdc in next ch, 1 sc in next ch, 3 sc in last ch. Do not turn. Working across the back of the ch, make 1 sc in next ch, 3 hdc in next ch [same ch as 1st 3-hdc group], 1 sc in last ch, complete this st with color Q, then, using color Q, join with a slst to 1st sc of 3-sc group. Ch 1.

Round 2: 1 sc in 1st st, *3 sc in center st of 3-sc group of previous rnd [corner st], 1 sc in each of next 3 sts. Repeat from *, ending with 3 sc in last corner st, 1 sc in each of last 2 sts. Using color N, complete last st, join with slst to 1st sc. Ch 1.

Round 3: 1 sc in 1st st, 1 sc in next st, *3 sc in corner st, 1 sc in each of next 5 sts. Repeat from *, ending with 3 sc in last corner st, 1 sc in each of last 3 sts, join with slst. Break the yarn.

Each subsequent rnd is worked in sc Tapestry st, using 2 colors. A color is used as the main color for 1 rnd, then as a secondary color in the next rnd and should then be cut. [Yarn tails should be tied to other tails, then hidden as you go along.] As you alternate the 2 colors of any row, carry the unused color along behind the piece. Before you join each rnd, be sure to give the piece a tug to loosen the Tapestry st. Except for the ch sts used to form peaks [in Round 8 and subsequent rnds], only sc is used. Therefore, only the color is needed to identify the st. [That is, 1M = 1 sc with color M.]

Round 4: Attach color M in the 1st sc after the final 3-sc group of Round 3. *1M in each of next 5 sts [do *not* count the joining slst of Round 3 as a st], 1N in next st, 3N in corner st, 1N in next st. Repeat from *, ending with 3N in last corner, 1N in last st. Using M, complete this st, join with slst. Ch 1. Break off N.

Round 5: 1M in 1st st, *1K in each of next 3 sts, 1M in each of next 3 sts, 3M in corner st, 1M in each of next 3 sts. Repeat from *, ending with 3M in last corner, 1M in each of last 2 sts. Using K, complete last st, join with slst. Ch 1. Break off M.

Round 6: 1K in 1st st, *1Q in each of next 3 sts, 1K in each of next 4 sts, 3K in corner, 1K in each of next 4 sts. Repeat from *, ending with 3K in last corner, 1K in each of last 3 sts. Using K, complete last st, join with slst. Ch 1. Break off K.

Round 7: 1Q in 1st st, *1P in each of next 3 sts, 1Q in each of next 5 sts, 3Q in corner st, 1Q in each of next 5 sts. Repeat from *, ending with 3Q in last corner st, 1Q in each of last 4 sts. Using O, complete last st, join with slst. Ch 1. Break off Q.

Round 8: [In this and subsequent rnds, it is assumed that the 1st st of the rnd is made in the 1st st of the previous rnd.] *1O in each of next 5 sts, 1P in each of next 5 sts, 1P in corner st, ch 4, 1P in 2nd ch from hk, 1P in each of next 2 chs, 1 more P in corner st [1 peak formed], 1P in each of next 5 sts, 1O in each of next 5 sts, 1P in each of next 5 sts, 3P in corner, 1P in each of next 5 sts. Repeat from * once, ending with 3P in last corner, 1P in each of last 5 sts. Using N, complete last st, join with slst. Ch 1. Break off P.

Round 9: *1N in each of next 5 sts, 1O in each of next 4 sts, 1O dec over next 2 sts, 1O in each of next 3 sts, 1O in top ch of peak, ch 3, 1O in 2nd ch from hk, 10 in next ch, 1 more O in peak, 1O in each of next 3 sts, 1O dec over next 2 sts, 1O in each of next 4 sts, 1N in each of next 5 sts, 1O in each of next 6 sts, 3O in corner, 1O in each of next 6 sts. Repeat from * once, ending with 3O in last corner, 1O in each of last 6 sts. Using M, complete last st, join with slst. Ch 1. Break off O.

Round 10: *1M in each of next 5 sts, 1N in each of next 4 sts, 1N dec over next 2 sts, 1N in each of next 5 sts, 1N in top ch of peak, ch 2, 1N in 2nd ch from hk, 1 more N in top of

131

peak, 1N in each of next 5 sts, 1N dec over next 2 sts, 1N in each of next 4 sts, 1M in each of next 5 sts, 1N in each of next 7 sts, 3N in corner st, 1N in each of next 7 sts. Repeat from * once, ending with 3N in last corner st, 1N in each of last 7 sts. Using L, complete last st, join with slst. Ch 1. Break off N.

Round 11: *1L in each of next 5 sts, 1M in each of next 12 sts, 1M in peak, ch 2, 1M in 2nd ch from hk, 1 more M in peak, 1M in each of next 12 sts, 1L in each of next 5 sts, 1M in each of next 8 sts, 3M in corner, 1M in each of next 8 sts. Repeat from * once, ending with 3M in corner, 1M in each of last 8 sts. Using K, complete last st, join with slst. Ch 1. Break off M.

Round 12: *1K in each of next 5 sts, 1L in each of next 14 sts, 1L in peak, ch 2, 1L in 2nd ch from hk, 1 more L in peak, 1L in each of next 14 sts, 1K in each of next 5 sts, 1L in each of next 9 sts, 3L in corner, 1L in each of next 9 sts. Repeat from * once, ending with 3L in last corner, 1L in each of last 9 sts. Using J, complete last st, join with slst. Ch 1. Break off L.

Round 13: *1J in each of next 5 sts, 1K in each of next 16 sts, 1K in peak, ch 2, 1K in 2nd ch from hk, 1 more K in peak, 1K in each of next 16 sts, 1J in each of next 5 sts, 1K in each of next 10 sts, 3K in corner, 1K in each of next 10 sts. Repeat from * once, ending with 3K in corner, 1K in each of last 10 sts. Using J, complete last st, join with slst. Ch 1. Break off K.

Round 14: 1J in each of next 23 sts, **3J in peak, 1J in each of next 34 sts, 3 sc in corner st,** 1J in each of next 34 sts. Repeat from ** to **, ending with 1J in each of last 11 sts, join with slst. Break off J.

You have completed 1 Motif A. Repeat until you have made 5 of this motif.

Motif B: Worked with all 8 colors.

Foundation chain: Ch 6 with color P.

Round 1: Repeat Round 1, Motif A. With N, complete last st and join with slst. Ch 1.

Round 2: Repeat Round 2, Motif A. With K, complete last st, join. Ch 1. Break off N.

Round 3: Repeat Round 3, Motif A, ending with 3 sc in last corner st, 1 sc in each of last 3 sts. Using Q, complete last st, join. Ch 1. Break off K.

Round 4: 1 sc in each of 1st 3 sc, *3 sc in corner st, 1 sc in each of next 7 sts. Repeat from *, ending with 3 sc in last corner, 1 sc in each of last 4 sts. Using P, complete last st, join. Ch 1.

Round 5: 1 sc in each of 1st 4 sts, *1 sc in corner st, ch 3, 1 sc in 2nd ch from hk, 1 sc in next ch, 1 more sc in corner st [peak formed], 1 sc in each of next 9 sts, 3 sc in corner, 1 sc in each of next 9 sts. Repeat from *, ending with 3 sc in last corner, 1 sc in each of last 5 sts, join with slst. Ch 1.

Each subsequent rnd is worked in Tapestry st, as in Motif A, but the "rays" of this motif are located on the peaks rather than the sides.

Round 6: 1P in each of 1st 4 sts, *1P dec over next 2 sts, 1O in each of next 2 sts, 1O in peak, ch 3, 1O in 2nd ch from hk, 1O in next ch, 1 more O in peak, 1O in each of next 2 sts, 1P dec over next 2 sts, 1P in each of next 10 sts, 3P in corner st, 1P in each of next 10 sts. Repeat from * once, ending with 3P in last corner, 1P in each of last 6 sts. Using O, complete last st, join. Ch 1. Break off P.

Round 7: 1O in each of 1st 5 sts, *1N in each of next 5 sts, 1O in peak, ch 2, 1O in 2nd ch from hk, 1 more O in peak, 1N in each of next 5 sts, 1O in each of next 12 sts, 3O in corner, 1K in each of next 12 sts. Repeat from *, ending with 3O in last corner, 1O in each of last 7 sts. Using N, complete last st, join. Ch 1. Break off O.

Round 8: 1N in each of 1st 5 sts, *1M in each of next 5 sts, 1N in each of next 2 sts, 1N in peak, ch 2, 1N in 2nd ch, 1 more N in peak, 1N in each of next 2 sts, 1M in each of next 5 sts, 1N in each of next 13 sts, 3N in corner, 1N in each of next 13 sts. Repeat from *, ending with 3N in last corner, 1N in each of last 8 sts. Using L, complete last st, join. Ch 1. Break off N.

Round 9: 1M in each of 1st 5 sts, *1L in each of next 5 sts, 1M in each of next 4 sts, 1M in peak, ch 2, 1M in 2nd ch, 1 more M in peak, 1M in each of next 4 sts, 1L in each of next 5 sts, 1M in each of next 14 sts, 3M in corner, 1M in each of next 14 sts. Repeat from *, ending with 3M in last corner, 1M in each of next 9 sts. Using L, complete last st, join. Ch 1. Break off L.

Round 10: 1L in each of 1st 5 sts, *1K in each of next 5 sts, 1L in each of next 6 sts, 3L in peak, 1L in each of next 6 sts, 1K in each of next 5 sts, 1L in each of next 15 sts, 3L in corner, 1L in each of next 15 sts. Repeat from * once, ending with 3L in corner, 1L in each of last 10 sts. Using K, complete last st, join. Ch 1. Break off L.

Round 11: 1K in each of 1st 5 sts, *1J in each of next 5 sts, 1K in each of next 7 sts, 3K in peak, 1K in each of next 7 sts, 1J in each of next 5 sts, 1K in each of next 16 sts, 3K in corner, 1K in each of next 16 sts. Repeat from * once, ending with 3K in last corner, 1K in each of last 11 sts. Join. Ch 1.

Round 12: 1K in each of 1st 5 sts, 1J in each of next 5 sts, 1K in each of next 8 sts, 3K in peak, 1K in each of next 8 sts, 1J in each of next 5 sts, 1K in each of next 17 sts, 3K in corner, 1K in each of next 17 sts. Repeat from *, ending with 3K in corner, 1K in each of last 12 sts. Using J, complete last st, join. Ch 1. Break off K.

Round 13: 1J in 1st 20 sts, *3J in peak, 1J in each of next 32 sts, 3J in corner, 1J in each of next 32 sts. Repeat from *, ending with 3J in last corner, 1J in each of last 12 sts. Join. Ch 1.

Round 14: 1J in each of 1st 21 sts, *3J in peak, 1J in each of next 34 sts, 3J in corner, 1J in each of next 34 sts. Repeat from *, ending with 3J in corner, 1J in each of last 13 sts. Join with slst. Break yarn.

You have completed 1 Motif B. Repeat until you have made 4 of this motif.

ASSEMBLING

The motifs will be quite distorted; block all 9 lightly according to the directions on page 35. Do not, however, attempt to do the final blocking until the motifs have been joined. Look at the photograph of the pillow on page 129 and join the motifs accordingly. Join them on the back side, with a slst thru the back lps only [see the section on joining on page 29]. Then reblock the pillow to the dimensions given at the beginning of the project. Complete the pillow following the directions on page 36.

Making Your Own Motifs

Now that you know how to make the basic geometric shapes, you can design your own motifs. The geometric shape you choose and the way you vary the colors and the stitchery will determine your design. Remember that a motif is seldom seen alone. You must consider not only how a single motif looks, but also how it will look when repeated. When you design a motif project, you can begin with a single motif and allow it to grow into an overall design, or begin with the design and then figure out how to create it with individual motifs.

Make the shape in single crochet and then double crochet to determine how it increases. Then you are ready to adapt the shape to a design. (If you incorporate fancy stitches into a square or rectangle, don't try to put the decorative stitches into the corners—use double crochet.) Not counting the increases, you should have an odd number of stitches on each side of the motif, so that you begin and end the side in the same way. (That is, a side that begins with 1 single crochet followed by 1 Hazelnut should end with 1 Hazelnut followed by 1 single crochet.)

Your motifs might be big or small, open or solid, identical or alternating patterns. You might repeat one motif using new colors each time—a great way to use up leftover yarn. Another decision to make is how to join your motifs. For example, crocheting the outside row of every motif in the same color adds to the overall design. Make your joining part of the design, rather than something to hide. How will the shapes fit together? You may need fill-in motifs, such as those in the Geometric Afghan (see page 174). What do you want to be the final shape of the completed project? If you want smooth edges, you may need to make partial motifs, such as C and D in the Floral Coverlet (see page 114). Sometimes, however, a jagged edge is quite effective.

Jute Rug

If you look closely, you'll see that our giant rug motifs are based on the center of a well-known traditional doily pattern. Doilies are an excellent source of beautiful designs that can be reproduced in all kinds of sizes and textures. These motifs, by the way, are easy to make and go faster than you might think; each takes only a few hours of your time—and what a satisfying result!

Materials:
- 6 balls 5-ply natural jute for each motif *or* any medium–heavy jute
- Trussing needle
- Several rolls carpet tape (strong, double-faced tape)

Hook: N

Gauge:
Round 1 = 3½" diameter, Rounds 1–4 = 12" diameter

Finished Size:
1 motif = 4' diameter
Finished rug = 12' diameter

Note: Put some adhesive tape around the index finger of your left hand so it will not be irritated by the jute.

When you are making a large circular project such as a rug, your work will be easier if you can learn to see the incs in each inc rnd, thereby eliminating the need to count many sts in each rnd. Since the circle is divided into 12 parts and you are increasing once in each part, the incs will be made one over another, with a non-inc rnd between each inc rnd. Look at Diagram 86. Each inc in Round A is made by working 2 sts into 1 st. Round B is a non-inc rnd and will therefore have 1 sc worked into each of the 2-sc groups of the previous rnd. On the next rnd, the 2-sc inc should be made in the st that was worked into the 2nd of the 2-sc inc group of Round A.

Instructions:
Foundation chain: Ch 5, join to 1st ch with slst.
Round 1: Ch 3 [= 1 dc], 11 dc in circle, join to top ch of ch-3 with slst.

Round 2: Ch 6 [= 1 dc, ch 3], *1 dc in next st, ch 3. Repeat from *, ending with ch 3, join with slst to 3rd ch of ch-6 [12 sps formed].
Round 3: Ch 6, *1 dc in next sp, 1 dc in dc of previous rnd, ch 3. Repeat from *, ending with ch 3, 1 dc in last sp, join with slst to 3rd ch of ch-6.
Round 4: Ch 6, *1 dc in next sp, 1 dc in each of next 2 dc, ch 3. Repeat from *, ending with 1 dc in last sp, 1 dc in last dc, join with slst to 3rd ch of ch-6.
Round 5: Ch 6, *1 dc in next sp, 1 dc in each of next 3 dc, ch 3. Repeat from *, ending with 1 dc in last sp, 1 dc in each of last 2 dc, join with slst to 3rd ch of ch-6.
Round 6: Ch 6, *1 dc in next sp, 1 dc in each of next 4 dc, ch 3. Repeat from *, ending with 1 dc in last sp, 1 dc in each of last 3 dc, join with slst to 3rd ch of ch-6.
Round 7: Ch 6, *1 dc in next sp, 1 dc in each of next 5 dc, ch 3. Repeat from *, ending with 1 dc in last sp, 1 dc in each of last 4 dc, join with slst to 3rd ch of ch-6.
Round 8: Ch 6, *1 dc in next sp, 1 dc in each of next 6 dc, ch 3. Repeat from *, ending with

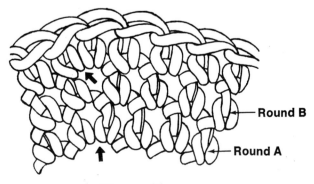

Diagram 86

1 dc in last sp, 1 dc in each of last 5 dc, join with slst to 3rd ch of ch-6.

Round 9: Ch 6, *1 dc in next sp, ch 3, skip 2 dc, 1 dc in each of next 5 dc, ch 3. Repeat from *, ending with 1 dc in last sp, ch 3, skip 2 dc, 1 dc in each of last 4 dc, join with slst to 3rd ch of ch-6.

Round 10: Ch 6, *2 dc in next sp, 1 dc in next dc, 2 dc in next sp, ch 3, skip 2 dc, 1 dc in each of next 3 dc, ch 3. Repeat from *, ending with 2 dc in next-to-last sp, 1 dc in next dc, 2 dc in last sp, ch 3, skip 2 dc, 1 dc in each of next 2 dc, join with slst to 3rd ch of ch-6.

Note: The 1st st of Round 11 will be in the *left* st of the 3-dc group of Round 10, while the same st will be in the *center* st of the 3-dc group for the rest of the rnd.

Round 11: Ch 6, *1 dc in next sp, 1 dc in each of next 5 dc, 1 dc in next sp, ch 3, skip 1st dc of 3-dc group, 1 dc in center dc, ch 3, skip last dc of 3-dc group. Repeat from *, ending with 1 dc in last sp, ch 3, join with slst to 3rd ch of ch-6.

Round 12: Slst into 1st sp, ch 3 [= 1 dc], 1 dc in 1st sp, *1 dc in each of next 7 dc, 2 dc in next sp, ch 3, 2 dc in next sp. Repeat from *, ending with 1 dc in each of next 7 dc, 2 dc in last sp, ch 3, join with slst to top ch of ch-3.

Round 13: 1 slst in each of 1st 2 sts, ch 3 [= skip 1 dc, 1 dc in next st], 1 dc in each of next 8 dc, skip next dc, *ch 3, 1 dc in next sp, ch 3, skip 1 dc, 1 dc in each of next 9 dc, skip next dc. Repeat from *, ending with ch 3, 1 dc in last sp, ch 3, join with slst to 3rd ch of ch-3.

Round 14: 1 slst in each of next 2 dc, ch 3 [= skip 1 dc, 1 dc in next st], 1 dc in each of next 6 dc, *(ch 3, 1 dc in next sp) 2 times, ch 3, skip 1 dc, 1 dc in each of next 7 dc, skip last dc. Repeat from *, ending with (ch 3, 1 dc in next sp) 2 times, ch 3, join with slst to 3rd ch of ch-3.

Round 15: 1 slst in each of next 2 dc, ch 3, 1 dc in each of next 4 dc, *(ch 3, 1 dc in next sp) 3 times, ch 3, skip 1 dc, 1 dc in each of next 5 dc, skip last dc. Repeat from *, ending with (ch 3, 1 dc in next sp) 3 times, ch 3, join with slst to 3rd ch of ch-3.

Round 16: 1 slst in each of next 2 dc, ch 3, 1 dc in each of next 3 dc, *(ch 3, 1 dc in next sp) 4 times, ch 3, skip 1 dc, 1 dc in each of next 3 dc, skip last dc. Repeat from *, ending with (ch 3, 1 dc in next sp) 4 times, ch 3, join with slst to 3rd ch of ch-3.

Round 17: 1 slst in each of next 2 dc, ch 6, *(1 dc in next sp, ch 3) 5 times, 1 dc in center dc of 3-dc group, ch 3. Repeat from *, ending with join with slst to 3rd ch of ch-6. Break the jute.

You have completed 1 motif. The rug as shown on page 135 has 7 motifs: 1 in the center with 6 around it. Other arrangements are possible. For example, you might arrange the motifs in a long, narrow row or use 3 to make a triangle. Arrange the motifs face down in the design you have chosen. Whatever the arrangement is, each motif should be joined to an adjoining motif for the length of 1 st pat; that is, 2 motifs should be joined from the dc of Round 17 made in the center of one 3-dc group [dc point] along the length of the (ch 3, 1 dc) pat to the next dc point. Pin or tie both sets of dc points tog, thread a trussing needle with jute, and sew the back lps tog between 1 set of dc points and the next.

Note: This rug will slide dangerously if strips of carpet tape are not placed on its back.

Kitchen Canisters

Add a cheery note to your kitchen with these canisters. Or use similar crocheted jute tubes to cover other household items—wastepaper baskets, pencil holders, or planters, for instance. If you prefer a sharp edge at the bottom, work a circle until it's a bit bigger than the can, then work a row of Post stitch to turn the corner, then work in rounds, without increasing.

Materials:
- 1 spool dark brown Lily jute for each canister *or* any thin jute
- ½ spool natural Lily jute for each canister *or* any thin jute
- 46-oz. metal juice can or the same size plastic container with snap-on lid
- Metal screw-on lid (approximately 3″ diameter, sides ½″ high)
- Heavy cardboard
- Metal-adhering glue
- Cotton balls

Hooks: N and H

Gauge:
Rounds 1–2 = 3″ diameter

Finished Size:
The cover fits a 46-fluid-oz. juice can (you can adjust the size to fit any can; see directions for making tubes on page 125).

Instructions:
Canister: Work the 1st 14 rows double, using 1 strand of dark brown and 1 strand of natural, and the N hk.
Foundation chain–Round 3: Repeat Rounds 1–3 of Joined Rounds Circles [page 122].
Round 4: Ch 1, 1 sc in 1st st, (1 sc in next st) 2 times, 2 sc in next st, *(1 sc in next st) 3 times, 2 sc in next st. Repeat from *, ending with 2 sc in last st, join to 1st sc with slst [30 sts].
Round 5: Ch 1, 1 sc in 1st st, *1 sc in next st. Repeat from *, ending with 1 sc in last st, join to 1st sc with slst [30 sts].
Round 6: Repeat Round 5.
Round 7: Ch 1, 1 sc in 1st st, (1 sc in next st) 3 times, 1 dec over next 2 sts, *(1 sc in next st) 4 times, 1 dec over next 2 sts. Repeat from *, ending with 1 dec in last 2 sts, join to 1st sc with slst [5 decs—25 sts].
Round 8: Repeat Round 5 [25 sts].
Round 9: Repeat Round 5 [25 sts].
Round 10: Ch 1, 1 sc in 1st st, *(1 sc in next st) 6 times, 1 dec over next 2 sts. Repeat from *, ending with 1 dec over last 2 sts [3 decs—22 sts].
Round 11: Repeat Round 5 [22 sts].
Round 12: Repeat Round 5 [22 sts].
Round 13: Ch 1, 1 sc in 1st st, (1 sc in next st) 8 times, 1 dec over next 2 sts, (1 sc in next st) 9 times, 1 dec over next 2 sts, join to 1st st with a slst [2 decs—20 sts].
Round 14: Repeat Round 5 [20 sts]. Break jute.
Note: Work the rest of the canister with 1 strand of dark brown and the H hk.
Round 15: Attach dark brown in 1st st, 1 sc in 1st st, *2 sc in next st, 1 sc in next st. Repeat from *, ending with 2 sc in last st, join to 1st sc with slst [10 incs—30 sts].
Rounds 16–21: Repeat Round 5 [30 sts].
Round 22: Ch 1, insert hk from back to front in the sp between the last st of the previous rnd and the 1st st of the previous rnd, bring hk across the post of the 1st st and out to the back between the 1st and 2nd sts, yo and pull up a lp, yo and complete sc. [1 sc Post st made; begin next sc Post st by inserting hk from back to front between 1st and 2nd sts of previous rnd.] *1 sc Post st around next st. Repeat from *, ending with 1 sc Post st around last st, join to 1st st with slst [1st rnd of lip made].
Round 23: Repeat Round 22 [2nd round of lip made].
Round 24: Repeat Round 22 [3rd round of lip made]. Break the jute.

Lid (top piece): Work with 1 strand of dark brown and the H hk.
Foundation chain: Ch 5, join with slst.
Round 1: Ch 1, 8 sc in center of ring, join with slst.
Round 2: Ch 1, 1 sc in 1st st, *1 sc in next st. Repeat from *, ending with 1 sc in last st, join with slst [8 sts].
Round 3: Ch 1, 1 sc dec in 1st and 2nd sts, *1 sc dec in next 2 sts. Repeat from *, ending with 1 sc dec in last 2 sts, join with slst [4 decs—4 sts].
Round 4: Ch 1, 2 sc in 1st st, *2 sc in next st. Repeat from *, ending with 2 sc in last st, join with slst [4 incs—8 sts].
Round 5: Repeat Round 4 [8 incs—16 sts].
Round 6: Repeat Round 2 [16 sts].
Round 7: Ch 1, 1 sc in 1st st, 2 sc in next st, *1 sc in next st, 2 sc in next st. Repeat from *, ending with 2 sc in last st, join with slst [8 incs—24 sts].
Round 8: Repeat Round 2 [24 sts].
Round 9: Repeat Round 7 [12 incs—36 sts].
Round 10: Repeat Round 2 [36 sts].
Round 11: Ch 1, 1 sc in 1st st, (1 sc in next st) 4 times, 2 sc in next st, *(1 sc in next st) 5 times, 2 sc in next st. Repeat from *, ending with 2 sc in last st [6 incs—42 sts]. Break the jute.
Lid (bottom piece): Work with 1 strand of dark brown and the H hk.
Rounds 1–3: Repeat Rounds 1–3 for the Joined Rounds Circles on page 122.
Round 4: Ch 1, 1 sc in 1st st, *1 sc in next st. Repeat from *, ending with 1 sc in last st, join with slst [24 sts].
Round 5: Repeat Round 22 of the canister [24 sc around post].
Round 6: Repeat Round 4 [24 sts].

Round 7: Ch 1, insert hk from *front to back* between last st and 1st st of previous rnd, across back of 1st st, and to the front between 1st and 2nd sts, yo and pull up a lp, yo and complete sc [1 sc Post st made; begin next st by inserting hk from front to back between 1st and 2nd sts], *1 sc Post st around next st. Repeat from *, ending with 1 sc Post st around last st, join with slst. [You have made the plug that will fit *into* the hole in the canister. Now you will complete the bottom piece of the lid by making a flat section that will lie on top of the lip of the canister.]
Round 8: Ch 1, 1 sc in 1st st, 2 sc in next st, *1 sc in next st, 2 sc in next st. Repeat from *, ending with 2 sc in last st [12 incs—36 sts].
Round 9: Repeat Round 11 of the top piece of the lid [6 incs—42 sts]. Break the jute.

To complete the lid, make a support for the bottom of the crocheted lid, put it inside the bottom, stuff the top of the crocheted lid with cotton balls, and join the 2 pieces.

The lid you use should fit snugly into the plug on the bottom of the crocheted lid. We used the lid from a large mayonnaise jar.

Cut a circle of the cardboard with the same circumference as that of the final rnd of the bottom of the crocheted lid. Center the metal lid on the circle, with the top of the metal lid facing up. Glue the rim of the metal top to the cardboard.

After the glue has dried, place the support in the bottom of the crocheted lid and stuff the top of the lid loosely with the cotton. Join the top and bottom crocheted pieces of the lid with a slst thru the 2 inside lps only [see page 29], to within 2 inches of completion. Finish stuffing the top so that it is firm but not bulging. Complete the joining. Break the jute.

Bathroom Accessories

Fortunately, fancy stitch patterns are not limited to straight rows of crochet. These richly colored bathroom accessories were made from basic shapes. The toilet seat cover is a modified oval and the wastepaper basket cover is a tube closed at one end. We selected some of our favorite stitches for these accessories to add interesting texture and a sense of movement to the overall design.

Materials:
- 10½ oz. UKI in the following amounts: dark purple #90 (color A), 3½ oz.; light orchid #70 (color B), 3½ oz.; dark green #28 (color C), 1 oz.; light green #57 (color D), 1 oz.; sea green #60 (color E), ½ oz.; dark blue #95 (color F), ½ oz.; light blue #94 (color G), ½ oz. *or* corresponding amounts of Coats & Clark's Knit Cro-Sheen in similar colors

Hook: F

Gauge:
10 sts = 2", 4 rows = 1"

Finished Size:
Toilet Seat Cover: 13½" long x 11½" wide
Wastepaper Basket Cover: 11" high x 9" wide
   Note: The above materials are enough for the toilet seat cover and wastepaper basket cover.

Toilet Seat Cover

Instructions:
Foundation chain: Color A—ch 51.
Row 1: Insert hk into 2nd ch from hk and make 1 sc, *1 sc in next ch, repeat from * until last ch, 3 sc in last ch, work back down other side of foundation ch, working 1 sc in each ch, ending with 1 sc in last ch. Ch 1, turn.
Row 2: 1 sc in 1st sc, **1 sc in next sc,** repeat from ** to ** until you reach the 3-sc group at the tip, make 1 sc in the 1st sc of this group, 2 sc in 2nd sc of the group, 1 sc in the 3rd sc of the group, repeat from ** to ** in each remaining sc, ending with 1 sc in last sc. Break yarn, turn.
Row 3: Color B—ch 2, 1 Popcorn st in next sc, **ch 1, skip 1 st, 1 Popcorn st in next st,** (repeat from ** to **) 23 times, (ch 2, 1 Popcorn in next st) 4 times, repeat from ** to **, ending with 1 dc in last st. Break yarn, turn.
Row 4: Color C—ch 1, 1 sc in 1st st, 1 sc in 1st Popcorn st of previous row, **2 sc in next ch-1 sp,** (repeat from ** to **) 23 times, (3 sc in next ch-1 sp) 5 times, repeat from ** to **, ending with 1 sc in last st. Ch 1, turn.
Row 5: 1 sc in 1st st, **1 sc in each of next 2 sts, 1 hdc in each of next 2 sts, 1 dc in each of next 3 sts, 1 hdc in each of next 2 sts, 1 sc in each of next 2 sts,** (repeat from ** to **) 3 times, 1 sc in each of next 2 sts, 1 hdc in each of next 2 sts, 3 dc in next st, 1 hdc in each of next 2 sts, 1 sc in each of next 2 sts, 2 sc in next st, 1 hdc in each of next 2 sts, 3 dc in next st, 1 hdc in each of next 2 sts, 1 sc in each of next 2 sts, (repeat from ** to **) 4 times, ending with 1 sc in last st. Ch 1, turn.
Row 6: 1 sc in 1st st, (repeat from ** to ** of Row 5) 4 times, 1 sc in each of next 2 sts, 1 hdc in each of next 2 sts, 1 dc in next st, 2 dc in next st, 1 dc in next st, 1 hdc in each of next 2 sts, 1 sc in each of next 4 sts, 1 hdc in each of next 2 sts, 1 dc in next st, 2 dc in next st, 1 dc in next st, 1 hdc in each of next 2 sts, 1 sc in each of next 2 sts, (repeat from ** to ** of Row 5) 4 times, ending with 1 sc in each of last 2 sts. Break yarn, turn.
Row 7: Color D—1 sc in 1st st, 1 sc in next st, **1 hdc in each of next 2 sts, 1 dc in next st, 2 dc in next st, 1 dc in next st, 1 hdc in each of next 2 sts, 1 sc in next st, 1 sc dec in next 2 sts, 1 sc in next st,** (repeat from ** to **) 3 times, 1 hdc in each of next 2 sts, 1 dc in next st, 2 dc in next st, 1 dc in each of next 2 sts, 1 hdc in each of next 2 sts, 1 sc in each of next 4 sts, 1 hdc in each of next 2 sts, 1 dc in next st, 2 dc in

next st, 1 dc in each of next 2 sts, 1 hdc in each of next 2 sts, 1 sc in next st, 1 sc dec in next 2 sts, 1 sc in next st, (repeat from ** to **) 4 times, ending with 1 sc in last 2 sts. Break yarn, turn.

Row 8: Color E—1 sc in 1st st, 1 sc in next st, (repeat from ** to ** of Row 7) 4 times, 1 hdc in each of next 2 sts, 1 dc in next st, 2 dc in next st, 1 dc in next st, 2 dc in next st, 1 dc in next st, 1 hdc in each of next 2 sts, 1 sc in each of next 3 sts, 1 hdc in each of next 2 sts, 1 dc in next st, 2 dc in next st, 1 dc in next st, 2 dc in next st, 1 dc in next st, 1 hdc in each of next 2 sts, 1 sc in next st, 1 sc dec in next 2 sts, 1 sc in next st, repeat from ** to ** of Row 7, ending with 1 sc dec in last 2 sts. Ch 1, turn.

Row 9: 1 sc in 1st st, 1 sc in next st, (repeat from ** to ** of Row 7) 4 times, 1 hdc in each of next 2 sts, 1 dc in next st, 2 dc in next st, 1 dc in each of next 2 sts, 2 dc in next st, 1 dc in next st, 1 hdc in each of next 2 sts, 1 sc in each of next 3 sts, 1 hdc in each of next 2 sts, 1 dc in each of next 2 sts, 2 dc in next st, 1 dc in each of next 2 sts, 2 dc in next st, 1 dc in next st, 1 hdc in each of next 2 sts, 1 sc in next st, 1 sc dec in next 2 sts, 1 sc in next st, repeat from ** to ** of Row 7, ending with 1 sc dec in last 2 sts. Ch 1, turn.

Row 10: 1 sc in 1st st, 1 sc in next st, (repeat from ** to ** of Row 7) 4 times, 1 hdc in each of next 2 sts, 1 dc in next st, 2 dc in next st, 1 dc in each of next 3 sts, 2 dc in next st, 1 dc in each of next 3 sts, 1 hdc in each of next 2 sts, 1 sc in each of next 3 sts, 1 hdc in each of next 2 sts, 1 dc in next st, 2 dc in next st, 1 dc in each of next 3 sts, 2 dc in next st, 1 dc in next st, 1 hdc in each of next 2 sts, 1 sc in next st, 1 sc dec in next 2 sts, 1 sc in next st, (repeat from ** to ** of Row 7) 4 times, ending with 1 sc dec in last 2 sts. Break yarn, turn.

Row 11: Color F—ch 3 [= 1st dc of row], 1 dc in next st, **1 hdc in each of next 2 sts, 1 sc in each of next 4 sts, 1 hdc in each of next 2 sts, 1 dc in each of next 3 sts,** (repeat from ** to **) 3 times, 1 hdc in each of next 2 sts, 1 sc in next st, 2 sc in next st, 1 sc in each of next 4 sts, 2 sc in next st, 1 sc in each of next 2 sts, 1 hdc in each of next 2 sts, 1 dc in each of next 3 sts, 1 hdc in each of next 2 sts, 1 sc in each of next 3 sts, 2 sc in next st, 1 sc in each of next 4 sts,

2 sc in next st, 1 sc in each of next 2 sts, (repeat from ** to **) 3 times, ending with 1 dc in each of last 2 sts. Ch 1, turn. Break yarn.

Row 12: [All sts of this row are worked in *loop B only* of each st of the previous row.] Color G—1 sc in 1st st, (**1 sc in next st**) 50 times, 2 sc in next st, 1 sc in each of next 3 sts, 2 sc in next st, 1 sc in each of next 3 sts, 2 sc in next st, 1 sc in each of next 10 sts, 2 sc in next st, 1 sc in each of next 3 sts, 2 sc in next st, 1 sc in each of next 3 sts, 2 sc in next st, (repeat from ** to **) 50 times, ending with 1 sc in top ch of ch-3. Break yarn, turn.

Row 13: [All sts of this row arc worked in *loop A only* of each st of the previous row.] Color A—ch 1, 1 hdc in 1st st, (**1 hdc in next st**) 49 times, 2 hdc in next st, 1 hdc in each of next 3 sts, 2 hdc in next st, 1 hdc in each of next 3 sts, (repeat from ** to **) 13 times, 2 hdc in next st, 1 hdc in each of next 3 sts, 2 hdc in next st, 1 hdc in each of next 3 sts, (repeat from ** to **) 49 times, ending with 1 hdc in last st. Ch 1, turn.

Row 14: 1 hdc in 1st st, *1 hdc in next st. Repeat from *, ending with 1 hdc in last st. Break yarn, turn.

Note: Rows 15–24 are worked with decs at the beg and end of each row to shape the piece to fit the seat of the toilet. This is accomplished by working slsts at the beg of each row and ending each row several sts before the end of the previous row. Shaping is further aided by not chaining at the end of each row.

Row 15: Color B—slst in 1st 2 sts, (**1 Pineapple st in next st, ch 1, skip 1 st**) 26 times, (1 Pineapple st in next st, ch 2, skip 1 st) 5 times, (repeat from ** to **) 8 times, (1 Pineapple st in next st, ch 2, skip 1 st) 5 times, (repeat from ** to **) 23 times, ending with 1 slst in each of last 3 sts. Break yarn, turn.

Row 16: Color C—attach in 1st ch-1 sp, 2 sc in same ch-1 sp, (**2 sc in next ch-1 sp**) 23 times, (3 sc in next ch-2 sp) 5 times, (repeat from ** to **) 8 times, (3 sc in next ch-2 sp) 8 times, (repeat from ** to **) 23 times, ending with 2 sc in last ch-1 sp. Ch 1, turn.

Row 17: Slst in 1st 2 sts, (repeat from ** to ** of Row 5) 5 times, 1 sc in each of next 28

sts, (repeat from ** to ** of Row 5) 5 times, ending with 1 sc in 3rd st from end. Do not ch. Turn.

Row 18: Slst into 1st 3 sts, **1 hdc in each of next 2 sts, 1 dc in each of next 3 sts, 1 hdc in each of next 2 sts, 1 sc in each of next 4 sts,** (repeat from ** to **) 4 times, 1 sc in each of next 30 sts, (repeat from ** to **) 4 times, ending with 1 slst in each of last 3 sts. Break yarn, turn.

Row 19: Color D—attach in *1st sc of the previous row,* ch 3 [= 1st sc of row], 2 dc in next dc, 1 dc in next dc, 1 hdc in each of next 2 sts, 1 sc in next st, 1 sc dec in next 2 sts, 1 sc in next st, (repeat from ** to ** of Row 7) 4 times, 1 sc in each of next 28 sts, (repeat from ** to ** of Row 7) 4 times, ending with 1 hdc in each of next 2 sts, 1 dc in next st, 2 dc in next st, 1 dc in next st. Break yarn, turn.

Row 20: Color E—attach in *2nd dc of previous row,* ch 3, 1 dc in next st, 1 hdc in each of next 2 sts, 1 sc in next st, 1 sc dec in next 2 sts, 1 sc in next st, (repeat from ** to ** of Row 7) 3 times, 1 hdc in each of next 2 sts, 1 dc in next st, 3 dc in next st, 1 dc in each of next 2 sts, 2 dc in next st, 1 dc in each of next 32 sts, 2 dc in next st, 1 dc in each of next 2 sts, 3 dc in next st, 1 dc in next st, 1 hdc in each of next 2 sts, 1 sc in next st, 1 sc dec in next 2 sts, 1 sc in next st, (repeat from ** to ** of Row 7) 3 times, ending with 1 hdc in each of next 2 sts, 1 dc in each of next 2 sts. Do not ch. Turn.

Row 21: Slst into 1st 2 sts, 1 sc in next st, 1 sc dec in next 2 sts, 1 sc in next st, (repeat from ** to ** of Row 7) 3 times, 1 hdc in each of next 2 sts, 1 sc in next st, 1 slst in next st. Break yarn. Skip 44 sts. Reattach yarn in next st, slst in same st, 1 sc in next st, 1 hdc in each of next 2 sts, 1 sc in next st, 1 sc dec in next 2 sts, 1 sc in next st, (repeat from ** to ** of Row 7) 3 times, ending with 1 sc in next st, 1 slst in each of last 3 sts. Do not ch. Turn.

Row 22: Skip the 1st slst and slst into each of the 2nd and 3rd slsts of the previous row, 1 sc in next st, 1 sc dec in next 2 sts, 1 sc in next st, (repeat from ** to ** of Row 7) 3 times, slst into next 3 sts. Break yarn. Skip 44 sts and reattach yarn in next st [this should be the reattached st of the previous row]. Slst into same st, slst in each of next 2 sts, 1 sc in next st, 1 sc dec in next 2 sts, 1 sc in next st, (repeat from ** to ** of Row 7) 3 times. Break yarn, turn.

Row 23: Color F—ch 1, 1 dc in each of next 2 sts, (**1 hdc in each of next 2 sts, 1 sc in each of next 4 sts, 1 hdc in each of next 2 sts, 1 dc in each of next 3 sts**) 3 times, 1 hdc in each of next 2 sts, 1 sc in each of next 4 sts, 1 hdc in each of next 2 sts, 1 dc in next st, 1 hdc in next st, 1 sc in next st and in each st until you reach the st in which you reattached the yarn in the previous row, 1 sc in same st, 1 sc in next st, 1 hdc in next st, 1 dc in each of next 3 sts, (repeat from ** to **) 2 times, 1 hdc in each of next 2 sts, 1 sc in each of next 4 sts, 1 hdc in each of next 2 sts, 1 dc in next st, 1 hdc in next st, 1 sc in next st. Break yarn, turn.

Row 24: Skip 1st 6 sts of previous row. Color G—attach in 7th st of previous row. All sts of this row are made in *loop B only* of each st of previous row. (**1 sc in next st**) 30 times, 2 sc in next st, 1 sc in each of next 6 sts, 2 sc in next st, 1 sc in each of next 6 sts, 2 sc in next st, 1 sc in each of next 20 sts, 2 sc in next st, 1 sc in each of next 6 sts, 2 sc in next st, 1 sc in each of next 6 sts, 2 sc in next st, (repeat from ** to **) 30 times, ending with 1 sc in last st. Break yarn. Weave in all loose ends.

EDGING

Follow the directions on page 25. However, this edging will be 4 rows, and you will be decreasing on each row so that a lip is formed that will secure the seat cover to the seat.

Row 1: Attach color A to Row 1 of the piece (center color A of seat) and edge the entire piece according to the directions on page 25, using hdc instead of sc. Dec 1 st every 4 sts. When you edge the part of the seat with the final color G, pick up loop B only of these sts. Join last edging st of this row to the 1st edging st with a slst.

Rows 2–3: Work a row of sc edging, making a dec every 5th st. Join last edging st of this row to the 1st edging st with a slst.

Row 4: Ch 1, work another row of sc edging, making 1 dec every 10th st. Join last edging st of this row to the 1st edging st with a slst. Break yarn.

143

Wastepaper Basket Cover

Foundation chain: Color A—ch 4, join with slst.

Round 1: Ch 1, 8 sc in ring, join with slst to 1st sc.

Round 2: Ch 1, 2 sc in same st, *2 sc in next st. Repeat from *, ending with slst in 1st sc [16 sts].

Round 3: Ch 1, 1 sc in same st, *2 sc in next st, 1 sc in next st. Repeat from *, ending with 2 sc in last st, join with slst to 1st sc [24 sts].

Round 4: Repeat Round 3 [36 sts].

Round 5: Ch 1, 1 sc in 1st st, *1 sc in next st. Repeat from *, ending with 1 sc in last st, join with slst to 1st sc.

Round 6: Ch 1, 1 sc in 1st st, 1 sc in next st, *2 sc in next st, 1 sc in each of next 2 sts. Repeat from *, ending with 2 sc in last st, join with slst to 1st sc [48 sts].

Round 7: Repeat Round 5.

Round 8: Ch 1, 1 sc in 1st st, 1 sc in each of next 2 sts, *2 sc in next st, 1 sc in each of next 3 sts. Repeat from *, ending with 2 sc in last st, join with slst to 1st sc [60 sts].

Round 9: Repeat Round 5.

Round 10: Ch 1, 1 sc in 1st st, 1 sc in each of next 3 sts, *2 sc in next st, 1 sc in each of next 4 sts. Repeat from *, ending with 2 sc in last st, join with slst to 1st sc [72 sts].

Round 11: Repeat Round 5.

Round 12: Ch 1, 1 sc in 1st st, 1 sc in each of next 4 sts, *2 sc in next st, 1 sc in each of next 5 sts. Repeat from *, ending with 2 sc in last st, join with slst to 1st sc [84 sts].

Round 13: Repeat Round 5.

Round 14: Ch 1, 1 sc in 1st st, 1 sc in each of next 5 sts, *2 sc in next st, 1 sc in each of next 6 sts. Repeat from *, ending with 2 sc in last st, join with slst to 1st sc [96 sts].

Round 15: Repeat Round 5.

Round 16: Ch 1, 1 sc in 1st st, 1 sc in each of next 6 sts, *2 sc in next st, 1 sc in each of next 7 sts. Repeat from *, ending with 2 sc in last st, join with slst to 1st sc [108 sts].

Round 17: Repeat Round 5.

Round 18: Ch 1, 1 sc in 1st st, 1 sc in each of next 7 sts, *2 sc in next st, 1 sc in each of next 8 sts. Repeat from *, ending with 2 sc in last st, join with slst to 1st sc [120 sts].

Round 19: Ch 1, 1 sc in same st, *1 sc in next st, repeat from *, ending with 1 sc in last st, join with slst.

Round 20: Repeat Round 19.

Round 21: Repeat Round 19. Break yarn, turn your piece.

Note: Until this point all rnds of the wastepaper basket cover were joined and *not turned,* and all work was being done on the *front of the piece.* However, the next rnd has Pineapple sts [see page 47], and these sts have more definition when seen from the back than they do when seen from the front. To accomplish this the piece is turned and worked from the *back of the piece.* It is then turned back to the front side at the completion of the rnd. It is not mandatory to do this, however. You can just join the rnd, ch up, and continue working on the front side if you wish.

Round 22: Color B—ch 3, *1 Pineapple st in next st, ch 1, skip 1 st, 1 Pineapple in next st. Repeat from *, ending with 1 Pineapple in last st, join with slst to top of ch-3. Turn your work so that the front faces you.

Round 23: Color C—ch 1, 1 sc in same st, 1 sc in next Pineapple, *2 sc in the next ch-1 sp. Repeat from *, ending with 1 sc in last Pineapple, join with slst to 1st sc [121 sts].

Round 24: Ch 1, 1 sc in 1st st, 1 sc in next st, 1 hdc in each of next 2 sts, 1 dc in each of next 3 sts, 1 hdc in each of next 2 sts, 1 sc in each of next 2 sts, *1 sc in each of next 2 sts, 1 hdc in each of next 2 sts, 1 dc in each of next 3 sts, 1 hdc in each of next 2 sts, 1 sc in each of next 2 sts. Repeat from *, ending with join to 1st sc with slst.

Round 25: Repeat Round 24.

Round 26: Color D—ch 1, 1 sc in same st, 1 sc in next st, **1 hdc in each of next 2 sts, 1 dc in next st, 2 dc in next st, 1 dc in next st, 1 hdc in each of next 2 sts, 1 sc in next st, 1 sc dec, 1 sc in next st.** (Repeat from ** to **) 9 times, ending with 1 hdc in each of next 2 sts, 1 dc in next st, 2 dc in next st, 1 dc in next st, 1 hdc in each of next 2 sts, 1 sc dec in last 2 sts, join with slst to 1st sc.

Round 27: Color E—ch 1, 1 sc in 1st st. (Repeat from ** to ** of Round 26) 10 times, ending with 1 hdc in each of next 2 sts, 1 dc in

144

next st, 2 dc in next st, 1 dc in next st, 1 hdc in each of next 2 sts, 1 sc in each of last 2 sts, join with slst to 1st sc.

Round 28: Ch 1, 1 sc in 1st st. (Repeat from ** to ** of Round 26) 10 times, ending with 1 hdc in each of next 2 sts, 1 dc in next st, 2 dc in next st, 1 dc in next st, 1 hdc in each of next 2 sts, 1 sc in next st, 1 sc dec, join with slst to 1st sc.

Round 29: Repeat Round 28.

Round 30: Color F—ch 3, **1 hdc in each of next 2 sts, 1 sc in each of next 4 sts, 1 hdc in each of next 2 sts, 1 dc in each of next 3 sts.** (Repeat from ** to **) 9 times, ending with 1 hdc in each of next 2 sts, 1 sc in each of next 4 sts, 1 hdc in each of next 2 sts, 1 dc in each of next 2 sts, join with slst to top of ch-3.

Round 31: Color G—ch 1, 1 sc in 1st st, *1 sc in loop B only of next st. Repeat from *, ending with 1 sc in loop B of last st, join with slst to 1st sc of rnd.

Round 32: Color A—ch 1, 1 hdc in same st, *1 hdc in loop B only of next st. Repeat from *, ending with 1 hdc in loop B of last st, join with slst to 1st hdc.

Round 33: Repeat Round 32, picking up both lps of st. Turn your work so that you will be looking at the inside of your piece.

Round 34: Color B—attach in ending slst of previous rnd and then repeat Round 22.

Round 35: Color C—repeat Round 23. [You should have 121 sts at the end of this rnd.]

Round 36: Repeat Round 24.

Round 37: Repeat Round 24.

Round 38: Color D—repeat Round 26.

Round 39: Color E—repeat Round 27.

Round 40: Repeat Round 28.

Round 41: Repeat Round 28.

Round 42: Color F—repeat Round 30.

Round 43: Color G—repeat Round 31.

Round 44: Color A—repeat Round 32.

Round 45: Repeat Round 33.

Round 46: Color B—repeat Round 22.

Round 47: Color C—repeat Round 23.

Round 48: Repeat Round 24.

Round 49: Repeat Round 24.

Round 50: Color D—repeat Round 26.

Round 51: Color E—repeat Round 27.

Round 52: Repeat Round 28.

Round 53: Repeat Round 28.

Round 54: Color F—repeat Round 30.

Round 55: Color G—repeat Round 31.

Round 56: Color A—repeat Round 32.

Round 57: Repeat Round 33.

Round 58: Color B—repeat Round 22.

Round 59: Color C—repeat Round 23.

Round 60: Ch 1, yo, insert hk from back to front in sp between 1st and last sts, across bar of 1st st and thru to the back in sp between 1st and 2nd sts, yo and draw lp back across bar of 1st st and out to the back, yo and draw a lp thru all 3 lps [1 hdc Post st made], insert hk from back to front in sp between 1st and 2nd sts, across the bar of the 2nd st, and thru to the back between the 2nd and 3rd sts, yo and draw a lp back across the bar of the 2nd st and out to the back, yo and draw a lp thru all 3 lps [2nd hdc Post st made]. Repeat hdc Post st in each st and join with slst to 1st hdc.

Round 61: Repeat Round 60.

Round 62: Ch 1, 1 hdc in same st, *1 hdc in each of next 7 sts, 1 hdc dec in next 2 sts. Repeat from *, ending with slst in 1st hdc.

Round 63: Repeat Round 62. [Rounds 60–63 will form a lip that will secure the cover to the wastepaper basket.] Break yarn.

Circular Tablecloth

The intricate patterns of this graceful tablecloth are formed by familiar basic and fancy stitches worked in a thin yarn with a very large hook. This unexpected combination of hook and yarn is one of our favorite ways to make simple stitches and shapes look unusual and impressive. The delicate, airy design looks best when placed over a liner. Choose a dark liner for a formal, traditional effect or a bright liner for a more modern effect. By the way, be sure to use a washable yarn.

Materials:
- 2½ lbs. flaxon #91 UKI 3/2 mercerized cotton *or* 24 balls cream Coats & Clark's Speed Cro-Sheen *or* any mercerized cotton that approximates the gauge

Hook: K

Gauge:
Rounds 1 and 2 = 3" (approximately), Rounds 1–6 = 9"

Finished Size:
52" diameter without fringe

   Note: Use small pieces of yarn or small safety pins as markers in the inc sts, as we suggest in the section on circles in this chapter [page 122]. After Round 7, incs will come directly over incs of the previous rnd.

Instructions:
Foundation chain: Ch 6, join with slst to 1st ch.
Round 1: Ch 1, 12 hdc in center of circle, join with slst to 1st hdc.
Round 2: Ch 1, 2 hdc in same st as joining, *2 hdc in next st. Repeat from *, ending with 2 hdc in last st, join with slst [24 sts].
Round 3: *Ch 4, skip next st, 1 sc in next st. Repeat from *, ending with ch 4, skip next st, join with slst to 1st ch of ch-4 [12 lps formed].
Round 4: 1 slst in 1st lp, ch 3 [= 1 dc], 3 dc in lp, *4 dc in next lp. Repeat from *, ending with 4 dc in last lp, slst in top ch of ch-3 [48 sts].
Round 5: *Ch 5, skip 4-dc group, 1 sc in sp between groups. Repeat from *, ending with 1 sc in last sp [12 lps].
Round 6: 1 slst in 1st lp, ch 4 [= 1 tr], 5 tr in lp, *6 tr in next lp. Repeat from *, ending with 6 tr in last lp, join with slst to 4th ch of ch-4 [72 sts].
Round 7: Ch 1, 1 hdc in *loop A only* of 1st st, *(1 hdc in loop A of next st) 5 times, 2 hdc in loop A of next st. Repeat from *, ending with 2 hdc in last st, join with slst in loop A and post lp of 1st hdc [1 inc every 6th st—84 sts].
Round 8: Ch 3 [= last dc of final Judith st], *1 Judith st in loop A and post lp of next 4 sts. Repeat from *, ending with skip 1 st, 1 dc in loop A and post lp of next 2 sts, slst in top ch of ch-3, put hk in front of 3-dc and thru missed st, draw up a long lp, put hk thru top of ch-3, yo, pull thru all lps.
Round 9: Ch 1, 1 sc in 1st st, (1 sc in next st) 5 times, 2 sc in next st, *(1 sc in next st) 6 times, 2 sc in next st. Repeat from *, ending with 2 sc in last st, join with slst to 1st sc [1 inc every 7th st—96 sts]. [Remember to make the sc that comes between complete Judith sts in the sp rather than the st.]
Round 10: Ch 3 [= 1 dc], (1 dc in loop B of next st) 6 times, 2 dc in loop B of next st, *(1 dc in loop B of next st) 7 times, 2 dc in loop B of next st. Repeat from *, ending with 2 dc in last st, join with slst to top ch of ch-3 [1 inc every 8th st—108 sts].
Round 11: Ch 4 [= 1 hdc, ch 1], skip 1 st, *(1 hdc in loop A of next st, ch 1, skip 1 st) 3 times, (1 hdc in loop A of next st, ch 1) 2 times. Repeat from *, ending with (1 hdc in loop A of next st, ch 1) 2 times, join with a slst to 3rd ch of ch-4 [1 inc every 9th st—120 sts].
Round 12: Ch 3 [= 1 hdc], 1 hdc in same st, *skip next st, 2 hdc in sp formed by ch-1. Repeat from *, ending with 2 hdc in last sp, slst in top of ch-3 [120 sts].
Round 13: Ch 1, repeat Row 1 of the Daisy st

directions on page 49, ending according to directions for Daisy st joined rnds [120 sts].

Round 14: Repeat Row 2 of Daisy st, ending according to directions for Daisy st joined rnds [120 sts].

Round 15: Repeat Row 2 of Daisy st, increasing 2 times every 10 sts. [Remember that in order to keep the Daisy st pat, 2 incs must be made at each inc point. Since the 1st st of the rnd is an eye, the 10th st is a non-eye. Make your incs in the eyes directly before and after the 10th st as follows: Complete Daisy directly preceding 10th st, *ch 1, insert hk thru eye, draw up lp, *yo*, draw up lp thru final st of just-completed Daisy, draw up lp thru next st [5 lps on hk], yo, draw thru 5 lps. Repeat from * once [2 incs every 10th st—144 sts].

Round 16: Repeat Row 2 of Daisy st, ending as for Round 13 [144 sts].

Round 17: Ch 1, 1 sc in 1st st, (1 sc in next st) 10 times, 2 sc in next st, *(1 sc in next st) 11 times, 2 sc in next st. Repeat from *, ending with 2 sc in last st, join with slst to 1st sc [1 inc every 12th st—156 sts].

Round 18: Ch 1, 1 sc in 1st st, *ch 4, skip 3 sts, 1 sc in next st. Repeat from *, ending with ch 4, skip 3 sts, join with slst to 1st sc [39 lps].

Round 19: [To simplify increasing on this rnd, tie markers into the lps that will get 5 sts before you begin. The lps that get 5 sts are numbers 4, 7, 10, 13, 17, 20, 23, 26, 30, 33, 36, and 39.] Slst into 1st lp, ch 1, *(4 sc in next lp) 3 times, 5 sc in next lp, [(4 sc in next lp) 2 times, 5 sc in next lp] 3 times. Repeat from *, ending with 5 sc in last lp, join with slst to 1st sc [1 inc every 13th st—168 sts].

Round 20: Ch 3 [= last dc of final Judith st], *1 Judith st in next 4 sts. Repeat from *, ending as in Round 8 [42 Judith sts—168 sts].

Round 21: Ch 1, 1 sc in 1st st, (1 sc in next st) 12 times, 2 sc in next st, *(1 sc in next st) 13 times, 2 sc in next st. Repeat from *, ending with 2 sc in last st, join to 1st sc with slst [1 inc every 14th st—180 sts].

Round 22: Repeat Round 20 [45 Judith sts—180 sts].

Round 23: Ch 1, 1 sc in 1st st, (1 sc in next st) 13 times, 2 sc in next st, *(1 sc in next st) 14 times, 2 sc in next st. Repeat from *, ending

with 2 sc in last st, join to 1st sc with slst [1 inc every 15th st—192 sts].

Round 24: Ch 2, 1 Pineapple st in same st, *ch 2, skip 1 st, 1 Pineapple in next st. Repeat from *, ending with ch 2, skip 1 st, join to 1st Pineapple with slst [96 Pineapples].

Round 25: Ch 3 [= 1 dc in *last* sp], skip 1st Pineapple st, *(2 dc in ch-2 sp, skip Pineapple) 7 times, 3 dc in next sp, skip next Pineapple. Repeat from *, ending with 2 dc in last sp, slst in top of ch-3 [1 inc every 16th st—204 sts].

Round 26: Ch 3 [= 1 dc], *1 dc in next st. Repeat from *, ending with 1 dc in last st, join with a slst to top ch of ch-3 [204 sts].

Round 27: Ch 1, 1 sc in loop A of 1st st, (1 sc in loop A of next st) 15 times, 2 sc in loop A of next st, *(1 sc in back lp of next st) 16 times, 2 sc in next st. Repeat from *, ending with 2 sc in loop A of last st, join with a slst to 1st sc [1 inc every 17th st—216 sts].

Round 28: Ch 3 [= 1 dc of final Judith st], *1 Judith st in loop A of each of next 4 sts. Repeat from *, ending with skip 1 st, 1 dc in loop A and post lp of next 2 sts, slst in top ch of ch-3, put hk in front of 3-dc and thru missed st, draw up a long lp, put hk thru top of ch-3, yo, pull thru all lps [54 Judith sts—216 sts].

Round 29: Ch 1, 1 sc in 1st st, (1 sc in next st) 16 times, 2 sc in next st, *(1 sc in next st) 17 times, 2 sc in next st. Repeat from *, ending with 2 sc in last st, join to 1st sc with slst [1 inc every 18th st—228 sts].

Round 30: Repeat Round 20 [57 Judith sts—228 sts].

Round 31: Ch 1, 1 sc in 1st st, (1 sc in next st) 17 times, 2 sc in next st, *(1 sc in next st) 18 times, 2 sc in next st. Repeat from *, ending with 2 sc in last st, join with slst to 1st sc [1 inc every 19th st—240 sts].

Round 32: Repeat Round 20 [60 Judith sts—240 sts].

Round 33: Ch 1, 1 sc in 1st st, (1 sc in next st) 18 times, 2 sc in next st, *(1 sc in next st) 19 times, 2 sc in next st. Repeat from *, ending with 2 sc in last st, join to 1st sc with slst [1 inc every 20th st—252 sts].

Round 34: Repeat Round 20 [63 Judith sts—252 sts].

Round 35: Ch 1, 1 sc in 1st st, (1 sc in next st) 19 times, 2 sc in next st, *(1 sc in next st) 20 times, 2 sc in next st. Repeat from *, ending with 2 sc in last st, join to 1st sc with slst [1 inc every 21st st—276 sts].

Round 36: Ch 1, 1 sc in 1st st, (1 sc in next st) 20 times, 2 sc in next st, *(1 sc in next st) 21 times, 2 sc in next st. Repeat from *, ending with 2 sc in last st, join with slst to 1st st [1 inc every 22nd st—276 sts].

Round 37: Ch 4 [= 1 tr], (1 tr in loop A of next st) 21 times, 2 tr in next st, *(1 tr in loop A of next st) 22 times, 2 tr in next st. Repeat from *, ending with 2 tr in last st, join with slst to top of ch-4 [1 inc every 23rd st—288 sts].

Round 38: Ch 1, 1 hdc in loop A of 1st st, (1 hdc in loop A of next st) 22 times, 2 hdc in loop A of next st, *(1 hdc in loop A of next st) 23 times, 2 hdc in loop A of next st. Repeat from *, ending with 2 hdc in loop A of last st, join to 1st sc with slst [1 inc every 24th st—300 sts].

Round 39: Ch 2, 1 Pineapple st in post lp of 1st st, *ch 2, skip 1 st, 1 Pineapple in post lp of next st. Repeat from *, ending with ch 2, skip last st, join to 1st Pineapple with slst.

Round 40: Ch 3 [= 1 dc in *last* sp], *skip Pineapple st, 2 dc in ch-2 sp. Repeat from *, ending with 1 dc in last sp, join with slst to top ch of ch-3 [300 sts].

Round 41: Ch 1, 1 hdc in 1st st, (1 hdc in next st) 23 times, 2 hdc in next st, *(1 hdc in next st) 24 times, 2 hdc in next st. Repeat from *, ending with 2 hdc in last st, join to 1st hdc with slst [1 inc every 25th st—312 sts].

Round 42: Repeat Round 28 [78 Judith sts—312 sts].

Round 43: Ch 1, 1 sc in 1st st, (1 sc in next st) 24 times, 2 sc in next st, *(1 sc in next st) 25 times, 2 sc in next st. Repeat from *, ending with 2 sc in last st, join to 1st sc with slst (1 inc every 26th st—324 sts].

Round 44: Ch 5 [= 1 dtr], *1 dtr in loop A of next st. Repeat from *, ending with 1 dtr in loop A of last st, join to top ch of ch-5 with slst [324 sts].

Round 45: Ch 1, 1 hdc in loop A of 1st st, *ch 1, 1 hdc in loop A of next st. Repeat from *, ending with ch 1, join to hdc with slst. Break yarn.

Follow the directions for making fringe on page 37, using a piece of cardboard 8½″ wide. Approximately 4 or 5 strands of cut yarn equal 1 fringe group. Put 2 fringe groups in each ch-1 sp. If you want heavy fringe, put 3 groups in each sp.

The tablecloth should be blocked from the center on a round table, according to the blocking directions on page 35. While the tablecloth is on the table, trim the fringe.

Adapting to Different Shapes

Both the Circular Tablecloth and the Shell Stitch Tablecloth were made for round tables. But if your table is another shape it is as easy to make an oval, square, or rectangular tablecloth as it is to make a round one. Turn to the section in this chapter that deals with the shape you'd like for your table (see pages 122–127 for specifics). Make a small practice swatch of the shape until you understand the increasing pattern necessary to keep the shape uniform and flat. You can then use the combination and order of the stitch pattern in the sample tablecloth, adjusting the increases to your shape. Don't be afraid to improvise. As you work, occasionally place the tablecloth on your table. You might be surprised at the different stitch possibilities that occur to you. Work the stitch patterns until the cloth drops over the edge of the table. We usually have a 5- to 7-inch drop on our tablecloths, but again, this is entirely up to you. You might prefer instead to have a floor-length drop or a short scalloped edge.

Note: Similarly, the rectangular shapes can be made into ovals, squares, or circles. The Rectangular Table Runner in this chapter (see page 150) can be adapted to any shape you like.

Rectangular Table Runner

This table runner is so simple to make that it presents the perfect opportunity for experimentation. Use whatever yarn you like—wool, cotton, or linen—and don't worry if your gauge is different from ours. The length can be adjusted, and table runners do vary considerably in width. We used the complementary colors of red and green. You might want to try other color combinations that are complementary—perhaps blue and orange or yellow and violet. Choose whatever combination that pleases you and will best harmonize with your furnishings.

Materials:
- 1 skein of CUM Gobelin in each of the following colors: burgundy, dark red, fuchsia, apricot (or rust), light chartreuse, dark chartreuse (or light olive) *or* corresponding amounts of any 2-ply wool, sport weight wool, or acrylic yarn

Hook: F

Gauge:
5 sts = 1″, 5 rows = 1″

Finished Size:
16″ wide; length is adjustable

Instructions:
Make the rectangle in sc according to the instructions on page 127. To determine how long to make the foundation ch, subtract 16″ [8″ at each end] from the desired finished length. Multiply your answer by 5 [there are 5 sts per inch], then add 1 for the 1st turning ch. Make a ch of this number of sts. The table runner as shown measures 54″: 54″ − 16″ = 38″; 38″ × 5 sts = 190 sts, + 1 = 191 sts in the foundation ch. Refer to the directions for changing colors in joined rounds on page 28 and change colors as follows:
Foundation chain: Burgundy.
Round 1: Burgundy.
Round 2: Dark red.
Round 3: Burgundy.
Round 4: Dark red.
Round 5: Dark red.
Round 6: Dark red.
Round 7: Burgundy.
Round 8: Burgundy.
Round 9: Fuchsia.
Round 10: Burgundy.
Round 11: Dark red.
Round 12: Dark red.
Round 13: Apricot.
Round 14: Fuchsia.
Round 15: Apricot.
Round 16: Apricot.
Round 17: Burgundy.
Round 18: Fuchsia.
Round 19: Fuchsia.
Round 20: Dark chartreuse.
Round 21: Fuchsia.
Round 22: Apricot.
Round 23: Dark chartreuse.
Round 24: Light chartreuse.
Round 25: Dark red.
Round 26: Burgundy.
Round 27: Burgundy.
Round 28: Dark red.
Round 29: Dark red.
Round 30: Dark red.
Round 31: Apricot.
Round 32: Light chartreuse.
Round 33: Apricot.
Round 34: Burgundy.
Round 35: Apricot.
Round 36: Light chartreuse.
Round 37: Light chartreuse.
Round 38: Dark chartreuse.
Round 39: Burgundy.
Round 40: Fuchsia.
Round 41: Dark chartreuse. Break yarn.
Round 42: Light chartreuse—edge the piece with Shrimp st [see page 50].

Block the piece according to the directions on page 35.

Copper Wire Birdcage

Any man-made fiber that is flexible enough to be wrapped around a hook can be crocheted. This project was worked in thin copper wire to make a gilded cage for a stuffed bird; if you prefer, use it as a showcase for lush green plants.

Materials:
- 1 spool #28 copper wire
- 15" square of ¼"-thick Plexiglas
- 9 lengths of ¼" plastic rod, 39" long
- 1 length of ¼" plastic rod, 42" long
- Duco cement (or comparable adhesive)
- Electric drill with ¼" and ¹⁄₁₆" bits
- Electric jigsaw with fine-toothed blade
- Rattail file

Hook: I

Gauge:
Motif 1, approximately 4" diameter
Motif 2, approximately 3" diameter
Motif 3, approximately 2¼" diameter
Motif 4, approximately 1¼" diameter

Finished Size:
3' high, 1' diameter

Note: Crocheting with wire requires very little special technique. Use a plastic crochet hk, as the friction between the wire and the hk will cause the coating of an aluminum hk to peel.

The wire may be a little unfamiliar to maneuver at first. Try running the wire up from the spool, across the palm of your hand, and over your index finger so that the wire lies in the crook of the finger. Also, the wire will flow with greater ease if you put a bandage or two over the part of your index finger that the wire crosses. The sts will not be as regular as those made with yarn, but this flexibility can enhance the design. After you complete each motif, pull on the edges slightly to even out the circle.

Instructions:
Motif 1: Make 48 of these motifs.
Foundation chain: Ch 5, insert hk into 5th ch from hk and make a slst to join the ring.
Round 1: Ch 1, work 8 sc over the ch into the ring, join last st to 1st st with slst [8 sts].

Round 2: Ch 1, 2 sc in same st, *2 sc in next st. Repeat from *, ending with 2 sc in last st, join last st to 1st st with slst [16 sts].
Round 3: Ch 1, 1 Pineapple st in same st, *ch 1, 1 Pineapple st in next st. Repeat from *, ending with 1 Pineapple st in last st, ch 1, join last st to 1st st with slst [32 sts].
Round 4: Ch 1, 2 sc in 1st ch-1 sp of previous rnd, *2 sc in next ch-1 sp. Repeat from *, ending with 2 sc in last ch-1 sp, join last st to 1st st with slst.
Round 5: Ch 1, 1 Pineapple st in same st, *ch 1, 1 Pineapple st in next st. Repeat from *, ending with 1 Pineapple st in last st, ch 1, join last st to 1st st with slst. Cut wire.

Motif 2: Make 8 of these motifs.
Foundation chain–Round 2: Repeat Foundation chain–Round 2 of Motif 1 [16 sts].
Round 3: Ch 1, 1 sc in same st, *2 sc in next st, 1 sc in next st. Repeat from *, ending with 2 sc in last st, join last st to 1st st with slst [24 sts].
Round 4: Ch 1, 1 Pineapple st in same st, *ch 1, 1 Pineapple st in next st. Repeat from *, ending with 1 Pineapple st in last st, ch 1, join last st to 1st st with slst.
Round 5: Ch 1, 2 sc in 1st ch-1 sp of previous rnd, *2 sc in next ch-1 sp. Repeat from *, ending with 2 sc in last ch-1 sp, join last st to 1st st with slst. Cut wire.

Motif 3: Make 8 of these motifs.
Foundation chain–Round 3: Repeat Foundation chain–Round 3 of Motif 1. Cut wire.

Motif 4: Make 8 of these motifs.
Foundation chain: Ch 6, insert hk into 6th ch from hk and make a slst, forming a ring.
Round 1: Ch 1, work 10 sc over the ch into the ring, join last st to 1st st with slst.
Round 2: Ch 1, 1 Pineapple st in same st, *ch 1, 1 Pineapple st in next st. Repeat from *, ending with 1 Pineapple st in last st, ch 1, join last st to 1st st with slst. Cut wire.

Strut covers: Make 8 of these.

Foundation chain: Ch 125.

Row 1: Insert hk into 2nd ch from hk and make a sc, *1 sc in next ch. Repeat from *, ending with 1 sc in last ch. Ch 1, turn.

Row 2: 1 sc in 1st st of previous row, *1 sc in next st. Repeat from *, ending with 1 sc in last st. Ch 1, turn.

Row 3: Repeat Row 2. Cut wire.

Fold the piece so that the heads of the sts of Row 3 lie next to the foundation ch row. You will form a tube by slip-stitching these 2 rows tog. Insert hk thru the head of the 1st st of Row 3 and the 1st foundation ch [pick up whichever strand of the foundation ch remains after working the 1st row] and make a slst. Repeat procedure down the row until all sts have been joined, ending with a slst in the last st of Row 3 and the foundation ch. Cut wire.

Ring support cover: Make 1 of these.

Foundation chain: Ch 125.

Repeat Rows 1–3 of the strut cover, but do not form a tube.

Door cover: Make 1 of these.

Foundation chain: Ch 50.

Repeat Rows 1–3 of the strut cover, but do not form a tube.

Door frame cover: Make 1 of these.

Foundation chain: Ch 20.

Repeat Rows 1–3 of the strut cover, then form a tube by slip-stitching the 3rd row to the foundation row.

Top support cover: Make 1 of these.

Foundation chain: Ch 5, insert hk into 5th ch from hk and make a slst, forming a ring.

Round 1: Ch 1, work 8 sc over the ch into the ring, join last st to 1st st with slst.

Round 2: Ch 1, 2 sc in same st, *2 sc in next st. Repeat from *, ending with 2 sc in last st, join last st to 1st st with slst. Cut wire [16 sts].

FORMING MOTIF STRIPS

Place 6 Motif 1's on a flat surface so that each motif is directly below the next. Each motif should touch the one directly below it for at least 3 pairs of opposing sts. Thread a blunt tapestry needle with a 12″ length of wire. Join these 6 motifs to each other by sewing thru the heads of the 3 pairs of opposing sts. Repeat this process 6 times for a total of 7 strips.

Make 1 strip consisting of 4 Motif 1's. This strip will be placed above the door frame. Make 1 strip consisting of 2 Motifs 1's. This strip will be placed inside the door.

Place 1 Motif 2, 1 Motif 3, and 1 Motif 4 on a flat surface. Motif 2 should be on the bottom, Motif 4 on top. Be sure that each motif is centered above the motif below. Again, attach these motifs thru the 3 pairs of opposing sts that touch each other. Repeat 7 times for a total of 8 strips for the top part of the cage.

The weight of the motif strips can cause the motif to elongate if held upright. Keep the strips lying on a flat surface until you are ready to attach them to the struts of the birdcage.

CONSTRUCTING THE BIRDCAGE

Cut a round of Plexiglas 13¼″ in diameter from the 15″ square with a jigsaw fitted with a fine-toothed blade. Save the remaining Plexiglas—it will be used later to help shape another part of the birdcage. Drill eight ¼″ holes in the round Plexiglas base, using an electric drill with a ¼″ bit; the holes should be ½″ from the edge of the base and 4¾″ from each other. [When measuring distances between holes, measure from the center of 1 hole to the center of the next.] Drill 2 small holes, using a $\frac{1}{16}$″ bit, equidistant between every two ¼″ holes. These holes will be 2⅛″ from each ¼″ hole, ½″ from the edge of the base, and ¼″ from each other. They will be used to secure the bottom-most motif to the base.

Struts: Make 8 of these.

Practice heating and bending the upright struts with an extra length of ¼″ plastic rod.

To heat and bend the 39″ rods, preheat your oven to 250°. With the oven door partially open, hold about 1′ of the rod in the oven. You'll notice that after a few seconds the plastic will soften and can be shaped by hand into any configuration. The shape you want is a gently curving arc. The edge of the Plexiglas base will serve as a template for this arc. When the end of the rod has softened, bend it around the Plexiglas base [Diagram 87]. Repeat the process with the remaining 39″ rods.

Ring support: Make 1 of these.

[See Diagram 88.] Heat the entire length of the 42″ plastic rod. When it's softened, form the

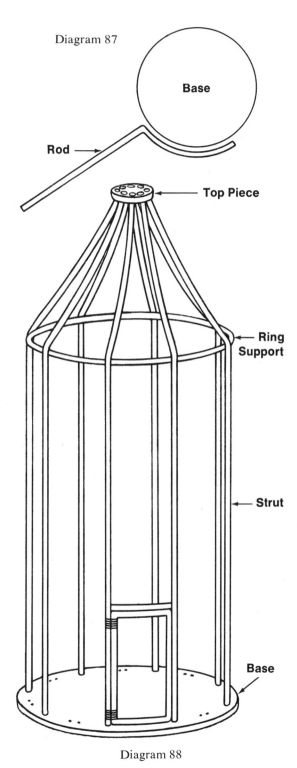

Diagram 87

Base

Rod

Top Piece

Ring Support

Strut

Base

Diagram 88

rod into a circle, using the remaining piece of Plexiglas as a template. The ends of the rod will overlap slightly. Trim the overlap with the jigsaw and then glue the ends tog with the cement. You should have a ring of ¼″ plastic rod the same size as the base. File the outside of the ring support with a rattail file at intervals of 4¾″, making slight indentations that will mark the placement of the struts.

Top piece: Make 1 of these.

[See Diagram 88.] With the jigsaw, cut a circle 1½″ in diameter from a corner of the Plexiglas that remained after the base was cut. Drill eight ¼″ holes ⅛″ from the edge. Each hole should be ⅜″ from the adjacent holes.

Door and door frame: Make 1 of each.

Cut the remaining plastic rod into 2 pieces measuring 8½″, 2 pieces measuring 4″, and 1 piece measuring 4½″. Glue the two 8½″ lengths to the 4″ lengths. This is the door. The remaining 4½″ length is the door frame.

COVERING THE STRUTS

Pull a long strut cover over a strut. The cover will come about halfway up the strut. With your right hand, hold the cover in place at the bottom of the strut, and with your left hand, gently push the cover up the strut. It will stretch as you push it. Work slowly, stretching a little at a time, until the cover is 3″ from the top. Dab on a little cement at the top, center, and bottom of cover to secure it to strut. Repeat with remaining 7 struts and covers.

COVERING DOOR AND DOOR FRAME

Fold the door cover around one of the long bars of the door so that Row 3 of the door cover lies next to the foundation ch row. Thread a blunt tapestry needle with an 18″ length of wire. Insert the needle thru the 1st st of Row 3 and the 1st st of the foundation ch and pull the wire thru. Insert the needle thru these same 2 sts and pull up a tight lp. Begin to join these 2 rows, following the directions for attaching by sewing on page 29. You will be sewing the cover into a tube around the rod. You can push the wire tog on the rod as you sew it. When the entire tube is sewn, gently push the cover around the door rectangle in the same way as you did the strut covers. When the end of the cover meets the beg, dab a little

155

cement on the front, middle, and ends to secure it to the door rods. Slip the door frame [the 4½″ rod] into the door frame cover. Stretch the cover the length of the door frame and dab a little cement on each end to secure the cover to the door frame.

COVERING RING AND TOP SUPPORTS

Fold the ring support cover around the ring support and follow the same joining instructions used for forming the door cover into a tube around the rod.

Place the top support cover on the top support and gently push the cover down over the edges of the top support. Dab a little cement around the edges and in the middle of the piece to secure it to the plastic piece.

ASSEMBLING BIRDCAGE

Slip the struts into the holes in the base. The tops of the struts fit into the holes of the top support [see Diagram 88]. Place the ring support inside the cage at the point where the struts begin to arc in toward the top piece. If any wire is covering the indentations on the ring support, push the wire away. The struts should rest on these indentations. When you are sure everything is in place, dab cement around the base strut holes, the indentation/strut points, and the strut holes in the top piece to secure the struts in place. Place the door frame rod between any 2 lower struts [lower struts are those between the base and the ring support] 9″ from the base [refer to Diagram 88]. Place the door in the rectangle formed by the door frame, the side struts, and the base. Secure the door to the left strut by making 2 hinges of wire wrapped around the strut and the door 1″ from the top and bottom of the left side of the door. The door will be able to be swung open and closed. To keep the door closed, wrap another small piece of wire around the right side of the door and the right strut.

SEWING MOTIFS INTO PLACE

Take 1 strip of 6 Motif 1's and fit it between two of the lower struts [not the struts with the door]. The center of the top motif should touch the center of the ring support. The center of the last motif will meet the center $1/16''$ holes between the struts. The sides of each motif will be sewn to the strut cover on either side. Be-

cause of the flexibility of the wire you can pull the motifs slightly so that they touch the side struts. However, be careful not to pull the motifs out of shape. Thread a blunt tapestry needle with wire and sew the top motif to the ring support. There should be 3 sts at the center of the top motif touching the ring support. Sew the sides of the top motif to the strut cover. The sides of each motif should meet the strut cover for 4 or 5 sts on each side. Next sew the bottom motif into place. First sew the sides of the bottom motif to the strut cover. The center of the bottom of the last motif should meet the 2 small holes in between the struts. Insert the tapestry needle thru one of these holes, pick up one of the sts that meets the hole, go back into the 2nd small hole, and pick up the next st of the motif which touches the 2nd $1/16''$ hole. When the top and bottom motifs are in place, sew the sides of the remaining motifs to the strut cover. Repeat this process with the 6 remaining strips of 6 Motif 1's. Sew the strip containing 4 Motif 1's into place above the door frame in the same manner, but attach the bottom motif to the jacket cover of the door frame. Sew the strip of 2 Motif 1's in place in the door. Sew the top motif to the top of the door, the bottom of the lower motif to the bottom of the door, and the sides of the motifs to the covers of the door.

ATTACHING MOTIFS TO UPPER STRUTS

[The upper struts are those between the ring support and the top piece.] Take one of the upper motif strips, consisting of Motifs 2, 3, and 4, and place it between 2 upper struts. The center of Motif 2 should touch the center of the ring support and should be sewn in place where the cover of the ring support touches the center of Motif 2. Sew the sides of Motif 2 to the upper strut covers on either side. Motif 4 should be 5″ from the top piece. Sew the sides of Motif 4 to the strut covers on either side. Last, sew the sides of Motif 3 to the strut cover. Repeat for remaining 7 upper motif strips.

Top wrap: Wind wire around the top 3″ of the struts. Every few yards dab a little cement on the wrapped wire; allow it to dry, then continue to wrap. Wrap until you have a thick covering and no part of any strut is visible.

Wall Organizer

Bright colors and simple shapes are the two elements of this project—a functional addition to any child's room. Each pocket of the train is worked in single crochet and then lined to make a tight fabric that can withstand a great deal of stretching and pulling. If you want to make an organizer that will accommodate larger objects just alter the size of each crocheted shape according to your needs.

Materials:
- 7 skeins Tahki Donegal in the following amounts: pink #809, 3 skeins; orange #807, 2 skeins; purple #812, 2 skeins *or* corresponding amounts of any worsted weight yarn
- 2 yards canvas
- 2 wood slats, 38x1½″
- Heavy-duty stapler
- 2 picture hooks

Hook: G

Gauge:
6 sts = 1″, 5 rows = 1″

Finished Size:
30x38″

Instructions:
   Note: The number for each shape corresponds to the numbers in Diagram 89.
Shape 1: Train cabin. Work with pink, purple, and then orange.
Foundation chain: Ch 41 with pink.
Row 1: Insert hk into 2nd ch from hk and make 1 sc, *1 sc in next st. Repeat from *, ending with 1 sc in last ch. Ch 1, turn [40 sts].
Row 2: 1 sc in 1st st, *1 sc in next st. Repeat from *, ending with 1 sc in last st. Ch 1, turn.
Rows 3–5: Repeat Row 2.
Row 6: Change to purple; repeat Row 2.
Row 7: Repeat Row 2.
Rows 8–12: Pink—repeat Row 2.
Rows 13–14: Orange—repeat Row 2.
Rows 15–19: Pink—repeat Row 2.
Rows 20–21: Purple—repeat Row 2.
Rows 22–26: Pink—repeat Row 2.
Rows 27–28: Orange—repeat Row 2.
Rows 29–33: Pink—repeat Row 2.
Rows 34–35: Purple—repeat Row 2.
Rows 36–40: Pink—repeat Row 2.
Rows 41–42: Orange—repeat Row 2.
Rows 43–47: Pink—repeat Row 2.
Rows 48–49: Purple—repeat Row 2.
Rows 50–54: Pink—repeat Row 2.
Rows 55–56: Orange—repeat Row 2.
Rows 57–61: Pink—repeat Row 2.
Rows 62–63: Purple—repeat Row 2.
Rows 64–68: Pink—repeat Row 2.
Rows 69–70: Orange—repeat Row 2.
Rows 71–75: Pink—repeat Row 2.
   Begin edging the piece by attaching purple in the side of Row 49, 1 sc in attaching st, 1 sc in side of each row [working toward the top of the piece]. Work around the shape, following the directions for edging on page 25. When you have made an edging st in the last st of the foundation ch, break yarn. The right side of Rows 1–48 are left unedged so that the shape can be placed next to Shape 2 and give the appearance of an unbroken shape.
Shape 2: Engine body. Work with pink, purple, and then orange.
Foundation chain: Ch 79 with pink.
Row 1: Insert hk into 2nd ch from hk and make 1 sc, *1 sc in next ch. Repeat from *, ending with 1 sc in last ch. Ch 1, turn [78 sts].
Rows 2–47: Repeat Rows 2–47 of Shape 1, including the color changes. Be sure you have 78 sts in each row of this shape. At the end of Row 47 break yarn.
   Edge with purple along both the top and bottom and the right side. The left side is left unedged.
Shape 3: Train headlight. Work with orange, pink, and then purple.
Foundation chain: Ch 10 with orange.
Row 1: Insert hk into 2nd ch from hk and

157

make 1 sc, *1 sc in next ch. Repeat from *, ending with 1 sc in last ch. Ch 1, turn [9 sts]. *Rows 2–21:* 1 sc in 1st st, *1 sc in next st. Repeat from *, ending with 1 sc in last st. Ch 1, turn. Break yarn after Row 21.

Edge the entire rectangle in pink and then work a 2nd edging row in purple.

Shape 4: Rounded valve cover. This shape is a semicircle and is made following the directions for semicircles in this chapter [page 124]. There are 13 rows in this semicircle and the color changes are as follows:
Foundation chain–Row 3: Purple.
Rows 4–8: Pink.
Rows 9–13: Purple.

This shape requires no edging.

Shape 5: Cabin roof. Work with purple.
Foundation chain: Ch 56 with purple.
Row 1: Insert hk into 2nd ch from hk and make 1 sc, *1 sc in next ch. Repeat from *, ending with 1 sc in last ch. Ch 1, turn [55 sts].
Rows 2–4: 1 sc in 1st st, *1 sc in next st. Repeat from *, ending with 1 sc in last st. Break yarn after Row 4.

Edge entire piece in purple.

Shape 6: Front wheels. Make 2 of this shape. Both front train wheels are semicircles and are made following the directions for semicircles. There are 9 rows in each semicircle. The color changes are as follows:
Foundation chain–Row 2: Purple.
Rows 3–4: Orange.

Row 5: Pink.
Row 6: Orange.
Row 7: Pink.
Rows 8–9: Purple. Break yarn after Row 9.
　These shapes require no edging.

Shape 7: Cattle pusher. Work with pink and then purple.
Foundation chain: Ch 26 with pink.
Row 1: Insert hk into 2nd ch from hk and make 1 sc, *1 sc in next ch. Repeat from *, ending with 1 sc in last ch. Ch 1, turn [25 sts].
Row 2: 1 sc in 1st st, *1 sc in next st. Repeat from *, ending with 1 sc dec over last 2 sts. Ch 1, turn [1 dec—24 sts].
Row 3: 1 sc dec over 1st 2 sts, *1 sc in next st. Repeat from *, ending with 1 sc in last st. Ch 1, turn [1 dec—23 sts].
Row 4: Repeat Row 2.
Row 5: Repeat Row 3.
Row 6: Repeat Row 2.
Row 7: Repeat Row 3.
Row 8: Repeat Row 2.
Row 9: Repeat Row 3.
Row 10: Repeat Row 2.
Row 11: Repeat Row 3.
Row 12: Repeat Row 2.
Row 13: Repeat Row 3.
Row 14: Repeat Row 2.
Row 15: Repeat Row 3.
Row 16: Repeat Row 2.
Row 17: Repeat Row 3.
Row 18: Repeat Row 2.
Row 19: Repeat Row 3.
Row 20: Repeat Row 2.
Row 21: Repeat Row 3.
Row 22: Repeat Row 2. Break yarn [1st left].
　Edge entire piece in purple.

Shape 8: Large back wheel. The wheel is made by following the directions for making a sc circle as given on page 122. There are 28 rnds in this circle, and the color changes are as follows:
Foundation chain–Round 2: Purple.
Rounds 3–4: Orange.
Round 5: Pink.
Rounds 6–7: Orange.
Round 8: Pink.
Rounds 9–10: Orange.
Round 11: Pink.

Rounds 12–13: Orange.
Round 14: Pink.
Rounds 15–16: Orange.
Round 17: Pink.
Rounds 18–19: Orange.
Round 20: Pink.
Rounds 21–28: Purple.
　This shape does not require edging.

Shape 9: Piston rod. Following the directions for making sc circles, make a circle with orange until it has 24 sts. Do *not* break yarn.
Row 1: Ch 1, 1 sc in same st, 1 sc in each of next 6 sts. Ch 1, turn [7 sts].
Row 2: 1 sc dec, 1 sc in each of next 4 sts of previous row, 1 sc dec. Ch 1, turn.
Rows 3–48: 1 sc in each st. Ch 1, turn. Break yarn after Row 48.
　Edge entire piece [including rounded part] in orange.

Shape 10: Front wheel cover plate. Work with orange and then purple.
Foundation chain: Ch 37 with orange.
Row 1: Insert hk into 2nd ch from hk and make 1 sc, *1 sc in next ch. Repeat from *, ending with 1 sc in last ch. Ch 1, turn [36 sts].
Rows 2–20: 1 sc in 1st st, *1 sc in next st. Repeat from *, ending with 1 sc in last st. Ch 1, turn. Break yarn after Row 20.
　Edge the entire piece in purple.

Shape 11: Bottom part of chimney. Work with orange and then purple.
Foundation chain: Ch 11 with orange.
Row 1: Insert hk into 2nd ch from hk and make 1 sc, *1 sc in next ch. Repeat from *, ending with 1 sc in last ch. Ch 1, turn [10 sts].
Row 2: 2 sc in 1st st, *1 sc in next st. Repeat from *, ending with 2 sc in last st. Ch 1, turn [2 incs—12 sts].
Row 3: 1 sc in 1st st, *1 sc in next st. Repeat from *, ending with 1 sc in last st. Ch 1, turn.
Row 4: Repeat Row 2.
Row 5: Repeat Row 3.
Row 6: Repeat Row 2.
Row 7: Repeat Row 3.
Row 8: Repeat Row 2.
Row 9: Repeat Row 3.
Row 10: Repeat Row 2.
Row 11: Repeat Row 3.
Row 12: Repeat Row 2.

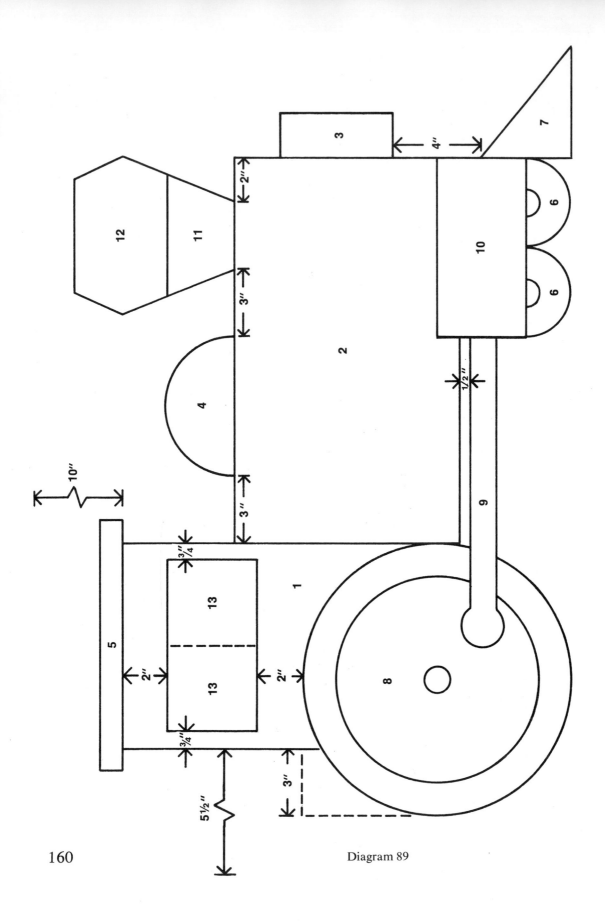

Diagram 89

Row 13: Repeat Row 3.
Row 14: Repeat Row 2.
Row 15: Repeat Row 3.
Row 16: Repeat Row 2.
Row 17: Repeat Row 3.
Row 18: Repeat Row 2.
Row 19: Repeat Row 3.
Row 20: Repeat Row 2.
Row 21: Repeat Row 3.
Row 22: Repeat Row 2 [32 sts].
Row 23: Repeat Row 3. Break yarn.
   Edge the entire piece in purple.

Shape 12: Top part of chimney. Work with pink and then purple.
Foundation chain: Ch 33 with pink.
Row 1: Insert hk into 2nd ch from hk and make 1 sc, *1 sc in next ch. Repeat from *, ending with 1 sc in last ch. Ch 1, turn [32 sts].
Row 2: 1 sc dec, *1 sc in next st. Repeat from *, ending with 1 sc dec. Ch 1, turn [2 decs—30 sts].
Row 3: 1 sc in 1st st, *1 sc in next st. Repeat from *, ending with 1 sc in last st. Ch 1, turn.
Row 4: Repeat Row 2.
Row 5: Repeat Row 3.
Row 6: Repeat Row 2.
Row 7: Repeat Row 3.
Row 8: Repeat Row 2.
Row 9: Repeat Row 3.
Row 10: Repeat Row 2 [22 sts].
Row 11: Repeat Row 3. Break yarn.
   Edge the entire piece in purple.

Shape 13: Cabin windows. Make 2 of this shape with orange, pink, and then purple.
Foundation chain: Ch 15 with orange.
Row 1: Insert hk into 2nd ch from hk and make 1 sc, *1 sc in next ch. Repeat from *, ending with 1 sc in last ch. Ch 1, turn [14 sts].
Rows 2–15: 1 sc in 1st st, *1 sc in next st. Repeat from *, ending with 1 sc in last st. Ch 1, turn. Break yarn after Row 15.
   Edge each square in pink and then make a 2nd edging row in purple. Following the directions for joining on page 29, join the squares along 1 edge.

LINING POCKETS
Shapes 2, 8, 10, 12, and 13 are pockets and therefore require a canvas lining to prevent stretching the crocheted fabric. For each of these shapes cut out a piece of canvas slightly larger than the shape. Turn each edge of the canvas ¼" to the back and pin in place. Turning back the edge of the circular lining for the back wheel requires special handling. With dressmaker's chalk, mark a circle on the back wheel lining ¼" in from the edge. At 1" intervals cut a ¼" slit from the edge of the canvas to the chalk-marked line. Then turn back each 1" piece and pin in place. When all the edges of each piece of lining are pinned in place, baste them with long basting sts. If you are going to handstitch seams, use a backstitch [see page 38]. If you are going to use a sewing machine, set your st gauge to 10 sts to the inch. Sew all edges ⅛" in from the edge of the lining. Place the lining on top of its corresponding shape so that the back side of the lining faces the back side of the crocheted shape. The crocheted piece should extend slightly beyond the piece of canvas lining. Pin the lining to the crocheted piece and then baste the lining to the shape about ½" in from the edge. [If you are handstitching, you can probably eliminate the basting stage.] Thread your needle or your machine with thread that closely matches the color of the crocheted fabric. With the lining facing you, either handstitch or machine st a seam ⅛" in from the edge of the lining on all sides of the shape. Remove basting sts or pins.

ASSEMBLING
To make the canvas back, cut a piece of canvas 38½x34½". Turn each edge ¼" to the back and pin in place. Baste the edges down, remove the pins, and either handstitch or machine st a seam ⅛" in from the edge on all sides. The piece should now measure 38x34". The longer edges are on the top and bottom. Turn the bottom edge 2" to the back, pin in place, and baste. Sew a seam ⅛" in from the original bottom edge. This will make a pocket at the bottom into which you will insert a wood slat to give weight to the bottom of the piece.
   Refer to the diagram for correct placing of each shape. Place Shape 1 on the canvas. Be sure that the semi-edged side of the crocheted piece is on the right. Pin the piece to the canvas and baste in place. Handstitch or machine st the shape to the canvas. When handstitching a

shape to the canvas, pick up the back lp of the edging st of the shape, insert the needle into the canvas, and then come back out thru the back lp of the next edging st. Make at least 1 hand-stitch in each edging st to ensure security; go back and make a 2nd seam by backstitching each shape ¼″ in from the edge, being sure the 2nd seam goes thru the crocheted fabric *and the lining*.

Place Shape 2 on the canvas. The top edging should just meet the edging of Shape 1. Be sure to match the stripes of Shape 2 to the stripes of Shape 1. Pin and baste Shape 2 along the sides and bottom only. Machine st or hand-stitch a seam along the 3 sides about ⅛″ in from the edge.

Shapes 3, 4, and 5 are not pockets and are sewn in place along all edges of each shape.

The two Shape 6's [the front wheels] are sewn in place approximately ¾″ below Shape 2 [the engine body].

Sew Shape 7 in place along all the edges.

Before attaching the large back wheel to the canvas, pin the rounded part of the piston rod to the large wheel. It should be about 4″ in from the edge of the wheel. Sew the rounded part of the piston rod to the wheel, using a blind st [see page 38]. Pin the large wheel in place. The bottom of the wheel should be even with the bottoms of the front wheels. The piston rod should run parallel to and ½″ below the engine body. Sew the wheel in place, leaving an 8″ opening on top to allow entry into the pocket. Pin the piston rod in place and sew a seam along both edges.

Pin Shape 10 [the wheel cover plate] in place, being sure that the right edge is even with right edge of the engine body. The wheel cover plate overlaps the engine body 1″ on top and should overlap the front wheels by ⅛″. Baste and sew the pocket in place along the sides and bottom edge.

Pin both the top and bottom chimney pieces [Shapes 11 and 12] in place. The bottom edge of Shape 11 should be pinned ⅛″ below the point where the top edge of the engine pocket ends. Baste and sew each piece along the top and bottom edges only, leaving the sides open so objects can be slid in and out.

Pin the cabin windows [Shape 13] in place. Baste and then sew a seam along the sides and bottom of the pocket.

Turn the canvas over and place a wood slat along the top, 2″ from the edge. Fold the top of the canvas over the slat and staple in place with a heavy-duty stapler. Place your staples ½″ apart. Place a picture hook 4″ in from each end of the wood slat. Insert the 2nd wood slat into the lower hem pocket and blind st the sides of the pocket closed.

Chapter 5 SHAPE DESIGNS

In nature and in art few forms have the sharp, clearly defined, symmetrical lines of geometry—instead, shapes curve and dip, expand and contract, curl and bulge. Many of our ideas come from the world around us. Color, patterns, and free-form shapes exist everywhere—in a garden or on a city street, from markings on animals to rolling landscapes. Wherever your eye rests there are design ideas. Free-form shapes and designs, often considered difficult, require nothing more than creative manipulations of the basic elements of crochet. Increasing, decreasing, and the basic stitches are the tools of free-form design. We'll describe several methods of constructing shapes and discuss combining shapes into larger designs. But every free-form shape or design is unique; perhaps the most important lesson you can learn is that anything goes—if it works, use it.

Free-Form Shaping

In Chapter 4 you learned about basic geometric shapes. Learning how to make these shapes is not a very difficult task. Everyone knows what a square looks like, for example, so there's common knowledge to begin with. Free-form shapes, however, are a bit different. They are just what you might expect them to be—non-geometric (shape A in Diagram 90 is a good example of what we mean), so by their very nature they pose a teaching problem. We won't be able to give you row-by-row instructions for all free-form shapes simply because they vary so much. We can, however, give you guidelines and point out methods we've devised to create interesting shapes. We've also given you some sample shapes with row-by-row directions; we hope these will serve as a starting point as well as give you an idea of how to go about creating your own free-form shapes. Generally speaking, what is required to make these shapes is the ability to combine your imagination with the skills you've already mastered.

Since there are several methods of crocheting free-form shapes and since they might all be used in the construction of a single shape, you must learn to select the appropriate method or methods for a particular shape.

You can work rows of single crochet back and forth, increasing and decreasing at the beginning and end of each row, so that the edges of your piece expand and contract. Since you build the piece 1 row at a time, your shape is not completely formed until the last row is finished. This is the best method for large, full shapes and allows optimum control over the shaping process. Shape A in Diagram 90 is an example of the shapes that are best formed by working row by row.

A second method establishes the shape of a piece on the first row by increasing or decreasing along the foundation chain. On subsequent rows you increase or decrease just enough to keep the shape lying flat. This method (foundation chain shaping), works best for thin, elongated shapes such as shape B.

Often the best way to form a shape may be to combine two or more geometric or free-form shapes. For instance, if you work triangles around the edge of a circle, you will have a star. Shape C would be made from a triangle and a rectangle, forming an arrow. The top curve of shape D would be made as a foundation chain shape, the teardrop tips worked back and forth.

You can also edge a geometric shape with stitches of varying heights to produce an irregular form. Shape E begins with a simple square. Then it is edged in stitches ranging from slip stitches to treble crochet.

Sometimes the shape you want to make fits quite clearly into one category or another. For example, the letters on the alphabet blocks on page 185 are obviously foundation chain shapes. (For more information about foundation chain shaping, see page 168.) If the shape is more complex, draw it first and try to break it down into its components. Do you see a triangle or an oval, a straight edge or a curve? Is it thin or thick? Are the edges regular or irregular? A complex shape usually has a number of diverse elements that combine to produce a total shape. Begin with any part and add the rest, using whatever techniques will best form each part. You can learn a great deal about the development of free-form design if you crochet a small shape, then allow it to grow organically. You might decide to repeat the same shape over and over again as we did in the Sunburst Place Mats (shown on page 202) and the Indian Motif Afghan (shown on page 182). A single free-form shape can become the focal point of the project when displayed against a simple background—the Trinket Box (shown on page 198) is an example of this approach. Perhaps the shape will suggest other shapes or stitches that might be added to it as you go along. Don't be afraid to rip out a piece and try again, and don't be afraid to experiment—a seemingly complex shape is never more difficult to crochet than any of its simple parts.

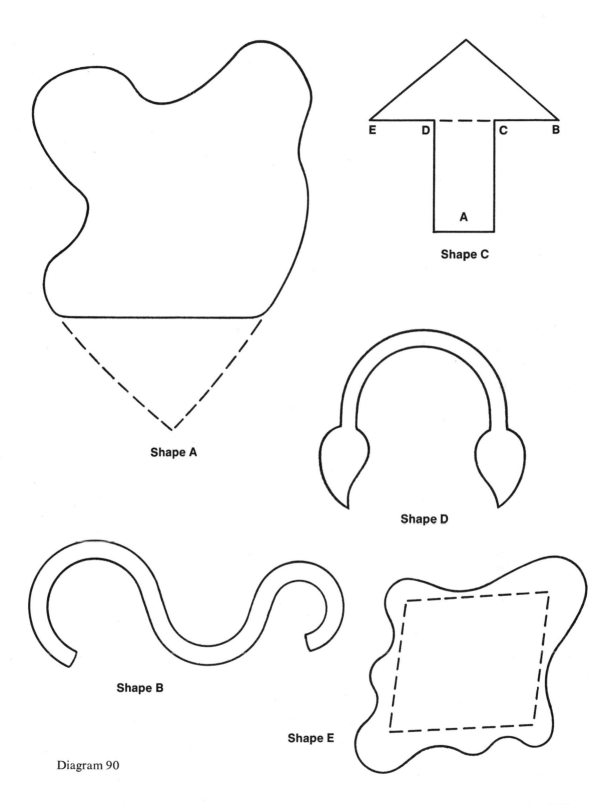

Shape C

Shape A

Shape D

Shape B

Shape E

Diagram 90

165

Row-by-Row Shaping

Before you begin to crochet, draw the desired shape to actual size on a piece of paper. Be sure to draw it carefully because you will use the drawing as a template for the crocheted shape. In other words, every time you finish crocheting a row, you will place the crocheted piece on the drawing to determine whether the row increased or decreased sufficiently. Since all shapes are edged when completed, keep in mind that your final shape will be slightly larger than the drawing.

You need a starting point. This could be a single stitch if your shape starts with a point, or a longer foundation chain if your shape has a straight edge. For a straight edge, make your foundation chain slightly longer than the edge. Work a row of single crochet. Hold the crocheted piece on the drawn form, matching the first row of crocheting to the straight edge of the drawing. If you have made too long a chain don't redo the whole thing. You can instead rip out any stitches that go beyond the length of the straight edge, undo the slip knot of the foundation chain, untie the unnecessary chain stitches, and close up the slip knot. While you are holding the crocheted piece against the drawing, you must decide how to begin the next row. If the drawing narrows on that side, you will need to decrease at the beginning of the next row; if the outline widens, you will have to increase. Now look at the opposite side of the drawing and decide if the end of this next row will need to expand or contract. It's important to remember that both ends of a free-form shape row are not necessarily the same. Next decide how much shaping will be necessary. If the edges of your drawing widen a lot, you can work 2 or even 3 increases at the end of a row. However, more than a few increases in one place will cause your piece to bulge on top. So if the piece widens very quickly, you might try chaining 2 or 3 after you complete the final stitch of a row. Then turn and work 1 or 2 single crochets in each chain stitch, then across the row. On the other hand, if the drawing narrows a

great deal, you can skip the turning chain stitch at the end of the row just completed and the 1st stitch of the previous row after turning your work. You would then make the 1st stitch of the new row in the 2nd stitch of the previous row. Sometimes a piece will narrow so much from one row to the next that you will need to break the yarn at the end of a row, turn your work, reattach the yarn in the stitch closest to the outline, and continue your work. If the outline remains straight, simply work an even row, without making increases or decreases.

After each row match your crocheted piece to the drawing. You will need to remember which is the front side of your work so that you always match the same side of the crochet to the same side of the drawing. A marker pulled through the post of a stitch will help. If after matching your piece to the drawing, you find the shaping isn't right, rip out the row and try again.

If the top of your shape ends in a rounded hump, you can work several increases along the last row, giving a slightly rounded shape to the top, or you can try using stitches of varying heights.

For practice we have given you a sample template (Diagram 91) and row-by-row directions for the shape as well. The shape begins with a straight edge. The superimposed dotted line shows a similar shape started from a point. To make the second shape you would work a triangle starting at the tip, as described on page 126, until its base was the length of the straight edge, then follow the directions as given.

Sample Shape

For this sample we used knitting-worsted–weight yarn and a G hook. The gauge is 5 sts = 1″, 6 rows = 1″.

Foundation chain: Ch 10.

Row 1: Insert hk into 2nd ch from hk and make 1 sc, *1 sc in next ch. Repeat from *,

ending with 1 sc in last ch. **Ch 1, turn** [9 sts].
Row 2: 1 sc in 1st st of previous row, *1 sc in next st. Repeat from *, ending with 2 sc in last st. Ch 1, turn [10 sts].
Row 3: 1 sc in 1st st of previous row, *1 sc in next st. Repeat from *, ending with 1 sc dec. Ch 1, turn [9 sts].
Row 4: 1 sc dec, *1 sc in next st. Repeat from *, ending with 2 sc in last st. Ch 1, turn [9 sts].
Row 5: 2 sc in 1st st of previous row, *1 sc in next st. Repeat from *, ending with 1 sc in last st. Ch 1, turn [10 sts].
Row 6: 2 sc in 1st st of previous row, *1 sc in next st. Repeat from *, ending with 1 sc in last st. *Do not chain,* turn [11 sts].
Row 7: 1 sc in *2nd* st of previous row, *1 sc in next st. Repeat from *, ending with 2 sc in last st. Ch 1, turn [11 sts].
Row 8: 2 sc in 1st st of previous row, *1 sc in next st. Repeat from *, ending with 1 sc dec. Ch 1, turn [11 sts].
Row 9: 1 sc in 1st st of previous row, *1 sc in next st. Repeat from *, ending with 1 sc in last st [no inc—11 sts].
Row 10: 1 sc in 1st st of previous row, *1 sc in next st. Repeat from *, ending with 2 sc in last st [12 sts].
Row 11: 1 sc in 1st st of previous row, 1 sc in each of next 4 sts. Break yarn. Skip 3 sts, re-attach yarn in next st, 1 sc in attaching st, 2 sc in next st, 1 sc in each of last 2 sts. Break yarn, turn [10 sts].
Row 12: Skip 1st 5 sts of previous row and the 3 sts of Row 10. Reattach yarn in 4th st from the end of row, 1 sc in attaching st, 2 sc in next st, 1 sc in each of last 2 sts. *Do not chain,* turn [5 sts].
Row 13: 1 sc in *3rd* st of previous row, 2 sc in next st, 1 sc in next st. Break yarn.

Pull all yarn tails to the back of the piece and hide them, following directions for weaving in yarn tails on page 24.

Edging

Your sample shape will not look complete until it has been properly edged. Before edging, it will have slightly jagged edges, and some of its features—curves, indentations, and corners—

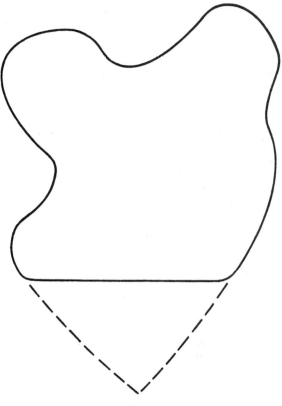

Diagram 91

will be unclear. Use the edging row to smooth off the rough edges and emphasize the overall form. It is probably best to use the same color yarn that you used for the piece itself. In general, you must increase where you want a bulge or curve, decrease where you want an indentation, and work even where you want a straight line. How many increases or decreases you make depends on the shape of your piece. Usually you would make an increase (2 stitches in the side of one row) for a small bulge and a 3-stitch increase (3 stitches in the side of one row) for a sharp angle. For a long curve, make an increase every few stitches. The same rules apply conversely for decreasing.

To edge the sample shape: Attach the yarn in the side of the 1st row of the piece. This will be the lower right-hand corner of the shape.

Make 1 st in attaching st, 1 sc in side of each

167

of next 2 rows, 1 dec [skip next row], 1 sc in side of next row, 2 sc in side of next row, 1 sc in side of next row, 1 dec, 1 sc in side of next row, 2 decs, 3 sc in side of next row, 1 dec [coming to top right of piece], 3 sc in 1st st of last row, 1 sc in each of next 2 sts, 2 sc in next st, 1 sc in side of next row, 1 dec, 1 sc in each of next 3 sts [coming to left-hand top bulges], 1 sc in each of next 4 sts, 3 sc in next st, 1 sc in side of each of next 3 rows, 2 dec, 1 sc in side of each of next 2 rows, 3 sc in side of next row, 1 sc in each of next 6 chs [pick up bottom strand], join with slst to 1st edging st of the piece.

Foundation Chain Shaping

You can establish the shape of a crocheted piece on the very first row. Start with a foundation chain. If you increase on Row 1, the piece will curve, with the foundation chain on the inside of the curve. If you decrease on Row 1, the piece will curve so that the foundation chain is on the outside of the curve. The number of increases and decreases determines how sharply the piece curves—a lot of increasing and decreasing gives a sharper curve. Subsequent rows widen the shape and require only enough increasing and decreasing to keep the shape lying flat.

As an example, we have given directions for a simple S-shape form.

Sample Shape (Curve)

Foundation chain: Ch 29.
Row 1: Insert hk into 2nd ch from hk and make a sc, (2 sc in next ch, 1 sc in next ch) 5 times, (1 sc dec, 1 sc in next ch) 5 times, ending with 1 sc dec over last 2 chs.

Note: If you want to add more rows to the S-shape, you will need to inc once over each inc of the previous row and dec once over each dec of the previous row. However, as you add rows to this shape, the curves move closer and closer to each other, so you are limited in the number of rows you can add and still maintain the integrity of the original shape.

Another type of foundation chain shape is formed by working down a foundation chain, making 1 single crochet in each chain stitch. When you reach the last chain stitch, you increase in it to bring you around the tip and then work back up the bottom strand of the foundation chain, forming a long, slender finger shape.

Sample Shape (Finger)

Foundation chain: Ch 16.
Row 1: Insert hk into 2nd ch from hk and make a sc, 1 sc in each of next 6 chs, ch 11, insert hk into 2nd ch from hk and make a sc, 1 sc in each of next 9 chs, back on original foundation ch, skip 1 ch, 1 sc in each of last 7 chs. Ch 1, turn.
Row 2: 1 sc in each of 1st 7 sts, skip the 1st st at the base of the finger [1 dec], make 1 sc in each st of the finger, make 3 sc in the tip when you reach it, work back up the other side of the finger, inserting your hk thru the bottom strand of each ch, skip the st on the other side of the base of the finger, 1 sc in each of the remaining 7 sts of the previous row. Ch 1, turn.
Row 3: 1 sc in each of the 1st 7 sts of the previous row, skip the st at the base of the finger, 1 sc in each st of the finger until you reach the 3-st group at the tip, work 1 sc in the 1st st of this group, 3 sts in the center st of the group, and 1 st in the 3rd st, continue working 1 sc in each st on the opposite side of the finger, skip 1 st at the base of the finger, 1 sc in each of the remaining 7 sts.

Repeat Row 3 until the finger is the desired size.

Note: As you add rows to the finger, the tip may begin to cup. If this occurs, add a few more incs on either side of the 3-st inc group at the tip.

Shaping by Combination

Many shapes and most designs are combinations of two or more smaller shapes. The shapes may all be of one kind or may each be formed by a different method. Usually you will need to complete one part of the shape, break your yarn, reattach the yarn at the point where you want to start the next portion of the shape, and continue.

Geometric Shapes

The easiest and most familiar shape combinations are geometric. *Stars* are easy to make by combining circles and triangles. Work a circle until you want to begin the points of the star. Count the number of stitches in the circle and break the yarn. Divide the number of stitches in the circle into equal parts. For example, if your circle has 36 stitches, you could divide it into 6 equal parts of 6 stitches each. Attach the yarn in any stitch. Make a stitch in the attaching stitch and in all of the stitches in the 1st segment. For a 36-stitch circle, you would make a single crochet in each of 6 consecutive stitches. Chain 1, turn the piece, and begin to form a triangle from the base, as described on page 126. When you have 1 stitch left, break the yarn. Reattach the yarn in the next stitch in the circle and repeat the process, working 1 triangle off each part of the circle. The 36-stitch circle will have 6 points (triangles) when completed. You control the width of the star points in the same manner as you do any triangle. If you want more star points, just divide the circle into a smaller number of equal parts. For example, you could have made 9 triangles (points) with a 4-stitch base on our 36-stitch circle.

An *arrow* is another interesting geometric shape that requires building one form on another. Look at shape C in Diagram 90. Make the shaft of the arrow, part A, as a simple rectangle, then break the yarn. Make a slip knot and chain the distance from point B to point C, insert your hook into the 1st stitch of the last row of the rectangle at point C, and make a

slip stitch. Slip-stitch across the entire last row of the rectangle, points C to D, then chain off 1 stitch more than you chained from B to C. Turn the piece, insert your hook into the 2nd stitch of the row, and work back across the row, picking up the chain stitches, and the slip stitches of the previous row, from point E to point B. Chain 1, turn. Begin to work a triangle from the base, decreasing 1 stitch each at the beginning and the end of each row. When you have 1 stitch left, break the yarn. Edge the entire shape, following the directions for edging on page 25.

The pattern of *overlapping diamonds* in Diagram 92 is interesting worked as a solid shape or a multicolored design. Work a diamond to any desired size. Break the yarn. Edge this diamond. Reattach the yarn at any point on the upper right side of the diamond, such as point A. Work up the right side of the diamond toward the tip, 3 single crochet in the tip, continue down the left side of the diamond until

Diagram 92

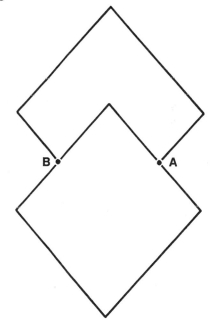

you reach the stitch directly opposite point A—point B on the diagram. Chain 1, turn. On Row 2 work 1 single crochet in each stitch of the previous row. When you reach the center stitch of the 3-single crochet increase group of the previous row, work 3 single crochet in it and continue down the opposite side, working 1 single crochet in each stitch of the previous row, ending with 1 single crochet in the last stitch of the previous row. Chain 1, turn. Repeat Row 2 until the 2nd diamond is the desired size. Break the yarn.

You could continue to add overlapping diamonds to the shape by attaching yarn at the right-hand corner of the previous diamond formed and repeating the pattern. If you change color for each diamond, you get the effect of a diamond behind a diamond.

Geometric and Free-Form Shapes

To make shape D in Diagram 90, first make the curved shape to the desired size using the foundation chain technique; break the yarn. Trace the lines of the curve on a piece of paper and draw the teardrop shapes onto the bottom of each leg of the curve. Hold the curved shape so that the arc is on the bottom and the legs point upward—in its U-shaped position. Attach the yarn in the 1st stitch on the right corner of the right leg and work across the top of the leg, making 1 stitch in each row. When you reach the end of the leg, turn the piece and begin to shape the teardrop, working rows back and forth as described on page 166. Remember to match the teardrop shape to the drawing after each row to ensure proper shaping. Repeat this shape on the other leg of the curve.

You can use this procedure—first forming one shape, tracing it on paper, and then shaping the next shape directly off the shape—for any shape that combines one geometric part and one free-form part.

Geometric Shapes with Irregular Edging

If you can draw a geometric shape inside your free-form shape, you may be able to create the undulating lines you desire by edging your piece with stitches of varying heights. This is a limited technique because it is most successful when you add only one row of edging. Subsequent rows of edging could be added but would require increasing to keep the piece lying flat, and in that case you would probably have more control and better luck working back and forth. Even with this qualification, there are instances where shaping by edging can be quite effective.

First make a geometric shape that just fits within the edges of the free-form shape. Start at any point where the crocheted shape almost touches the edge of the drawing. Attach your yarn and work a slip stitch or single crochet into the piece. Continue to work around the piece, working higher and higher stitches (half double, double, half treble, treble crochets) as the piece widens and lower stitches as it narrows. Work the stitches in sequence—slip stitch, single crochet, half double crochet, double crochet, half treble, and treble crochet. Don't skip, say, from single to double crochet or from treble to half double crochet. If you do, the edge will not be smooth and the taller stitches will buckle. However, you can work as many or as few of each stitch as the design requires before going on to the next higher or lower stitch. Place the piece on the drawing every few stitches, as you did in row-by-row shaping, to check your work.

Developing Shape Designs

Just as individual shapes can be broken down into simple parts, entire designs can be seen in terms of their individual components. Draw your design on a piece of paper, then try to break it down into its component shapes. The drawing needn't be exact and complete—our designs inevitably grow and change as we work —but it should give you an idea of the best way to proceed.

You can start with a central shape and then crochet secondary shapes off it, or you can crochet each individual shape and then lay the shapes next to each other on a flat surface, re-forming the original design. You will be able to see where the edging stitches of one shape meet the edging stitches of the shapes adjoining it.

Connecting Shapes

You can join the shapes by sewing or crocheting them together (see page 29 for sewing crocheted pieces together and for slip-stitching pieces together), picking up and joining opposing pairs of edging stitches wherever one shape meets another.

Edging Connected Shapes

Several shapes can be set off from the rest of the design by edging them before adding more shapes. Look at Diagram 93. It is a drawing of a butterfly wing. If you were to crochet this design, you would first crochet and join shapes A and B, then edge them in another color. The result would be that shapes A and B would appear to be floating inside the edging.

To edge connected shapes think of the connected forms as one large shape, and edge this large shape as you would any free-form shape (see page 25).

Filling In

Working shapes together will sometimes result in spaces left between them. Since the

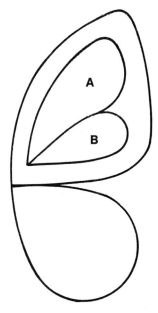

Diagram 93

spaces between various shapes will **not always** be the same, you will need to learn a **general** method for filling in.

Think of the space to be filled in as another shape. If you wanted to fill in the space between points A and C in Diagram 94, you could make either a square or a triangle in reverse.

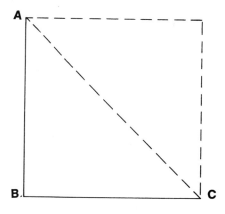

Diagram 94

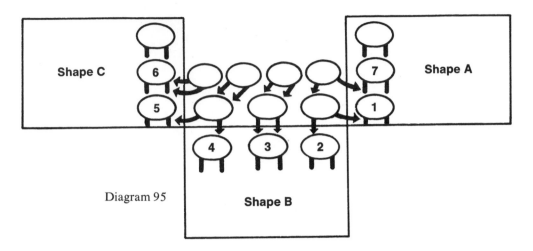

Diagram 95

Shape C

Shape A

Shape B

For a square, attach the yarn at point A, make a single crochet in the attaching stitch, work toward point B, making 1 decrease on both sides of point B, and continue working up toward point C, 1 single crochet in stitch at point C. Chain 1, turn. On Row 2 make 1 decrease at the beginning of the row, 1 decrease directly over point B, and a decrease at the end of the row. Repeat Row 2 until you have 1 stitch left. Break the yarn.

If you eliminate the increases at the beginning and end of each row, you will form a triangle in the space.

If the space to be filled in is more irregular than that in our example, follow any of the shaping techniques we have discussed in this book to make that form, either crocheting it directly onto the bordering edges of the space or crocheting it separately and sewing it into the space.

Row-by-Row: A second method of filling in allows you to fill the space row by row. You begin at the bottom of the space by attaching the yarn in the lower right-hand corner of the area to be filled. Then work across the space, ending the row by making the last stitch in the side of the left-hand corner. On subsequent rows, begin each row by picking up the side of the stitch just above the last row completed. Turn your work, skip the next stitch, and continue making stitches across the row. End each row by making a single crochet decrease in the last stitch of the previous row and the side of the row just above the 1st stitch of the previous row. As you build row upon row, working the 1st and last stitches into the sides of the area to be filled, the rows will eventually become even with the top of the side shapes, thus filling the space.

Look at Diagram 95. The following directions explain how to fill the space between shapes A, B, and C:

Row 1: Attach yarn in side of stitch 1, insert hk into the same st, yo and pull up a lp, insert hk into stitch 2, yo and pull up a lp, yo and close all 3 lps tog, 1 sc in next st. Insert hk into stitch 4, yo and pull up a lp, insert hk into side of stitch 5, yo and pull up a lp, yo and close all 3 lps tog.

Row 2: 1 sc in side of stitch 6. Turn your work. Skip the 1st st, 1 sc in each of next 3 sts, skip next st, 1 sc in side of Row 2A.

Row 3: 1 sc in side of Row 3A. Ch 1, turn your piece. Skip 1st st, 1 sc in each of next 4 sts, 1 sc in side of Row 3B. Break yarn.

Blocking

Building shapes often results in ruffling or cupping over some part of the design. It is a well-known secret that blocking as you work will eliminate these problems. If you notice some curling or ruffling as you build the design, block the piece flat (see page 35 for specific blocking instructions) and then continue crocheting your design. Although you should always shape all the parts of your design carefully, this blocking-as-you-go technique will help ensure a perfectly flat finished design.

Completing Your Project

Imagine that your design is crocheted, connected, and completed—now what? To fit into your home as a blanket, lampshade, planter, or whatever you want, it will need a functional shape. You can sew the entire crocheted design onto a background piece of fabric or crochet that is already the desired shape for your project—definitely the simplest solution. Or you could fill out the piece by working back and forth and in rounds, shaping the piece into a square, circle, rectangle, or whatever final form you wish. If you fill out your design with one color, the design will appear to be sitting on a background of that color.

The first phase of filling out involves evening out the edges of the design. With the background color, fill in any indentations the design may have. Then work one row of edging after another, gradually eliminating the increases and decreases that would be necessary to maintain the shape of the design. You may find it easier to work back and forth along one side of the piece at a time until the piece has relatively regular sides.

After you have evened out the edges of the piece, you can reshape the piece into its final form. The more closely related the form of the design is to the final form, the easier this task will be. If the two forms are quite different, you may need to build pieces onto the design in the background color. If you want a geometric shape, check the directions for making that particular shape in Chapter 4 (pages 122–127) and form your piece so that you will eventually be able to follow those directions. For instance, if you want to make a square, you will need to create four equal sides that meet in right-angled corners.

Once your piece has become a basic shape you can make it as large as you wish.

Crochet as an Art Form

Over the past few years, crochet has grown immensely in both popularity and scope. Young as well as old, men as well as women, are rediscovering a traditional craft. With more and more people picking up hook and yarn and joining our ranks, it is not at all surprising that changes are coming about. New techniques, designs, and uses for crochet have emerged, adding a dimension to our craft that can only be called art. Crocheted free-form sculpture, fantasy creatures, exotic tapestry-stitch wall hangings, miniatures, human figures, and pillows crocheted with "paintings" worked into their surfaces have been displayed in art galleries, craft exhibits, and museums all over the country. Many art schools have already established courses, if not entire curriculums, based on "fiber art," an academic term that refers to working with yarns. Crochet is a strong contender in this new movement. Lately we've been seeing more and more evidence of this new trend in the more traditional crochet outlets, such as women's interest magazines, craft magazines, craft club publications, and the all inclusive craft kits that are sold in retail stores and hobby shops. Both the quantity and the quality of crochet items available today is definitely on the upswing, with no peak in sight.

The fortunate aspect of this profusion of ideas is that the techniques required to make many of these exciting new pieces are nothing more than variations and extensions of the traditional crochet skills taught in this book. When you come right down to it, probably the only essential skill is the development of your imagination. Many of the skills taught in this chapter will give you a solid background in this area. Where you go from here is entirely a matter of individual choice.

Geometric Afghan

Sit down with a pencil, paper, and a ruler and see how diamonds, squares, rectangles, triangles, and their variations work together. Geometric shapes can be fitted together like pieces of a jigsaw puzzle, creating very appealing and unusual patterns. Case in point: this afghan, which we see as a kind of geometric patchwork quilt, attractive and versatile enough to fit any decor.

Materials:
- 50 skeins Unger Britannia in the following amounts: rose #496, 15 skeins; burgundy #557, 15 skeins; dark blue #93, 10 skeins; light blue #541, 10 skeins *or* corresponding amounts of any sport weight yarn

Hook: G

Gauge:
4 sts = 1″, 3 rows = 1″

Finished Size:
60x58″

Instructions:
Motif A: Make 14 of these motifs with burgundy and 14 with rose.
Foundation chain: Ch 2.
Row 1: Insert hk into 2nd ch from hk, make 3 sc. Ch 1, turn [3 sts].
Row 2: 2 sc in 1st st of previous row, 1 sc in next st, 2 sc in last st. Ch 1, turn [5 sts].
Row 3: 1 sc in 1st st of previous row, 2 sc in next st, 1 sc in next st, 2 sc in next st, 1 sc in last st. Ch 1, turn [7 sts].
Row 4: 1 sc in 1st st of previous row, 2 sc in next st, *1 sc in next st. Repeat from *, ending with 2 sc in next-to-last st, 1 sc in last st. Ch 1, turn [9 sts].
Rows 5–12: Repeat Row 4. [You will be increasing 2 sts each row; Row 12 will have 25 sts.]
Row 13: 1 sc in 1st st of previous row, 1 sc dec, *1 sc in next st. Repeat from *, ending with 1 sc dec [over 2nd and 3rd sts from the end], 1 sc in last st. Ch 1, turn [23 sts].
Rows 14–16: Repeat Row 13. [You will be making 2 decs in each row; Row 16 will have 17 sts.]

Rows 17–28: Repeat Row 4. [Row 28 will have 41 sts.]
Rows 29–40: Repeat Row 13. [Row 40 will have 17 sts.]
Rows 41–44: Repeat Row 4. [Row 44 will have 25 sts.]
Rows 45–54: Repeat Row 13. [Row 54 will have 5 sts.]
Row 55: 1 sc in 1st st of previous row, 2 sc decs over last 4 sts [3 sts].
Row 56: (Insert hk into next st, yo and pull up a lp) 3 times, yo and close all 4 lps tog [1 st]. Break yarn.
Motif B: Make 49 of these motifs with dark blue.
Foundation chain: Ch 2.
Row 1: Insert hk into 2nd ch from hk, make 3 sc. Ch 1, turn [3 sts].
Row 2: 2 sc in 1st st of previous row, 1 sc in next st, 2 sc in last st. Ch 1, turn [5 sts].
Row 3: 1 sc in 1st st of previous row, 2 sc in next st, 1 sc in next st, 2 sc in next st, 1 sc in last st. Ch 1, turn [7 sts].
Row 4: 1 sc in 1st st of previous row, 2 sc in next st, *1 sc in next st. Repeat from *, ending with 2 sc in next-to-last st, 1 sc in last st. Ch 1, turn [9 sts].
Rows 5–12: Repeat Row 4. [You will be increasing 2 sts each row; Row 12 will have 25 sts.]
Row 13: 1 sc in 1st st of previous row, 1 sc dec, *1 sc in next st. Repeat from *, ending with 1 sc dec [over 2nd and 3rd sts from the end], 1 sc in last st. Ch 1, turn [23 sts].
Rows 14–22: Repeat Row 13. [Row 22 will have 5 sts.]
Row 23: 1 sc in 1st st of previous row, 2 sc decs over last 4 sts [3 sts].
Row 24: (Insert hk into next st, yo and pull

174

up a lp) 3 times, yo and close all 4 lps tog [1 st]. Break yarn.

Motif C: Make 49 of these motifs with light blue.

Foundation chain: Ch 2.

Row 1: Insert hk into 2nd ch from hk, make 3 sc. Ch 1, turn [3 sts].

Row 2: 2 sc in 1st st of previous row, 1 sc in next st, 2 sc in last st. Ch 1, turn [5 sts].

Row 3: 1 sc in 1st st of previous row, 2 sc in next st, 1 sc in next st, 2 sc in next st, 1 sc in last st. Ch 1, turn [7 sts].

Row 4: 1 sc in 1st st of previous row, 2 sc in next st, *1 sc in next st. Repeat from *, ending with 2 sc in next-to-last st, 1 sc in last st. Ch 1, turn [9 sts].

Rows 5–8: Repeat Row 4. [You will be increasing 2 sts each row; Row 8 will have 17 sts.]

Row 9: 1 sc in 1st st of previous row, *1 sc in next st. Repeat from *, ending with 2 sc in next-to-last st, 1 sc in last st. Ch 1, turn [18 sts].

Row 10: 1 sc in 1st st of previous row, 2 sc in next st, *1 sc in next st. Repeat from *, ending with 1 sc in last st. Ch 1, turn [19 sts].

Row 11: Repeat Row 9 [20 sts].

Row 12: Repeat Row 10 [21 sts].

Row 13: 1 sc in 1st st of previous row, *1 sc in next st. Repeat from *, ending with 1 sc dec over 2nd and 3rd sts from the end, 1 sc in last st. Ch 1, turn [20 sts].

Row 14: 1 sc in 1st st of previous row, 1 sc dec, *1 sc in next st. Repeat from *, ending with 1 sc in last st. Ch 1, turn [19 sts].

Row 15: Repeat Row 13 [18 sts].

Row 16: Repeat Row 14 [17 sts].

Row 17: 1 sc in 1st st of previous row, 1 sc dec, *1 sc in next st. Repeat from *, ending with 1 sc dec [over 2nd and 3rd sts from the end], 1 sc in last st. Ch 1, turn [23 sts].

Rows 18–22: Repeat Row 13. [Row 22 will have 5 sts.]

Row 23: 1 sc in 1st st of previous row, 2 sc decs over last 4 sts [3 sts].

Row 24: (Insert hk into next st, yo and pull up a lp) 3 times, yo and close all 4 lps tog [1 st]. Break yarn.

EDGING

Motif A is edged following the directions for edging shapes in this chapter [see page 167]. Whenever an inc row follows a dec row, an indentation is formed. Be sure to emphasize this indentation by making a dec whenever you reach this indented part of your shape. Motifs B and C are edged as you would any simple shape, making a 3-st inc at all points [corners].

ASSEMBLING

Block each piece according to the directions on page 35 before assembling.

You will first need to attach pairs of Motif C tog along the straight side. Do this following the directions on page 29. Then arrange all the motifs in the pat shown in the photograph on page 175 and join motifs tog.

Victorian Lampshade

A beautiful hanging lamp is often just the final touch needed for a well decorated room. Our Victorian Lampshade is an amalgam of several crochet techniques: a simple circle, finger-shaped spokes, and oval motifs sewn in between the spokes. It is fitted over a frame that can be easily constructed with coat hangers. You could make this shade in any color that harmonizes with your room.

Materials:
- 1 skein Golden Fleece Xochitl, white (yarn A)
- 2 skeins (each 10 oz.) Bucilla Paradise, white #428 (yarn B)
- 3 skeins Bucilla Wondersheen (each 400 yds.), white #11 (yarn C)
- 2 oz. ¼" rayon ribbon, off white (yarn D)
- 6 wire coat hangers
- #28 copper wire
- 1 light socket
- Cord with plug, brass ring, and chain

Hook: G

Gauge:
4 sts = 1", 2 rows = 1"

Finished Size:
12¾" diameter, 38" circumference
   Note: Work with 2 strands of yarn B; work with 3 strands of yarn C.

Instructions:
Shade: Work with yarns A, B, and D.
Foundation chain: Ch 15 with yarn A, insert hk into 15th ch from hk and make a slst to join the ring tog.
Round 1: Ch 3 [= 1st dc of rnd], work 23 dc over ch into ring, join last dc of rnd to 1st dc of rnd with slst into top ch of ch-3 [24 sts].
Round 2: Ch 3, 1 dc in same st [top ch of ch-3 of previous rnd], *2 dc in next st. Repeat from *, ending with 2 dc in top ch of ch-3 of rnd. Break yarn [48 sts].
Round 3: Attach yarn B, ch 1, 1 sc in 1st st of previous rnd, *1 Hazelnut st in next st, 1 sc in next st. Repeat from *, ending with 1 Hazelnut in last st, join with slst to 1st sc of rnd. Break yarn.

Round 4: Attach yarn A, ch 3, 1 dc in each of next 2 sts, *2 dc in next st, 1 dc in each of next 3 sts. Repeat from *, ending with 2 dc in last st, join with slst to top ch of ch-3. Break yarn [12 incs—60 sts].
Round 5: Attach yarn B, repeat Round 3. Break yarn.
Round 6: Attach yarn D, ch 1, 1 sc in 1st st of previous rnd, 1 sc in each of next 11 sts, *ch 26, insert hk into 2nd ch from hk and make 1 sc, 1 sc in each of next 24 chs [1 finger formed], 1 sc in each of next 12 sts. Repeat from *, ending with 1 sc in each of last 12 sts, join with slst to 1st sc of rnd [5 fingers formed].

   Note: Rounds 7–10 are worked with the fingers as a part of the rnd. The 13th st of Round 7 will actually become the 1st st of the 1st finger.
Round 7: Ch 1, 1 hdc in 1st st of previous rnd, 1 hdc in next st, *1 sc in each of next 6 sts, 1 hdc in each of next 2 sts, 1 dc in next st, 1 dc dec over next 2 sts, 1 hdc in each of next 2 sts, 1 sc in each of next 20 sts, 3 sc in next st [tip of finger], 1 sc in each of next 19 sts, 1 hdc in each of next 2 sts, 1 dc in next st, 1 dc dec over next 2 sts, 1 hdc in each of next 2 sts. Repeat from *, ending with 1 dc dec, join with slst to 1st hdc of rnd. Break yarn.
Round 8: Attach yarn C, ch 1, 1 hdc in 1st st of previous rnd, 1 hdc in next st, *1 sc in each of next 6 sts, 1 hdc in each of next 2 sts, 1 dc in next st, 1 dc dec over next 2 sts, 1 hdc in each of next 2 sts, 1 sc in each of next 39 sts [around finger], 1 hdc in each of next 2 sts, 1 dc in next st, 1 dc dec over next 2 sts, 1 hdc in each of next 2 sts. Repeat from *, ending with 1 dc dec, join with slst to 1st hdc of rnd.
Round 9: Ch 1, 1 hdc in 1st st of previous rnd, 1 hdc in next st, *1 sc in each of next 6

sts, 1 hdc in each of next 2 sts, 1 dc in next st, 1 dc dec over next 2 sts, 1 hdc in each of next 2 sts, 1 sc in each of next 18 sts, 2 sc in next st, 1 sc in next st, 2 sc in next st, 1 sc in each of next 17 sts, 1 hdc in each of next 2 sts, 1 dc in next st, 1 dc dec over next 2 sts. Repeat from *, ending with 1 dc dec, join with slst to 1st hdc of this rnd. Break yarn.

Round 10: Attach yarn D, ch 1, 1 sc in 1st st of previous rnd, 1 sc in next st, *1 sc in each of next 8 sts, 1 sc dec in next 2 sts, 1 sc in each of next 42 sts, 1 sc dec in next 2 sts. Repeat from *, ending with 1 sc dec, join with slst to 1st sc of rnd. Break yarn.

Motif pattern: Work with yarns A, B, C, and D.
Foundation chain: Ch 13 with yarn A.

Note: Round 1 is worked down the foundation ch, around the bottom of the ch, and back up the other side of the ch, picking up the bottom strand of each foundation ch st.

Round 1: Insert hk into 2nd ch from hk and make 1 sc, 1 sc in each of next 10 chs, 3 sc in last ch [around tip of ch], 1 sc in each of next 11 chs, 3 sc in last ch [actually the bottom strand of the 1st ch st you picked up], join with slst to 1st sc of rnd.

Round 2: Ch 1, 1 sc in 1st st of previous rnd, 1 sc in each of next 11 sts, 3 sc in next st, 1 sc in each of next 13 sts, 3 sc in next st, 1 sc in next st, join with slst to 1st sc of rnd. Break yarn.

Round 3: Attach yarn B, ch 1, 1 sc in 1st st of previous rnd, *1 Hazelnut st in next st, 1 sc in each of next 2 sts,* repeat from * to * 3 times, (1 Hazelnut in next st, 1 sc in next st) 2 times, repeat from * to * 3 times, (1 Hazelnut in next st, 1 sc in next st) 3 times, join with slst to 1st sc of rnd. Break yarn.

Round 4: Attach yarn D, ch 1, 1 hdc in 1st st of previous rnd, 1 hdc in each of next 12 sts, 2 hdc in each of next 4 sts, 1 hdc in each of next 11 sts, 2 hdc in each of next 4 sts, join with slst to 1st hdc of rnd. Break yarn.

Round 5: Attach yarn C, ch 1, 1 sc in 1st st of previous rnd, *ch 2, skip 1 st, 1 sc in next st. Repeat from *, ending with 1 sc in next-to-last st, ch 2, join with slst to 1st st of rnd.

Round 6: Ch 2, 1 sc in 1st ch-2 sp, (ch 2, 1 sc in next ch-2 sp) 6 times, ch 2, 1 sc in next ch-2 sp, ch 2, 1 sc in same ch-2 sp as previous st [1 inc], ch 2, 1 sc in next ch-2 sp, ch 2, 1 sc in next ch-2 sp, ch 2, 1 sc in same ch-2 sp as previous st [1 inc], (ch 2, 1 sc in next ch-2 sp) 7 times, ch 2, 1 sc in next ch-2 sp, ch 2, 1 sc in same ch-2 sp as previous st [1 inc], ch 2, 1 sc in next ch-2 sp, ch 2, 1 sc in next ch-2 sp, ch 2, 1 sc in same ch-2 sp as previous st [1 inc], join with slst to top ch of 1st ch-2 of rnd.

Round 7: Ch 2, 1 sc in 1st ch-2 sp of previous rnd, *ch 2, 1 sc in next ch-2 sp. Repeat from *, ending with 1 sc in last ch-2 sp, join with slst to 1st ch-2 sp of rnd. Break yarn.

Round 8: Attach yarn D, ch 1, 3 hdc in 1st ch-2 sp of previous rnd, *3 hdc in next ch-2 sp. Repeat from *, ending with 3 hdc in last ch-2 sp, join with slst to 1st hdc of rnd. Break yarn.

Round 9: Attach yarn A, ch 1, 1 sc in 1st hdc of previous rnd, *1 sc in next st. Repeat from *, ending with 1 sc in last hdc, join with slst to 1st sc of rnd. Break yarn.

Repeat the motif pat 4 more times to make a total of 5 motifs.

ATTACHING MOTIFS

Each motif is sewn into place between 2 fingers of the shade. Pin the motif to the shade so that the center oval of the motif is vertical and parallel to the fingers on either side. You will notice that only the top two thirds of the motif sts meet the sts of the shade. The bottom third of the motif will hang freely. The motif will be joined by sewing, as explained in Chapter 1 [page 29]. For this project we prefer sewing the motif to the shade thru the center strands of opposing pairs of sts.

EDGING AND FRINGE

When all motifs are sewn into place, attach yarn B to any edge st not used for joining the motifs to the shade. Edge the lampshade in sc sts, picking up only those sts that were not used for joining.

Following the directions for making fringe on page 37, count the number of edging sts just made and make 5″ fringe with yarn A for each edging st [1 strand of fringe per st]. After the shade is attached to the frame, you can even the fringe out with a pair of scissors, or if you like the effect, leave it uneven.

MAKING FRAME

Straighten all 6 coat hangers by hand. Cut 1 hanger to measure 42″ and the remaining 5 to measure 21″. Bend the 42″ wire into a circle 12¾″ in diameter and 38″ in circumference [there should be a 4″ overlap where the ends of the wire meet]. Wrap this overlapping area tightly with the copper wire, forming the circle base. Bend a 1″ lp on both ends of one of the 21″ pieces of wire. Then bend the entire piece into a semicircle so that a radius from the center of the arc to the center of the semicircle measures 6″ [see Diagram 96]. Do the same with the remaining 4 pieces of wire. Attach each of the 5 wire semicircles to the circle frame by placing each lp around the wire of the base. Sp the semicircles so that each lp end is 4″ away from the next lp end. When the semicircles are in place, squeeze the lp ends tightly in place with pliers and secure them by wrapping each lp end with the copper wire. Wrap the point of intersection at the top with the copper wire. Screw the brass ring into the light socket and secure it to the point of intersection with the copper wire so that the

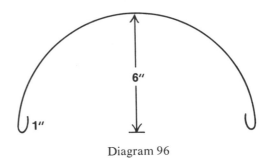

Diagram 96

socket hangs inside the frame. The wire plug will be pulled out thru the top of the frame and shade.

Slide the shade onto the frame so that the center of each finger and the center of each motif rests on a wire arm of the frame. Using 1 strand of yarn C, pull pieces of yarn thru to the inside of the frame close to an arm. Tie a tight knot. Repeat this procedure along each inside arm of the frame until the shade is tied securely in place. Turn the shade upside down and hide all loose yarn tails according to the directions in Chapter 1 [page 23].

Use a low-wattage bulb in the socket.

Crocheting with Different Yarns

When we created the Victorian Lampshade we found particular pleasure in working with different yarns of the same color. The various tones of white complement the textural differences of the yarn. The oval motifs are further enhanced by the soft white background.

Working with different yarns has been part of our crocheting method for many years. The most important factor to consider is the gauge of each yarn or combination of yarns (see page 34 for more about gauge). If you were to use a yarn of one thickness for a row and then switch to a yarn of another thickness for the next, the new row might not be the same length as the preceding row. For example, let's say that you started out with a yarn that gave a 3-stitch-to-the-inch gauge. You would then need to know the gauge of the new yarn so that you could work a proper number of stitches in the

new row. Your new yarn might be thin and give a 6-stitch-to-the-inch gauge. In that case, you would need to work 2 stitches of the new yarn into each stitch of the old yarn.

Another alternative would be to work with a combination of thinner yarns that would, when worked together, give the same gauge as the thick yarn. This way you would not have to alter the number of stitches in the new row.

Once you understand the relationship between yarn and gauge, you can play with and interchange yarns freely. We have found that working rows of basic stitches in various yarn combinations has eliminated the need for more complex designs or fancy stitch patterns and, therefore, recommend this for beginning crocheters. It's a good way to make projects look unique. It also reflects individuality since the combinations are your own choice.

Indian Motif Afghan

Repeated central motifs are the hallmark of the famous Bokhara rug designs of the Middle East; these designs served as inspiration for our afghan. Basically, the motifs are simple shapes, filled in and joined together. The decorative border is crocheted in Tapestry stitch, which is alternated with rows of single crochet. You can add or eliminate rows of motifs to alter the size of the afghan.

Materials:
- 18 skeins Paternayan Tapestry yarn in the following amounts: burgundy #841, 5 skeins; purple #614, 1 skein; tan #472, 10 skeins; brown #957, 2 skeins; black #050, 1 skein *or* corresponding amounts of any worsted weight yarn

Hook: G

Gauge:
5 sts = 1", 5 rows = 1"

Finished Size:
60x54" (approximately)

Instructions:
Note: The motif is broken down into its component parts, beg with the main rectangle and then followed by the top and bottom squares, filling in, and finally the edging for the motif.

Main rectangle: Work with burgundy.

Foundation chain: Ch 16.

Row 1: Insert hk into 2nd ch from hk and make 1 sc, *1 sc in next ch. Repeat from *, ending with 1 sc in last ch. Ch 1, turn [15 sts].

Rows 2–4: 1 sc in 1st st, *1 sc in next st. Repeat from *, ending with 1 sc in last st. Ch 1, turn.

Note: Rows 5 and 6 require changing to purple mid-row for 9 sts and back to burgundy for the last 3 sts of the row. This is done in the same way as changing colors for Tapestry st worked back and forth, as explained on pages 84–86. Be sure to carry the unused color along the back of the piece, working over the unused yarn as you make your sc. On Row 6 [back of the piece] hold the unused yarn in front of the head of the st and work over the strand of unused yarn as you make your sc. When you break off the purple yarn, be sure to leave a 3–4" tail to be woven in later on. To facilitate the written directions for these rows we refer to a st worked in burgundy as Bsc and a st worked in purple as Psc.

Rows 5 and 6: 1 Bsc in each of 1st 3 sts. 1 Psc in each of next 9 sts, 1 Bsc in each of last 3 sts. Ch 1, turn. Break off purple yarn after Row 6.

Rows 7–10: Repeat Row 2, using burgundy.

Rows 11 and 12: Repeat Row 5. Break off purple yarn after Row 12.

Rows 13–16: Repeat Row 2, using burgundy.

Rows 17 and 18: Repeat Row 5. Break off purple yarn after Row 18.

Rows 19–22: Repeat Row 2, using burgundy.

Rows 23 and 24: Repeat Row 5. Break off purple yarn after Row 24.

Rows 25–28: Repeat Row 2, using burgundy. Break yarn.

Weave all loose yarn tails into the back of the piece, following the directions on page 24.

Top and bottom squares: Hold the piece so that the front faces you, with Row 1 on the bottom edge and Row 28 on top. Skip the 1st 5 sts of the last row [Row 28] and attach burgundy yarn in the next st. This is the 1st st of the square and will be referred to as such in the written directions.

Row 1: 1 sc in same st, 1 sc in each of next 4 sts. Ch 1, turn [5 sts].

Rows 2–4: 1 sc in 1st st, 1 sc in each of next 4 sts. Ch 1, turn. Break yarn after Row 4.

Turn the piece upside down. The front should still be facing you, with the foundation ch and Row 1 of the main rectangle on top. Depending on which strands you picked up from the foundation ch, you will have 1 or 2

unused strands remaining. Use the remaining strands to work your square. Skip the 1st 5 chs and attach burgundy in the next st.

Repeat Rows 1–4 of the square. Break yarn after Row 4.

Weave in loose yarn tails.

You will now fill in the sp formed by the top and bottom edges of the main rectangle and the sides of the small squares.

Top right space: Hold the piece so that the front faces you. Attach tan yarn in the upper right-hand corner. This is the 1st st of the last row of the main rectangle.

Row 1: 1 sc in attaching st, 1 sc in each of next 3 sts, insert hk into next st, yo and pull up a lp, insert hk into side of Row 1 of the same square, yo and pull up a lp [3 lps on hk], insert hk into side of Row 2 of the square and pull up a lp, yo and close all 4 lps tog, 1 sc in side of each of next 2 rows of the square. Ch 1, turn.

Note: The remaining 3 filling-in rows refer only to those sts worked in the previous row.
Row 2: 1 sc in 1st st, (insert hk into next st, yo and pull up a lp) 3 times, yo and close all 4 lps tog, 1 sc in each of last 3 sts. Ch 1, turn.
Row 3: 1 sc in each of 1st 2 sts, (insert hk into next st, yo and pull up a lp) 3 times, yo and close all 4 lps tog. Ch 1, turn.
Row 4: (Insert hk into next st, yo and pull up a lp) 3 times, yo and close all 4 lps tog. Break yarn.

Top left space: Attach tan yarn in the left side of Row 4 of the top square.
Row 1: 1 sc in attaching st, 1 sc in side of next row, insert hk into side of next row, yo and pull up a lp, insert hk into side of next row [Row 1 of the square], yo and pull up a lp, insert hk into the 11th st of the last row of the main rectangle, yo and pull up a lp, yo and close all 4 lps tog, 1 sc in each of last 4 sts. Ch 1, turn.

The remaining filling-in rows refer only to those sts worked in the previous row.
Row 2: 1 sc in each of 1st 2 sts, (insert hk into next st, yo and pull up a lp) 3 times, yo and close all 4 lps tog, 1 sc in each of last 2 sts. Ch 1, turn.
Row 3: 1 sc in 1st st, (insert hk into next st, yo and pull up a lp) 3 times, yo and close all 4 lps tog, 1 sc in last st. Ch 1, turn.
Row 4: (Insert hk into next st, yo and pull up a lp) 3 times, yo and close all 4 lps tog. Break yarn.

Turn the piece upside down. The front should still be facing you. Attach tan yarn in the upper right-hand corner. This will be the 1st foundation ch on the left side of Row 1 of the main rectangle.

Repeat Rows 1–4 of the top right space. Break yarn.

Attach tan yarn in the left side of Row 4 of the small square and repeat Rows 1–4 of the top left space. Break yarn.

Weave all loose yarn tails into the back of the piece.

You now have a rectangular piece.

In order to widen the rectangle the long sides will be edged in dc and the short sides in sc. Hold the piece so that the front faces you and the short edges are on top and bottom. Attach tan yarn in the center st of the small square.
Round 1: 1 sc in attaching st, 1 sc in each of next 2 sts, *work 3 sc across the top of the left fill-in sp [which should bring you to the corner], in the corner work (1 sc, 1 hdc, 1 dc), work 3 dc down the side of the filled-in sp, 1 dc in the side of each of the next 29 rows of the main rectangle [this includes the foundation ch of the main rectangle], 3 dc along the side of the next filled-in sp [which should bring you to the next corner]. In the corner work (1 dc, 1 hdc, 1 sc), 3 sc along the top of the filled-in sp,* 1 sc in each of the 5 sts of the small square. Repeat from * to *, ending with 1 sc in each of the last 2 sts, join rnd with slst.
Round 2: Ch 1, 1 sc in same st, 1 sc in each of next 7 sts, in next st work (1 sc, 1 hdc, 1 dc), *1 dc in each of next 35 sts, in next st work (1 dc, 1 hdc, 1 sc),* 1 sc in each of next 15 sts, in next st work (1 sc, 1 hdc, 1 dc). Repeat from * to *, ending with 1 sc in each of last 7 sts, join with slst.
Round 3: Ch 1, 1 sc in same st, 1 sc in each of next 9 sts, in next st work (1 sc, 1 hdc, 1 dc), *1 dc in each of next 35 sts, in next st work (1 dc, 1 hdc, 1 sc),* 1 sc in each of next 19 sts,

in next st work (1 sc, 1 hdc, 1 dc). Repeat from * to *, ending with 1 sc in each of last 9 sts, join rnd with slst. Break yarn.

Repeat 29 more times for a total of 30 motifs.

ATTACHING MOTIFS

The motifs are joined following the directions for joining on page 29. There should be 5 rows, with 6 motifs in each row. The rows of motifs are joined tog in the same way as the individual motifs.

Decorative border: After all motifs are joined, attach tan yarn in any st on the edge of the piece.

Round 1: 1 sc in same st, 1 sc in each st on the edge of the piece, work 3 sc in corner when you reach it, continue around piece, joining the last st to the 1st st of the rnd with a slst.

Note: Rounds 2–4 of the border are worked in Tapestry st [see pages 84–86 for instructions for working Tapestry st in 1 direction]. The colors used are tan and brown: A tan st is designated Tsc and a brown st is designated Bsc.

Round 2: 1 Tsc in each of 1st 5 sts, *1 Bsc in each of next 5 sts, 1 Tsc in each of next 5 sts. Repeat from * to end. [When you reach the 3-sc group in the corners, work 3 sc in the center st in whichever color is required in that st—that is, if the center st of the 3-sc group is the 4th tan st of the 5-st group, work 3 sc in it in tan and then make a tan st in the next st and continue. Your corners will therefore have more than 5 sts of a color group, but the pat will appear to be even.] Join last st to 1st st with slst.

Note: Since everyone's 1st edging rnd may not have the same number of sts, you may not be able to end the rnd with 5 sts of 1 color. If that occurs, inc or dec in the last few sts of the rnd so that there are 5 sts of 1 color at the end of the rnd. For example, if your rnd ends with 3 tan sc, add 2 sts in tan or make 2 decs with brown.

Round 3: 1 Tsc in each of 1st 4 sts, *1 Bsc in each of next 5 sts, 1 Tsc in each of next 5 sts, (for corner see Note on previous rnd). Repeat from *, ending with 1 Tsc in last st, join with slst.

Round 4: 1 Tsc in each of 1st 3 sts, *1 Bsc in each of next 5 sts, 1 Tsc in each of next 5 sts, (for corner see Note on Round 2). Repeat from *, ending with 1 Tsc in each of last 2 sts, join with slst. Ch 1. Break yarn.

Round 5: Ch 1 with tan, 1 sc in 1st st, 1 sc in each st of the previous rnd. When you reach a corner, work 3 sc in the center st of the 3-sc group. Join rnd with slst.

Round 6: Repeat Round 5, using black.

Round 7: Repeat Round 5, using purple.

Round 8: Repeat Round 5, using black.

Round 9: Repeat Round 5, using burgundy.

Round 10: Repeat Round 5, using black.

Round 11: Repeat Round 5, using tan.

Round 12: Repeat Round 2.

Round 13: Repeat Round 3.

Round 14: Repeat Round 4.

Round 15: Repeat Round 5, using tan.

Round 16: Repeat Round 5, using black.

Round 17: Repeat Round 5, using purple.

Round 18: Repeat Round 5, using black.

Round 19: Repeat Round 5, using burgundy.

Round 20: Repeat Round 5, using black.

Rounds 21–23: Repeat Round 5, using tan.

Round 24: Using brown, 1 Shrimp st in 1st st, 1 Shrimp st in each st, work 3 Shrimp sts in the center st when you reach the 3-sc group in each corner, join last st to 1st st with slst. Break yarn.

Weave in all loose yarn tails.

If necessary, block the piece to the correct finished size [see page 35].

Alphabet Seat Blocks

Want to learn the ABC's of foundation chain shaping? Constructing these giant alphabet blocks will give you the experience you need to master this method of free-form design. Light, soft, and washable, the blocks are marvelous stools or footrests, and we've found that children, not content with such ordinary uses, turn them into wonderful fantasy towers, castles, caves, and houses.

Materials:
- 15 skeins of Aunt Lydia's Rug Yarn in each of the following colors: medium blue, light blue, coral, buttercup (yellow), orchid *or* corresponding amounts of any bulky cotton-acrylic blend
- Foam rubber slabs for stuffing
- White glue

Hook: I or J or smallest hk you can comfortably use (see Instructions)

Gauge:
3 sts = 1″, 3 rows = 1″ (or smaller gauge if possible—see instructions)

Finished Size:
1 square (1 side of 1 block) = 11½″ before edging, 12″ after edging. Each block is a 12″ cube with 6 sides.
   Note: Materials given are for five 12″ cubes.

Instructions:
For each side follow the directions for making a sc square by working back and forth [see page 123].The squares that form the sides of the blocks must be as stiff as possible. The smaller the gauge, the stiffer your fabric will be. [More sts per inch makes a smaller gauge; see page 34.] Find the smallest gauge you can produce, then make a ch of the length necessary to produce a piece approximately 11½″ wide or a bit smaller. Remember that you can make extra ch sts, then simply cut off the ch sts you don't need after you have completed the 1st row and then pull on the tail to retighten the end. Work rows of sc back and forth until the piece reaches approximately 11½″ square. Break yarn. Edge the piece in sc, according to the directions for edging on page 25. For 5 blocks, make 6 squares of each color—30 squares all together.

As you make the letters, you will follow directions that, although not complicated, could be confusing if the terms are not clear. Right and left always mean your right and left. The top and bottom of a letter are the top and bottom as the letter would be written. So the point of an A is the top and the point of a V is the bottom. A one-sided post, used in letters such as P and D, is straight on 1 side and has curves on the top and bottom on the other side. The curved side is the outside edge and always faces left, so the inside is always on the right. You are not told to edge the top and bottom of every letter; you can do so if you wish. There are 26 letters and 5 colors. Make 5 letters of each color and the extra letter of any color you like. Instructions for the letters are grouped by similarities in construction.

V

Foundation chain: Ch 54.
Row 1: (1 sc, ch 3, 1 dc, 1 hdc) all in 2nd ch from hk, 1 sc in each of next 25 sts, 5 sc in next st, 1 sc in each of next 25 sts, (1 hdc, 1 dc, 1 htr) in last ch. Break yarn.
Row 2: With front of piece facing you, attach yarn in exposed lp or lps of foundation ch opposite last 3-st group. 1 slst in 1st ch and in each of next 24 chs, skip next 2 sts, 1 hdc in each of next 25 chs, 1 hdc dec over last ch and side of 1st sc of Row 1. Break yarn.

A

Repeat directions for V. Then with front of piece facing you and point away from you,

attach yarn in 11th st from bottom on the inside of the left leg [point is top of letter]. Ch 6, 1 sc in 11th st from bottom on opposite leg, 1 sc in 12th st from bottom, do *not* ch or turn, 1 sc in each ch, 1 slst in 12th st from bottom on left leg. Break yarn.

W

Repeat directions for making the V [see page 185]. For 2nd piece of the W, start out by chaining 42.

Row 1: (1 sc, ch 3, 1 dc, 1 hdc) all in 2nd ch from hk, 1 sc in each of next 25 chs, 5 sc in next ch, 1 sc in each of next 14 chs. Break yarn.

Row 2: Attach yarn in exposed lp or lps of foundation ch opposite last sc. 1 slst in 1st ch and in each of next 12 chs, skip next 2 sts, 1 hdc in each of next 25 chs, 1 hdc dec in last ch and side of 1st sc of Row 1.

Note: W is the widest letter, stretching all the way across the square when sewn.

M

Repeat directions for V. This V is the center of the M. For the left leg, start by chaining 22.

Row 1: With back of V facing you and point of V toward you, make 1 sc in 5th st from top on outside of left bar of V, 1 slst in 4th st from top [st directly before 3-st group], turn, do *not* ch, 1 sc in 1st ch and each of next 18 chs, 1 hdc in next ch, 1 dc in next ch, 1 htr in last ch. Break yarn.

Row 2: Attach yarn in exposed lp or lps of foundation ch opposite last htr. 1 slst in 1st st and in each of next 21 sts. Break yarn.

eg of the M, attach yarn in
p on outside leg of V with
u; ch 23.

) in 2nd ch from hk [= 1
h, 1 hdc in next ch, 1 sc in
s, 1 slst into 4th st from top

facing you, attach yarn in
of ch opposite the 18th sc of
ttaching st and in every ch.

Ch 28.

nd ch from hk, (1 sc in next
hdc, 1 dc, 1 htr) in last ch.

yarn in exposed lp or lps
ch opposite last htr. 1 hdc in
of next 24 sts (1 hdc, 1 dc,
eak yarn.

ost, start by chaining 22.
of center bar facing you and
make 1 sc in 3rd hdc before
t in 2nd hdc from end, ch 1,
h and in each of next 17 chs,
1 dc in next ch, 1 htr in next

yarn in exposed lp or lps of
opposite last htr. 1 slst in 1st
next 21 chs. Break yarn.
t post, start by chaining 22.
ter bar facing you and sc row
on top, attach in 3rd sc from left of center bar.
Repeat directions for left post.

I

Foundation chain: Ch 24.
Row 1: 1 sc in 2nd ch from hk and in each of
next 22 chs. Ch 1, turn.
Row 2: 1 sc in 1st st, ch 3 [= 1 htr], 1 dc in
next ch, 1 hdc in next ch, 1 sc in each of next
17 chs, 1 hdc in next ch, 1 dc in next ch, 1 htr
in last ch. Break yarn.
Row 3: With front of piece facing you, attach
yarn in exposed lp or lps of foundation ch opposite last htr. Repeat Row 2.

H

Repeat directions for I to make 2 posts. The
bar that connects the 2 posts is closer to the
top of the letter than the bottom. Decide which
ends of the posts are the tops. Then with the
fronts of the posts facing you, attach the yarn
in the 11th st from the top on the inside of the
left post. Ch 8, 1 sc in 11th st from top on the
inside of the opposite post, 1 sc in 10th st from
the top, do *not* ch or turn, 1 sc in each ch, 1 slst
in 10th st from top of left post. Break yarn.

K

Repeat directions for I.
To start top bar, decide which end of the
post is the top. With front facing you, attach
yarn in 16th st from the top, ch 20. 1 htr in 5th
ch from hk, 1 dc in next ch, 1 hdc in next ch, 1
sc in each of next 11 chs, 1 slst in last ch, 1 slst
in 14th st from top of post. Break yarn.
To do the bottom bar, ch 12. With front facing you, 1 sc in exposed lp or lps of 3rd foundation ch from post of top bar, 1 sc in 4th st from
post, ch 1, turn, 1 sc in each of next 12 chs, ch
4, turn, 1 htr in 1st st, 1 dc in next st, 1 hdc in
next st, 1 sc in each of next 9 sts, 1 slst in 5th
ch from post of top bar. Break yarn.

L

Repeat Rows 1 and 2 of I to make a one-
sided post.
With front of post facing you, attach yarn
in exposed lp or lps of ch opposite last htr for
the bar. Ch 10, 1 sc in 2nd ch from hk, ch 3
[= 1 htr], 1 dc in next ch, 1 sc in each of next
6 chs, 1 slst in 3rd st from bottom of post. Reattach yarn in side of the head of the last htr of
Row 2 of post, 1 sc in sides of sts along bottom
of post, 1 sc in each ch along bottom of bar.
Break yarn.

E

Repeat Rows 1 and 2 of I to make a one-
sided post. Repeat bar of L on bottom of post.
For the top bar, ch 8. With back of post facing

187

you, make 1 sc in top st of inside of post, 1 sc in next st of post, ch 1, turn, 1 sc in each of 1st 5 chs, 1 hdc in next ch, 1 dc in next ch, 1 htr in last ch. Break yarn. With front facing you, attach yarn in side of head of last htr, 4 sc in side of htr, 3 sc in corner, 1 sc in each ch of bar and in sides of sts along top of post. Break yarn.

Counting only the exposed lps of the foundation ch along the inside of the post and with the front facing you, attach yarn in 9th st from the top bar for the center bar. Ch 9. 1 sc in 2nd ch from hk, ch 3 [= 1 htr], 1 dc in next ch, 1 hdc in next ch, 1 sc in each of next 4 chs, 1 slst in 7th st from the bottom of the top bar. Break yarn.

F

Repeat Rows 1 and 2 of I directions [see page 187] for a one-sided post. Repeat directions for the top bar and center bar of E [see above].

P

Repeat Rows 1 and 2 of I directions for a one-sided post.

With back facing you, attach yarn in top st of inside [right side] for post for the curve. Ch 21, 1 sc in 11th st from top of post, 1 sc in 12th st from top of post, ch 1, turn, 1 sc in 1st ch, [**1 sc in each of next 3 chs, 1 hdc in next ch, 1 hdc inc in next ch,** (1 dc in next ch, 1 dc inc in next ch) 4 times, 1 dc in next ch, repeat from ** to ** *in reverse order*], ending with 1 sc in last ch, 1 sc in each of the 5 sts across the top of the post.

B

Repeat directions for P.

With back of the piece facing you, attach the yarn in 2nd st from the post on the bottom of the top curve of P to make the bottom curve of B. Ch 19. 1 sc in 2nd st from bottom of post, 1 sc in 1st ch, repeat within brackets in P from top curve, ending with 1 hdc in next st, 1 sc in next st, 1 sc in 3rd st from post of top curve.

R

Repeat directions for P. To do the bottom post of the R, start by chaining 11.

With front facing you, attach yarn to 4th st from post on bottom of top curve, 1 sc in 5th st, 1 sc in 6th st. Ch 1, turn.
Row 1: 1 sc in 1st ch and in every ch. Ch 1, turn.
Row 2: (1 sc, ch 3, 1 dc) in 1st st, 1 hdc in next st, 1 sc in each of next 10 sts, 1 sc dec in last ch and 7th st from post on top lp. Break yarn.

D

Repeat Rows 1 and 2 of I to make a one-sided post.

With front facing you, attach yarn in 3rd st from top on inside, 1 sc in 2nd st from top, 1 sc in top st, ch 1, turn, 1 sc in 1st sc, ch 43 for the curve. With back facing you, 1 sc in 3rd st from bottom on inside of post, 1 sc in 2nd st from bottom, 1 sc in bottom st, do not ch, turn, 1 hdc in 1st ch, **1 sc in each of next 3 chs, 1 sc inc in next ch, (1 hdc in each of next 2 sts, 1 hdc inc in next st) 2 times,** (1 dc in next st, 1 dc inc in next st) 5 times, 1 dc in next st, repeat from ** to ** *in reverse order*, 1 sc in side of 1st st.

O

Foundation chain: Ch 61. (1 sc in each of next 3 sts, 1 sc inc in next st) 2 times, **1 hdc in each of next 3 sts, 1 hdc inc in next st, 1 dc in each of next 13 sts, 1 hdc inc in next st, 1 hdc in each of next 3 sts,** (1 sc inc in next st, 1 sc in each of next 3 sts) 2 times, 1 sc inc in next st, repeat from ** to **, 1 sc inc in last st, join to 1st st with slst. Break yarn.

Note: Both the O and the Q should be tilted slightly when you sew them in position so that the thin part of the top is to the left of center.

Q

Repeat directions for O.

To do the bar of the Q start by chaining 14.

1 hdc in 2nd ch from hk and next 3 chs, 1 sc in each of next 6 chs, 1 slst in next ch, 1 slst dcc over next 2 sts. Break yarn.

Note: The tail portion of the letter should lie under the circle on the right bottom of the square when you sew it on. Curve the bottom of the bar to make a slight curl before pinning the Q in place.

C

Foundation chain: Ch 49.
Row 1: 1 sc, ch 3 in 2nd ch from hk [= 1 htr], 1 dc in next ch, 1 hdc in next ch, 1 sc inc in next ch, 1 sc in each of next 3 chs, 1 sc inc in next ch, repeat from ** to ** of directions for O twice, 1 sc inc in next ch, 1 sc in each of next 3 chs, 1 sc inc in next ch, 1 sc in each of next 3 chs, 1 sc inc in next ch, 1 sc in each of next 4 chs, 1 dc in last ch. Break yarn.

Note: The bottom part of the C should extend a little bit further to the right than the top part does when you position and sew it in place.

G

Foundation chain: Ch 58. Repeat directions for C until final sc of C, then 1 sc in each of next 5 chs, 3 dc in next ch, 1 dc in each of next 7 chs, 1 htr in last ch. Break yarn. Edge last htr with 5 sc to emphasize bar.

U

Foundation chain: Ch 60.
Row 1: 1 sc in 2nd ch from hk, ch 3 [= 1 htr], 1 dc in each of next 19 chs, 1 hdc inc in each of next 3 sts, 1 sc inc in next ch, 1 sc in each of next 9 chs, 1 sc inc in next ch, 1 sc in each of next 17 sc, 1 hdc in next st, 1 dc in next st, 1 htr in last st. Break yarn.
Row 2: Attach yarn in exposed lp or lps of ch opposite last htr, 1 slst in 1st ch and in each of next 19 chs, 1 slst dec over next 2 sts, 1 slst in each of next 2 chs, 1 slst dec, 1 slst in each of next 7 chs, 1 slst dec, 1 slst in each of next 2 chs, 1 slst dec, 1 slst in each of last 20 chs. Break yarn.

J

Foundation chain: Ch 39.
Row 1: 3 dc in 4th ch from hk, 1 hdc in next ch, (1 sc in each of next 3 chs, 1 sc inc in next ch) 2 times, 1 hdc in each of next 2 chs, 1 dc in each of next 21 chs, 1 htr in each of next 2 chs, 1 tr in last ch. Break yarn.
Row 2: With front facing you, attach yarn in exposed lp or lps opposite tr, 1 slst in 1st st and in each of next 24 sts, skip next st [opposite inc of Row 1], 1 slst in each of next 3 sts, skip next st, 1 slst in each of next 5 sts. Break yarn.

Note: Keep the post of the J straight, up to the 1st inc when you sew it in position.

S

Foundation chain: Ch 48.
Row 1: 1 sc, ch 3 [= 1 htr] in 2nd ch from hk, 1 dc in next st, 1 hdc in next st, 1 sc inc in next st, 1 sc in each of next 7 sts, 1 sc inc in next st, 1 hdc in each of next 3 sts, 1 hdc inc, 1 dc in each of next 14 chs, 1 hdc dec, 1 hdc in each of next 3 sts, 1 sc dec, 1 sc in each of next 7 sts, 1 sc dec, (1 hdc, 1 dc, 1 htr) in last ch.
Row 2: With front facing you, attach yarn in exposed lp of foundation ch opposite last htr, 1 slst in 1st 3 sts, 1 slst inc in next st, 1 slst in each of next 7 chs, 1 slst inc in next st, 1 slst in each of next 3 chs, 1 slst inc in next ch, 1 slst in each of next 14 chs, 1 slst dec over next 2 sts, 1 slst in each of next 2 sts, 1 slst dec, 1 slst in each of next 6 chs, 1 slst dec, 1 slst in each of last 4 sts. Break yarn.

T

Foundation chain: Ch 22.
Row 1: 1 sc in 2nd st from hk and in each ch [21 sc], ch 1, turn, 1 sc in 1st st, ch 3 [= 1 htr], 1 dc in next st, 1 hdc in next st, 1 sc in each of next 18 sts. Break yarn.
Row 2: With front facing you, attach yarn in exposed lp or lps opposite last st. Repeat Row 1 *in reverse order,* ending with 1 htr in last ch. Break yarn.

To do top bar, ch 18.

Row 1: 1 sc in 2nd ch from hk, ch 3 [= 1 htr], 1 dc in next ch, 1 sc in each of next 11 chs, 1 hdc in next ch, 1 dc in next ch, 1 htr in last ch. Break yarn.

Row 2: With front facing you, attach yarn in side of head of last htr, 4 sc in side of htr, 3 sc in corner, 1 sc in each exposed lp or lps of foundation ch, 3 sc in next corner, 4 sc in side of htr. Break yarn.

Note: The post should lie under the top bar when the T is sewn in place.

Y

Foundation chain: Ch 30.

Row 1: (1 sc, ch 3, 1 dc, 1 hdc) in 2nd ch from hk, 1 sc in each of next 11 chs, one 3-st sc dec over next 3 sts, 1 sc in each of next 11 chs, 1 hdc in next st, 1 dc in next st, 1 htr in next st. Break yarn.

Row 2: Attach yarn in exposed lp or lps of foundation ch opposite the final htr of Row 1. 1 sc in 1st st and in each of next 14 sts, ch 13, 1 slst in 2nd ch from hk and in each of next 11 chs, skip next ch and 1st st on left fork, 1 sc in each of next 11 sts, 1 sc dec over next 2 sts. Break yarn.

X

To do the thick bar, ch 31.

Row 1: (1 sc, ch 3, 1 dc, 1 hdc) in 2nd ch from hk, 1 sc in each of next 27 chs, 1 sc dec over last 2 sts. Break yarn.

Row 2: With front facing you, attach yarn in exposed lp or lps of foundation ch opposite last sc, (1 sc, ch 3, 1 dc, 1 hdc) all in 1st st, 1 hdc in each of next 27 sts, 1 hdc dec over last 2 sts. Break yarn.

To do the thin bar, ch 31.

Row 1: 1 sc in 2nd ch from hk and in each of next 29 chs, (1 hdc, 1 dc, 1 htr) in last st. Break yarn.

Row 2: With front facing you, attach yarn in exposed lp or lps of foundation ch opposite last htr, 1 slst in 1st st and in each of next 29 sts, (1 sc, 1 hdc, 1 dc) in last st.

Note: The top of the thick bar should point to the left when the X is sewn in place.

Z

To do the center post, ch 28.

Row 1: 1 sc in 2nd ch from hk and in each of next 25 chs, (1 hdc, 1 dc, 1 htr) in last st. Break yarn.

Row 2: With front facing you, attach yarn in exposed lp or lps opposite last htr, 1 hdc dec over 1st 2 sts, 1 hdc in each of next 25 sts, (1 dc, 1 htr) in last st. Break yarn.

For the top bar, with front facing you, attach yarn in 1st st of Row 1, ch 14, (1 sc, ch 3) in 2nd st [= 1 htr], 1 dc in next st, 1 hdc in next st, 1 sc in each of next 8 sts, 1 sc dec in 9th ch and 3rd st from top of post. Break yarn.

With front facing you, attach yarn in 1st st of Row 2, ch 16, (1 sc, ch 3) in 1st st [= 1 htr], 1 dc in next st, 1 hdc in next st, 1 sc in each of next 10 sts, 1 sc dec in next ch and 3rd st from bottom of post for the bottom post. Break yarn.

SEWING

Divide the squares into individual blocks. Each block should have 6 squares: 2 squares of each of 3 colors—1 color for the top and bottom, 1 color for the front and back sides, and 1 color for the other sides. [The front and back sides are those at the top and bottom of the letter on the top of the block.] Four of the blocks will have a letter on each of the 5 visible surfaces and a blank square on the bottom. The 5th block will have letters on every side. The letters on the blocks in the photograph on page 186 are matched to the squares in the following way: The color of the square on top of the block is the color of the letters on all 4 sides. [That is, if the square on top is yellow, the letters on the 4 sides are also yellow.] The letter on the top square is the color of the front and back side squares. [That is, if the front and back side squares are light blue, the letter on top is light blue as well.] However, you can match squares and letters any way you like.

The care you take in placing the letters on the squares will determine the success of the project, so take some time pinning each letter carefully to its square before you sew it on. Turn the squares sideways so that the ridges formed by the rows of sc run vertically, then use these ridges both to center the letter on the squares and as guidelines for vertical posts such as those in D, T, E, and so on. Center the letter on the square. There should be about an inch above and below each letter and several inches on each side. The letters will look best if they are stretched a bit, so pin the inside of the post first, then stretch the outside edge before you pin it. Make sure that the bottoms of all the straight bars or posts, including those of slanting bars, such as in the A, K, and R, are exactly horizontal. Curves should be stretched and pinned first along the foundation ch and then along the outside. Curves connected to posts, such as the curves in the B, D, and P, usually lie flat along the very top and bottom of the letter. For example, the curve of the letter D is flat for about an inch on both top and bottom after it leaves the post. The axis of a circular letter, such as O, Q, C, or G, should be tilted slightly to the left. That is, the thin part at the top tilts slightly toward the top left-hand corner of the square. Corners that are not right angles, such as those in the V, W, and N, should be stitched tog on the inside edges.

After a letter is placed as you want it, thread a large blunt tapestry needle with yarn the same color as the letter and sew the letter to the square using the st described in overlap joining on page 30. Begin with the inside edge, stretching and shaping the letter as you sew. Check your work every so often—it's easy to pull out a few sts and correct a curve if necessary.

After all the letters are sewn on, block the squares, following the directions on page 35.

ASSEMBLING

You could make a muslin cube and stuff it, according to the directions for making pillows [page 36]. However, foam rubber slabs cut to size and glued tog are much easier. Foam rubber can be found in many thicknesses. Buy whatever thickness you want and cut the foam rubber into enough 12x12″ squares to equal 13″ in height. For example, 1 block would need 3 pieces of foam cut 4x12x12″ and 1 piece cut 1x12x12″. Glue the pieces into a stack to make a cube 12x12x13″ [the extra inch keeps it firm when used as a seat].

Join 5 squares of each of the blocks [top and 4 sides] on the front side with a slst thru the 2 inside lps only, according to the directions on page 29. Insert a foam rubber block into each of the crocheted covers [the extra inch should be on the top or bottom]. With the tapestry needle, sew the bottom square of the cover to the sides thru the 2 inside lps.

Making an Alphabet Afghan

If you want to decorate a child's room with alphabet letters but don't want to make the blocks, why not make an alphabet afghan?

The first step is to plan it out. Here's a suggestion: Make thirty-six 9-inch squares and arrange them in 9 rows of 4 squares each. (This will fit a standard 35x75-inch twin bed.) Next plan the color scheme. You may want to alternate the colors of each square or to make each square the same color, using contrasting yarns for the letters. Following the directions for single crochet squares worked in rows (page 123), crochet the squares with a worsted yarn and an F or G hook.

Using the same hook and yarn, crochet the letters (pages 185–190). Place each letter on a square in the arrangement of your choice. We did it this way: A and B on the first row of squares; C–F on the second; G and H on the third; I–L on the fourth; M and N on the fifth; O–R on the sixth; S and T on the seventh; U–X on the eighth; and Y and Z on the ninth. Leave the 10 empty squares blank or crochet free-form or geometric shapes and sew them on. Attach letters to squares with tapestry needle and thread, using the method described in overlap joining on page 30. Edge and block each square (see pages 25 and 35). Join the squares (page 29) and edge the entire afghan in same or contrasting yarn.

Desk Accessories

An illusion of depth is created when you work concentric shapes in graduated shades of one color. We used this effect in a set of desk accessories that are as appropriate for a modern chrome and glass desk as they are for an old rolltop. Our desk pad base was made with a piece of Plexiglas but heavy-duty cardboard or leather would work equally well and give a different look.

Materials:
- 50 oz. Borgs i Lund linen in the following amounts: black, 10 oz.; dark gray, 10 oz.; medium gray, 10 oz.; light gray, 10 oz.; raspberry, 10 oz. *or* corresponding amounts of any linen that gives a comparable gauge
- One 10x24″ piece black Plexiglas
- One 12-oz. juice can
- One tube of Duco Cement

Hook: #1 steel

Gauge:
6 sts = 1″, 6 rows = 1″

Finished Size:
Blotter sides, 19x5″
Pencil holder, size of 12-oz. juice can

Blotter

Instructions:
Main rectangle: The central raspberry rectangle of the blotter is made by following the directions for rectangles worked from the center on page 127. Make a foundation ch of 81 sts with raspberry. Work the rectangle for 3 rnds. Break yarn.

You will now begin to build 4 concentric rectangles around each end of the main raspberry rectangle. To do so you will need to pick up sts from the main rectangle and, as you add rectangles, the preceding rectangle. To avoid confusion we will refer to a st of the main rectangle as Mst. All other st directions refer to sts of the previous row [on the previous concentric rectangle].
Concentric Rectangle 1: Hold the main rectangle with the front facing you and the short sides on the top and bottom. Locate the 3-sc group in the upper right-hand corner. Counting the 1st sc of this group as 1, count back down the right side of the main rectangle 26 sts and attach the black yarn in the 26th st.
Row 1: 1 sc in same st, 1 sc in each of next 25 sts, 3 sc in next st, 1 sc in each of next 5 sts, 3 sc in next st, 1 sc in each of next 26 sts. Ch 1, turn.
Row 2: 1 sc in 1st st, 1 sc in each of next 26 sts, 3 sc in next st, 1 sc in each of next 7 sts, 3 sc in next st, 1 sc in each of next 27 sts. Break yarn.
Row 3: Hold the piece so that the front faces you. Attach the black yarn in the center st of the 3-sc group in the right-hand corner, 1 sc in same st, 1 sc in each of next 10 sts. Break yarn.
Concentric Rectangle 2: Attach dark gray yarn in the Mst just before the Mst in which you attached the black yarn to make the 1st concentric rectangle.
Row 1: Insert hk in same st, yo and pull up a lp, insert hk into side of 1st black sc of Row 1 of the 1st concentric rectangle, yo and pull up a lp, yo and close all 3 lps tog, 3 sc in side of next sc [this is the last sc of Row 2 of the 1st concentric rectangle—the 3-sc group you just made will bring you around the corner of the 1st concentric rectangle], 1 sc in each of the next 28 sts. [The 28th st just made is actually the side of the corner sc of Row 2 of the 1st concentric rectangle. From now on this side st will be treated as a regular st in the directions.] 3 sc in next st, 1 sc in each of next 9 sts, 3 sc in next st, 1 sc in each of next 28 sts, 3 sc in next st, insert hk into side of last sc of Row 1 of 1st concentric rectangle, yo and pull up a lp, insert hk into next Mst, yo and pull up a lp, yo and close all 3 lps tog, 1 sc in next Mst. Ch 1, turn.

Row 2: Skip 1st st, 1 sc dec over next 2 sts. Break yarn. Reattach yarn in the center st of the 3-sc group in the upper right-hand corner, 1 sc in same st, 1 sc in each of next 12 sts. Break yarn. Skip 30 sts, reattach yarn in next st, 1 sc in same st, 1 sc in next st, 1 sc dec over next st and next Mst, 1 sc in next Mst. Ch 1, turn.

Row 3: Skip 1st st, 1 sc in each of next 2 sts, 3 sc in next st, 1 sc in each of the next 31 sts, 3 sc in next st, 1 sc in each of next 11 sts, 3 sc in next st, 1 sc in each of the next 31 sts, 3 sc in next st, 1 sc dec over next st and next Mst. Change to medium gray yarn, following the directions for changing yarn mid-row on page 23, 1 sc in next Mst. Ch 1, turn.

Concentric Rectangle 3: Work with medium gray.

Row 1: Skip 1st st, 1 sc in each of next 2 sts, 3 sc in next st, 1 sc in each of next 33 sts, 3 sc in next st, 1 sc in each of next 2 sts, 1 sc dec over next st and next Mst, 1 sc in next Mst. Ch 1, turn.

Row 2: Skip 1st st, 1 sc in each of next 5 sts. Break yarn. Skip next 35 sts, reattach yarn in next st, 1 sc in same st, 1 sc in each of next 16 sts. Break yarn. Skip next 35 sts, reattach yarn in next st, 1 sc in same st, 1 sc in each of next 2 sts, 1 sc dec over next st and next Mst, 1 sc in next Mst. Ch 1, turn.

Row 3: Skip 1st st, 1 sc in each of next 2 sts, 3 sc in next st, 1 sc in each of next 37 sts, 3 sc in next st, 1 sc in each of next 15 sts, 3 sc in next st, 1 sc in each of next 37 sts, 3 sc in next st, 1 sc in each of next 3 sts, 1 sc dec over next st and next Mst. Change to light gray yarn, 1 sc in next Mst. Ch 1, turn.

Concentric Rectangle 4: Work with light gray.

Row 1: Skip 1st st, 1 sc in each of next 5 sts, 3 sc in next st, 1 sc in each of next 39 sts, 3 sc in next st, 1 sc in each of next 17 sts, 3 sc in next st, 1 sc in each of next 39 sts, 3 sc in next st, 1 sc in each of next 3 sts, 1 sc dec over next st and next Mst, 1 sc in next Mst. Ch 1, turn.

Row 2: Skip 1st st, 1 sc in each of next 6 sts. Break yarn. Skip next 41 sts, reattach yarn in next st, 1 sc in same st, 1 sc in each of next 20 sts, break yarn. Skip next 41 sts, reattach yarn in next st, 1 sc in same st, 1 sc in each of next 5 sts, 1 sc dec over next st and next Mst, 1 sc in next Mst. Ch 1, turn.

Row 3: Skip 1 st, 1 sc in each of next 5 sts, 3 sc in next st, 1 sc in each of next 43 sts, 3 sc in next st, 1 sc in each of next 19 sts, 3 sc in next st, 1 sc in each of next 43 sts, 3 sc in next st, 1 sc in each of next 4 sts, 1 sc dec over next st and next Mst. Break yarn.

Weave in all loose yarn ends on the back of the piece [see page 24].

Hold the piece so that the front faces you and the end with concentric rectangles is on the right. Repeat Concentric Rectangles 1–4 on the left side of the main rectangle.

FILLING IN

Following the directions for row-by-row filling in [page 172], fill in the sps between the rectangles on both sides of the main rectangle. There are 12 sts on each side of the main rectangle in between the 2 shapes and 7 sts on either side. These 7 sts are treated as if they were the sides of 7 rows. After filling in both sps, break yarn.

EDGING

The shape is now a rectangle and needs to be edged. Following the directions for edging on page 25, edge the piece with black yarn in sc. Make 3 rows of edging sts. Break yarn.

Lip: Holding the piece so that the concentric rectangles are on the top and bottom, attach black yarn in the upper right-hand corner, make 1 Post st [see directions on page 43] in the same st, 1 Post st in each st, when you reach a corner make 3 Post sts in the center of the 3-sc group. Continue to make 1 Post st in each st until you reach the lower right-hand corner. Break yarn.

Top and bottom flaps: Work with black.

Row 1: Reattach black yarn in upper right-hand corner. Make 1 sc in same st, 1 sc in each st until you reach the center st of the 3-sc group of the upper left-hand corner, make 1 sc in this st. Ch 1, turn.

Rows 2–8: 1 sc in 1st st, *1 sc in next st. Repeat from *, ending with 1 sc in last st of previous row. Ch 1, turn. Break yarn after you have completed Row 8.

Turn the piece upside down [the front is

still facing you] and repeat Rows 1–8 of the flap. Weave in all loose yarn tails [see directions on page 24].

Repeat entire procedure to make another blotter piece for the other edge [see photograph on page 193].

Block both blotter pieces to the appropriate size, following the directions for blocking on page 35. When blocking, always be sure that the edges of your piece are absolutely straight.

ASSEMBLING

Hold 1 long piece with the short ends on the top and bottom. The lip should be on the long right-hand side and the flaps are on the top and bottom. Place the piece on the right-hand side of the plastic so that the lip lies over the edge on the right-hand side and the top and bottom flaps overlap the plastic by about 2″. When you have the piece placed correctly, turn the plastic piece over, holding the crocheted piece in place. Spread a thin line of Duco cement along the edge and the top and bottom. Press the flaps over, pulling them to make the piece taut, and hold in place on the back side. Repeat along the edge. Allow the piece to dry. Repeat on the left-hand side with the 2nd long crocheted piece.

Pencil Holder

Instructions:

Main Rectangle: Make a rectangle from the center following directions for rectangles on page 127. Make a foundation ch of 33 sts with the raspberry yarn. Work the rectangle for 3 rnds.

Concentric Square 1: Work with black.

Row 1: Holding the piece with the front facing you, and the short edges on the top and bottom, locate the 3-sc group in the upper right-hand corner—counting the 1st st of this group as 1, count back down the right-hand side for 5 sts and attach black linen in the 5th st, 1 sc in same st, 1 sc in each of next 4 sts, 3 sc in next st, 1 sc in each of next 5 sts, ch 1, turn.

Row 2: 1 sc in each of 1st 6 sts, 3 sc in next st, 1 sc in each of next 7 sts, 3 sc in next st, 1 sc in each of next 6 sts. Break linen. Turn.

Row 3: Skip the 1st 7 sts, attach yarn in the next st, 1 sc in same st, 1 sc in each of next 10 sts. Break linen.

Concentric Square 2: Work with dark gray.

Row 1: Attach yarn in the Mst just before the one in which you attached the black linen on Row 1 of Concentric Square 1, insert hk into same st, yo and pull up a loop, insert hk into side of Row 1 of Concentric Square 1, yo and pull up a lp, yo and close all 3 lps tog, 3 sc in side of Row 2 of Concentric Square 1. [This will turn the corner of the black square; therefore we will not make a st thru the head of the 1st black st. Instead, skip the 1st st and make the next st in the 2nd st of the 2nd black row.] 1 sc in each of next 7 sts, 3 sc in next st, 1 sc in each of next 9 sts, 3 sc in next st, 1 sc in each of next 7 sts, 3 sc in next st, 1 sc dec over side of next row and next Mst, 1 sc in next Mst, ch 1, turn.

Row 2: Skip 1st st, 1 sc in each of next 3 sts, break linen. Skip next 10 sts, reattach yarn in next st, 1 sc in same st, 1 sc in each of next 12 sts, skip next 9 sts, reattach yarn in next st, 1 sc in next st, 1 sc dec over next st and next Mst, 1 sc in next Mst, ch 1, turn.

Row 3: Skip 1st st, 1 sc in next st, 3 sc in next st, 1 sc in each of next 11 sts, 3 sc in next st, 1 sc in each of next 11 sts, 3 sc in next st, 1 sc in each of next 11 sts, 3 sc in next st, 1 sc in next st, 1 sc dec over next st and next Mst, complete st with medium gray linen, 1 sc in next Mst, ch 1, turn.

Concentric Square 3: Work with medium gray.

Row 1: Skip 1st st, 1 sc in each of next 3 sts, 3 sc in next st, 1 sc in each of next 13 sts, 3 sc in next st, 1 sc in each of next 13 sts, 3 sc in next st, 1 sc in each of next 13 sts, 1 sc in next st, 1 sc dec over next st and next Mst, 1 sc in next Mst, ch 1, turn.

Row 2: Skip 1st st, 1 sc in each of next 4 sts, break linen. Skip next 15 sts, reattach yarn in next st, 1 sc in same st, 1 sc in each of next 16 sts, break linen. Skip next 15 sts, reattach yarn in next st, 1 sc in same st, 1 sc in each of next 3 sts, 1 sc dec over next st and next Mst, 1 sc in next Mst, ch 1, turn.

Row 3: Skip 1st st, 1 sc in each of next 3 sts, 3 sc in next st, 1 sc in each of next 17 sts, 3 sc in next st, 1 sc in each of next 15 sts, 3 sc in next st, 1 sc in each of next 17 sts, 3 sc in next st, 1 sc in each of next 2 sts, 1 sc dec over next st and next Mst, complete last st with light gray linen, 1 sc in next Mst, ch 1, turn.

Concentric Square 4: Work with light gray.

Row 1: Skip 1st st, 1 sc in each of next 4 sts, 3 sc in next st, 1 sc in each of next 19 sts, 3 sc in next st, 1 sc in each of next 17 sts, 3 sc in next st, 1 sc in each of next 19 sts, 3 sc in next st, 1 sc in each of next 4 sts, 1 sc dec over next st and next Mst, 1 sc in next Mst, ch 1, turn.

Row 2: Skip 1st st, 1 sc in each of next 17 sts, break linen. Skip next 21 sts, reattach yarn in next st, 1 sc in same st, 1 sc in each of next 20 sts, break linen. Skip next 21 sts, reattach yarn in next st, 1 sc in same st, 1 sc in each of next 4

sts, 1 sc dec over next st and next Mst, 1 sc in next Mst, ch 1, turn.

Row 3: Skip 1st st, 1 sc in each of next 5 sts, 3 sc in next st, 1 sc in each of next 23 sts, 3 sc in next st, 1 sc in each of next 19 sts, 3 sc in next st, 1 sc in each of next 23 sts, 3 sc in next st, 1 sc in each of next 5 sts, 1 sc dec over next st and next Mst. Break linen.

Fill in the space in between the squares following directions for row-by-row filling in on page 172. Edge the piece with 3 rows of black.

ASSEMBLING

Spread Duco cement around top and bottom of can. Fold the pencil holder around the can so that the 2 long edges of the crocheted piece meet the top and bottom of the can evenly. Press and hold. Allow to dry.

Crocheting with Beads

Just as they are used to ornament craft objects, beads can be used to enhance crochet items as well. The method is simple. It's just a matter of stringing the beads onto your yarn and moving them into place as you crochet.

Crochet your piece until you have completed the row just before the first row to be beaded. Break the yarn and end off. String the beads for the row you are about to crochet onto the uncrocheted yarn, trying not to string too many or too few. (If you end up having to add more beads in the middle of the row, you will have to break the uncrocheted yarn and slide the additional beads onto it. The fabric will be weakened and the knots may make it difficult to slide the beads.) The fastest way to string the beads is to thread a needle with the uncrocheted yarn and insert it through the holes in the beads. If the needle won't pass through the hole, dip the yarn tip in clear, fast-drying glue. After it has dried, use the hardened tip of yarn as you would a needle and insert it through the hole in the bead.

With the back side of the piece facing you, attach the beaded yarn and begin to crochet. Make single crochets, sliding the beads down toward the skein and out of the

way as you go. When you want to add a bead, pull it along the yarn until it is resting snugly next to the stitch just completed; make a single crochet in the next stitch. The bead will be held firmly in place by the 2 single crochets. Continue until all the beads have been added.

Today you can find all kinds of interesting and inexpensive beads in your local novelty shops and craft outlets. Even so, the most difficult part of crocheting with beads is the search for beads that have holes large enough to accommodate your yarn. Even very large beads are frequently made with tiny holes. If you are adding only a few beads, you might be able to force the yarn through holes that are slightly too small. However, this won't work if you plan to use many beads. The more you plan to add, the more important it is that the beads slide easily along the yarn. Constantly having to force the beads down toward the skein as you work will damage your yarn. As an alternate method you can simply work the beaded rows with a thinner yarn; or you can attach both a thin yarn and a thick yarn to the piece, string the beads onto the thin yarn, and then crochet with both the thick and the thin.

Trinket Box

This special box will keep your most treasured possessions safe and accessible. The motifs on the top and sides of the box were crocheted separately, then "appliquéd" onto the single crochet box covering. By sewing the motifs onto the background we eliminated the need to fill in and shape out around the central designs. The box covering provides a tight background fabric for these motifs.

Materials:
- 44 oz. DMC #3 Pearl Cotton in the following amounts: black, 20 oz.; silver-blue, 8 oz.; copper, 8 oz. *or* corresponding amounts of any pearl cotton that gives a comparable gauge
- Felt, fabric, or contact paper for lining (optional)
- 1 cigar box
- White glue
- 1 mirror, 2″ diameter

Hook: #1 steel

Gauge:
8 sts = 1″, 8 rows = 1″

Finished Size:
This is dependent on the size of the cigar box you'll be using.

Instructions:
Note: Since all cigar boxes are not a uniform size, you will need to make 5 rectangles that fit the top and sides of your cigar box. Following directions for rectangles worked row by row on page 127, make 1 rectangle for the top of your cigar box, 2 rectangles of the same size for the front side and the back side, and 2 rectangles of the same size for the right and left sides of the box. They should be $\frac{1}{16}$″ smaller than the surfaces they will cover on all sides. When you edge the rectangles, they will cover their respective surfaces exactly.
Central motif: Following the directions for sc circles on pages 122–123, make a circle with copper until there are 24 sts in a rnd [or 3 rnds].
Round 4: Ch 1, 1 sc in 1st st, 1 sc in each of next 4

sts. Repeat from *, ending with 1 sc dec [4 decs—20 sts].
Round 5: Ch 1, 1 sc in same st, 1 sc in each of next 2 sts, *1 sc dec, 1 sc in each of next 3 sts. Repeat from *, ending with 1 sc dec. Break yarn [4 decs—16 sts].

You now have a case into which you will insert your mirror [however, do not do so at this time].
Casing rim: Work with black, silver-blue, and copper.
Row 1: Hold the casing with the lip side facing you. Go back to Round 3. You will be working Post sts around each st of Round 3 to form a rim around the casing. Insert hk from front to back in the sp between any 2 sts of Round 3 and make a Post st. Inc once *in every st.* Join the last st to the 1st st with a slst [24 incs 48 sts].
Row 2: Using black, ch 1, 1 sc in same st, 1 sc in each of next 2 sts, 2 sc in next st, (1 sc in each of next 3 sts, 2 sc in next st) 2 times, 1 sc in each of next 2 sts. Ch 1, turn [17 sts].
Row 3: 2 dc in 1st st, 1 dc in each of next 2 sts, 1 hdc in each of next 3 sts, 1 sc in each of next 4 sts, 3 sc in next st, 1 sc in each of next 4 sts, 1 hdc in each of next 3 sts, 1 dc in each of next 2 sts, 2 dc in next st. Ch 1, turn.
Row 4: 2 sc in 1st st, 1 sc in each of next 11 sts, 3 sc in next st, 1 sc in each of next 11 sts, 2 sc in last st. Ch 1, turn.
Row 5: 2 sc in 1st st, 1 sc in each of next 13 sts, 3 sc in next st, 1 sc in each of next 13 sts, 2 sc in last st.
Row 6: Attach silver-blue yarn in the st just before the st in which you attached the black yarn on Row 2. Insert hk into same st, yo and pull up a lp, insert hk into side of Row 2, yo and pull up a lp, insert hk into side of Row 3,

yo and pull up a lp, yo and close all 4 lps tog, 1 sc in side of same row, 1 sc in side of next 2 rows, 3 sc in side of Row 5 [this will turn the corner], 1 sc in each of next 15 sts, 3 sc in next st, 1 sc in each of next 15 sts, 3 sc in last st, 1 sc in side of each of next 3 rows, insert hk into side of next row, yo and pull up a lp, insert hk into side of Row 1, yo and pull up a lp, insert hk into next st on rim, yo and pull up a lp, yo and close all 4 lps tog. Ch 1, turn.

Row 7: Insert hk into 1st st, yo and pull up a lp, (insert hk into next st and pull up a lp) 2 times, yo and close all 4 lps tog, 1 sc in each of next 2 sts, 3 sc in next st, 1 sc in each of next 17 sts, 3 sc in next st, 1 sc in each of next 17 sts, 3 sc in next st, 1 sc in each of next 3 sts, (insert hk into next st, yo and pull up a lp) 2 times, insert hk into next st on rim, yo and pull up a lp, yo and close all 4 lps tog. Break yarn.

Skip 3 sts on the rim. Attach black yarn in next st and repeat Rows 1–6 of the central motif.

There are 3 unused sts left on each side of the rim in between the top and bottom of the central motif. Holding the piece with the front facing you, attach copper yarn in the center st of one of these 3-st groups.

Row 1: Insert hk into same st, yo and pull up a lp, insert hk into next st, yo and pull up a lp, insert hk into next st [this is a silver-blue st], yo and pull up a lp, yo and close all 4 lps tog, 1 sc in each of next 5 sts, 3 sc in next st, 1 sc in each of next 19 sts, 3 sc in next st, 1 sc in each of next 19 sts, 3 sc in next st, 1 sc in each of next 4 sts, insert hk into next st [last silver-blue st], yo and pull up a lp, (insert hk into next copper st on rim, yo and pull up a lp) 2 times, yo and close all 4 lps tog. Ch 1, turn.

Row 2: 1 sc dec over 1st 2 sts, 1 sc in each of next 4 sts, 3 sc in next st, 1 sc in each of next 21 sts, 3 sc in next st, 1 sc in each of next 4 sts, 1 sc dec. Break yarn.

Still holding the piece so that the front is facing you, reattach the copper yarn in the center st of the 3-sc group that is on the opposite side of the motif. The center st of this group has already been used, but it will be used again for the 2nd fill-in row.

Repeat Rows 1 and 2 of the fill-in with copper yarn.

Turn the motif over and slst the bottoms of opposing motifs tog [see page 29].

Small motifs: Ch 2 with black.

Row 1: Insert hk into 2nd ch from hk and make 1 sc. Ch 1, turn.

Row 2: 3 sc in 1st st. Ch 1, turn [3 sts].

Row 3: 2 sc in 1st st, 1 sc in next st, 2 sc in last st. Ch 1, turn [5 sts].

Row 4: 1 sc in 1st st, 2 sc in next st, 1 sc in next st, 2 sc in next st, 1 sc in last st. Break yarn [7 sts].

Row 5: Attach silver-blue yarn in side of Row 1, 1 sc in same st, 1 sc in side of next 2 rows, (1 hdc, 2 dc, 1 hdc) in side of next row, 1 sc in each of next 2 sts, 3 hdc in next st, 1 sc in side of next 2 rows, 2 sc in side of next row, join with slst to 1st st of row.

Row 6: With copper, ch 1, 1 sc in same st, 1 sc in each of next 4 sts, 3 sc in next st, 1 sc in each of next 4 sts, 3 sc in next st, 1 sc in each of next 4 sts, 3 sc in next st, 1 sc in each of next 5 sts, 2 sc in last st, join with slst.

Row 7: Ch 1, 1 sc in same st, 1 sc in each of next 5 sts, 3 hdc in next st, 1 sc in each of next 6 sts, 3 hdc in next st, 1 sc in each of next 6 sts, 3 hdc in next st, 1 sc in each of next 7 sts, 3 sc in next st, join with slst.

Repeat 7 times for a total of 8 small motifs.

EDGING

Edge the large top piece in copper on all sides. The side rectangles are edged in 2 colors: The long sides of the rectangles are edged in copper, and the short sides are edged in black. To do this edge 1 side of the piece, following the directions for edging on page 25. When you reach the corner, work the 1st 2 sts of the 3-st group in the 1st color, then change to the 2nd color, following the directions for changing yarn mid-row on page 23, and make the 3rd st in the new color. Continue down the side in the 2nd color.

ASSEMBLING

Lay the 4 side pieces on a flat surface in the following order: front side, right side, back side, left side. Following the directions for joining in Chapter 1 [page 29], join each piece to the one next to it. Then join the last piece to the 1st piece, forming a sleeve. Hold 1 long edge of the top piece next to the top edge of the back-side piece and join these 2 pieces tog along the inside with copper. Pin 1 small motif in each corner of the top piece so that the edges of the motifs are exactly even with the edges of the top piece [see the photograph on page 198]. Thread a needle with copper and sew these motifs to the corner by inserting the needle thru the bottom of the top piece close to the edge, coming up thru the motif, passing over the post of the st directly to the right or left, and inserting the needle back thru to the bottom of the top piece. Make all your sts close to the edge of the motif. Repeat in all corners. Pin the large motif in the center of the top piece and sew in place in the same manner. Pin one of the remaining 4 small motifs in the center of each side piece and sew in place.

If you plan to line the box, do so now. Cut [and seam if you are using fabric] pieces of the lining material so that they fit inside the box and come up to $\frac{1}{16}''$ below the inside edges of the box. [If you line the box above this edge, the lid won't close properly.]

Slip the crocheted cover over the box. Be sure all the edges of the piece are matched to the edges of the box. The joining seams should be directly over the corners of the box. Lift the top piece and put a small amount of glue along all 4 edges of the top of the box about $\frac{1}{16}''$ from the edge. Spread a little glue over the surface of the top, then carefully press the top piece in place. Push straight pins thru the top piece into the box all along the edges of the top to keep the piece in place while drying. Hold the top edges of the side pieces slightly away from the box. Spread a little glue along each edge, then press and pin the edge to the box. Allow to dry. Turn the box upside down and repeat the gluing and pinning process along the bottom edge. Allow to dry. Remove all pins.

Insert the mirror into the casing.

Making and Decorating Toys

Here's a way to combine some of the techniques you learned in Chapters 4 and 5, and make great gifts for children at the same time. Make animal figures from basic shapes; decorate them by crocheting and then appliquéing free-form and geometric shapes. As we've shown in the Trinket Box, appliquéing shapes onto a solid background is an easy way to create interesting shape designs.

Refer to the basic shape instructions (pages 122–127). With a little imagination you'll see how these shapes can be transformed into simple animal figures. Circles—1 big and 1 small —become the body and head of a bear, 4 tubes make his limbs, and 2 semicircles become his ears. One big, long tube makes a great snake, while a big oval and 4 tubes will do very nicely for a Humpty Dumpty. Work 2 triangles from the base, stopping 2 or 3 rows before the tip, and you've got 2 butterfly wings; make an oval for its body and sew the pieces together. As you can see, the possibilities are endless—octo-puses, starfish, caterpillars, and turtles are just a few more. To make flat animals (for wall hangings or framed pictures) simply make one of each shape needed and glue or sew the piece to a background. To make stuffed animals, make 2 of each piece. Sew the pieces together, leaving a small opening, and then stuff. (Keep in mind that these are children's toys and no doubt will have to be washed quite often. You might want to choose your stuffing material on the basis of its washability.) Finish sewing the 2 pieces together.

Once you've made the basic shape, appliqué free-form or geometric shapes to create special features. Circles are fine for eyes, noses, and buttons; semicircles can be used for mouths; and free-form shapes in general make great spots for snakes and giraffes. For a bit more dimension, leave a small opening when you appliqué the shape onto the animal, stuff with a small amount of absorbent cotton, and then sew it on completely.

Sunburst Place Mats

The subtle, curved lines of many free-form shapes are often best displayed in combination with yarns that are easily handled. For these place mats, worked in machine-washable mercerized cotton, we repeated one small shape around the edge of a single crochet circle. This heightens the "ray-like" effect of the design as well as providing you with a large, smooth area for tableware and glasses.

Materials:
- 6 balls of Joseph Galler Parisian Cotton in the following amounts: cassis (magenta), 3 balls; orange, 1½ balls; saffron (dark orange), 1½ balls *or* corresponding amounts of any thin cotton or linen

Hooks: 00 steel and G

Gauge:
Single strand: 6 sts = 1"; 7 rows = 1"
Double strand: 4 sts = 1"; 4 rows = 1"

Finished Size:
18" diameter
   Note: Materials given are for 1 place mat.
   The great number of yarn tails in each place mat makes it essential that you hide tails as you crochet. See the directions on page 23.

Instructions:
Motif: Use single strand and 00 hk.
Foundation chain: Ch 11 with magenta.
Row 1: *1 sc in 2nd ch from hk and in each of next 4 chs,* ch 6, repeat from * to *, 1 sc in *side* of final sc of 1st 6-sc group, skip ch in which this final sc was made, 1 sc in each of last 5 chs. Ch 1, turn.
Row 2: 1 sc in each of 1st 3 sts, skip 2 sts, one 5-dc Shell st in next st, skip 2 sts, 1 sc in each of last 3 sts. Break yarn.
Row 3: Look at Diagram 97. With the front of Row 2 facing you and the 5-dc Shell on the bottom, stitch A will be the 1st st of the ch row on your right and stitch C will be the last st on your left. Point B is not a st; it is the turning ch between the foundation ch and Row 1. Skip stitch A and attach orange in next st. 1 sc in attaching st, work over the ch row and make one 6-dc Shell st in the same st of Row 1 in

which the 5-dc Shell was made, 1 sc in the 3rd st of Row 1 from point B, ch 1, bring hk and yarn behind point B, 1 sc in 3rd st from point B on other side of piece, one 6-dc Shell in same st as other Shells, 1 sc in st directly before stitch C. Break yarn.
Row 4: Attach dark orange in stitch A. 1 sc in stitch A, 1 sc in 1st sc of Row 3 and in each of next 6 dc and next sc of Row 3, 1 sc in 2nd st from point B of Row 1, ch 1, bring hk and yarn behind point B, 1 sc in 2nd st from point B on other side, 1 sc in every st of Row 3, 1 sc in stitch C. Break yarn [10 sc on either side of ch-1].

   You have completed 1 motif. Make 20 motifs for each place mat.
Center of place mat: Use double strand and G hk.
Rounds 1–18: With magenta, follow the directions for making a spiral circle on page 122. On the last st of Round 18 change to orange

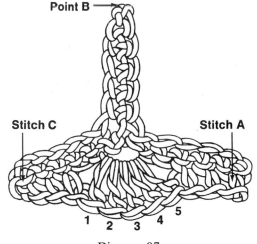

Diagram 97

201

and slst into the 1st st of Round 18. Break yarn [120 sts].

Rounds 19–21: Work in joined, rather than spiral, rnds, following the directions on page 122. Work in Tapestry st, carrying both the orange and the dark orange yarn, and crocheting over the yarn not in use [see pages 84–85]. Remember to give the piece a bit of a tug before you join each rnd to loosen up the carried yarn.

Round 19: Ch 1 with orange. 1 orange sc in 1st st and in each of next 9 sts, *1 dark orange sc in each of next 10 sts, 1 orange sc in each of next 10 sts. Repeat from *, ending with 1 dark orange sc in each of the last 10 sts, join to 1st st with a slst. Ch 1.

Round 20: 1 dark orange sc in 1st st and in each of next 8 sts, 1 dark orange inc in next st, *1 orange sc in each of next 9 sts, 1 orange inc in next st, 1 dark orange sc in each of next 9

sts, 1 dark orange inc in next st. Repeat from
*, ending with 1 orange sc in each of last 9 sts,
1 orange inc in last st, join with slst to 1st st. Ch
1 [1 inc every 10th st—132 sts].

Round 21: 1 orange sc in 1st st and in each of
next 10 sts, *1 dark orange sc in each of next
11 sts, 1 orange sc in each of next 11 sts. Repeat from *, ending with 1 dark orange sc in
each of last 11 sts, change to magenta on last
st, join. Ch 1 with magenta. Break yarn.

Round 22: With magenta, 1 sc in 1st st and in
each of next 9 sts, 1 inc in next st, *1 sc in each
of next 10 sts, 1 inc in next st. Repeat from *,
ending with 1 inc in last st, join with slst. Ch 1
[1 inc every 11th st—144 sts].

Round 23: Attach motifs on this row. Insert
hk in 1st st and draw up a lp [2 lps on hk].
With front of motif facing you, insert hk thru
point B of motif from front to back [make sure
that hk is inserted thru at least 2 strands at
point B], yo and draw thru all lps on hk [1
motif attached]. *(1 sc in each of next 6 sts,
attach motif in next st) 4 times, 1 sc in each of
next 7 sts, attach motif in next st. Repeat from
*, ending with 1 sc in each of last 7 sts, change
to orange on last st, join to 1st st with slst. Ch
1, using orange. Break yarn.

Allow motifs to hang behind piece while you
work Rounds 24–25.

Round 24: With orange, 1 sc in 1st st and in
each of next 10 sts, 1 inc in next st, *1 sc in
each of next 11 sts, 1 inc in next st. Repeat
from *, ending with 1 inc in last st, change to
dark orange on last st, join to 1st st. Ch 1,
using dark orange. Break yarn.

Round 25: With dark orange, 1 Shrimp st in
every st, join with slst. Break yarn.

OUTSIDE EDGING
Use single strand and 00 hk.

Round 1: Join motifs on this rnd. Attach
magenta in 1st st of Row 2 of any motif. This
is the st directly above stitch C in Diagram 97.
*3 sc in 1st st of Row 2, one 3-st dec over the
next 3 sts, 1 sc in next st, 3 sc in center st of
5-dc Shell, 1 sc in next st, one 3-st dec over
next 3 sts, 3 sc in last st of Row 2, ch 2. Repeat
from *, ending with 3 sc in last st of Row 2 of
last motif, ch 2, join to 1st sc with slst. Break
the yarn.

Round 2: Attach dark orange in center st of
any 3-sc group above center of 5-dc Shell. *3
sc in center st of 3-sc group, ch 3, 1 sc in center
st of next 3-sc group [above stitch A], 1 Bar
st sc over the ch-2 and into the side of the 1st
st of Row 4 of motif [the dark orange row], 5
dc over ch-2, 1 Bar st sc over ch-2 and into
side of last st of Row 4 of new motif, 1 sc in
center st of 3-sc group [above stitch C], ch 3.
Repeat from *, ending with ch 3, join to 1st st
with slst. Break yarn.

Round 3: Attach orange in 2nd st of Round 2
[center sc of 3-sc group]. *1 sc in center st of
3-sc group, one 5-dc Shell st in ch-3 sp, skip
next st, one 3-st dec over the next 3 sts, 1 sc in
next st, one 3-st dec over next 3 sts, skip next
st, one 5-dc Shell in next ch-3 sp. Repeat from
*, ending with 5 dc in last ch-3 sp, join to 1st st
with slst. Break yarn.

Round 4: Attach magenta in center st of last
5-dc Shell of Round 3 [over stitch C]. 1 sc in
attaching st, *one 5-dc Bar st Shell over Round
3 and into center st of 3-sc group of Round 2,
1 sc in center st of next 5-dc Shell, 1 sc in each
of next 8 sts. Repeat from *, ending with 1 sc
in last 5-dc Shell, 1 sc in each of last 7 sts, join
to 1st st with slst. Break yarn.

Round 5: Attach dark orange in center st of
5-dc Bar st Shell of Round 4. *3 sc in center
st of 5-dc Shell, 1 sc in each of next 13 sts. Repeat from *, ending with 1 sc in each of last 13
sts, change to orange on last st, join with slst.
Ch 1 with orange. Break yarn.

Round 6: 1 sc in 1st st, *3 sc in center of 3-sc
group of Round 5, 1 sc in each of next 15 sts.
Repeat from *, ending with 1 sc in each of last
14 sts, change to magenta on last st, join with
slst. Ch 1 with magenta. Break yarn.

Round 7: With magenta, 1 sc in each of 1st 2
sts, *3 sc in center of 3-sc group of Round 6,
1 sc in each of next 17 sts. Repeat from *,
ending with 1 sc in each of last 15 sts, join with
slst. Break yarn.

Round 8: Attach dark orange in 1st st. 1
Shrimp st in every st, join with slst. Break yarn.

Block the place mat [see page 35]. You
may want to block directly on the back of the
place mat, without an intervening cloth, to ensure that the motifs are blocked correctly.

Materials and Suppliers

Below is a list of manufacturers and stores from which you can obtain materials and information. Almost all of the manufacturers carry sport weight, worsted weight, bulky weight, and novelty yarns, and will be glad to send you the names of stores in your area that serve as outlets. Some will even sell and ship materials directly to you on request. The retail stores listed below on the right are in the New York City area. They all fill mail order requests for yarn and some will also send sample cards of their yarn inventory for a small fee.

Manufacturers

American Thread
High Ridge Park
Stamford, Conn. 06905

Emile Bernat
Depot and Mendon St.
Uxbridge, Mass. 01569

Stanley Berrocco
140 Mendon St.
Uxbridge, Mass. 01569

Coats and Clark's
P.O. Box 1966
Stamford, Conn. 06904

Columbia Minerva
Box 500
Robesonia, Pa. 19551

Joseph Galler, Inc.
156 Fifth Ave.
New York, N.Y. 10010

Golden Fleece
Radio City Station
P.O. Box 1142
New York, N.Y. 10019

Lily Mills Co.
Handweaving Dept.
Shelby, N.C. 28150

Paternayan Brothers
312 E. 95 St.
New York, N.Y. 10028

Reynolds Yarn
International Creations
Box 55
Great Neck, N.Y. 11023

Spinnerin
30 Wesley St.
South Hackensack, N.J. 07606

Tahki Imports
336 West End Ave.
New York, N.Y. 10023

Berga Ullmann, Inc.
59 Demond Ave.
P.O. Box 918
North Adams, Mass. 01247

Bernhard Ullmann
30-20 Thompson Ave.
Long Island City, N.Y. 11101

Retail Stores

Coulter Studios
(Importer of Borgs i Lund cowshair, wool, and linen)
118 E. 59 St.
New York, N.Y. 10002

Quickit
238 E. 53 St.
New York, N.Y. 10022

School Products
(Importer of CUM yarns)
1201 Broadway
New York, N.Y. 10001

Threadbare, Unlimited
20 Cornelia St.
New York, N.Y. 10014

Yarn Center
866 Sixth Ave.
New York, N.Y. 10009

Acknowledgments

Many thanks to everyone who helped—especially Jim
Ramsay and Bill Arp. And . . . Rachel Arp, Dorrie Bernstein,
Ceal DeLaurier, Arie deZanger, Joan Hammes, Carol Hines,
Jeanne McClow, Evelyn Miller, Roz Miller, Kathleen
Moore, Bob Reiter, Elizabeth Rice, Susan Rosenthal,
F.A.O. Schwarz, Risa Steinberg, Chris Swirnoff, Roslyn Targ,
Jos. Trautwein, Mildred Waters.

Index